D1025674

Blending
Qualitative&
Quantitative
RESEARCH METHODS in
THESES and DISSERTATIONS

Blending Qualitative & Quantitative

RESEARCH METHODS in
THESES and DISSERTATIONS

R. MURRAY THOMAS

CORWIN PRESS, INC.
A Sage Publications Company
Thousand Oaks, California

For information:

Corwin Press, Inc.
A Sage Publications Company
2455 Teller Road
Thousand Oaks, California 91320
www.corwinpress.com

Sage Publications Ltd.
6 Bonhill Street
London EC2A 4PU
United Kingdom

Sage Publications India Pvt. Ltd.
B-42, Panchsheel Enclave
Post Box 4109
New Delhi 110 017 India

Printed in the United States of America

Library of Congress Cataloging-in-Publication Data

Thomas, R. Murray (Robert Murray), 1921-
Blending qualitative and quantitative research methods in theses and dissertations / R. Murray Thomas.
      p. cm.
Includes bibliographical references and index.
ISBN 0-7619-3931-8 (cloth) — ISBN 0-7619-3932-6 (pbk.)
    1. Dissertations, Academic—United States. 2. Research—United States—Methodology. I. Title.
LB2369.T4575 2003
001.4′2—dc211

                          2003000852

This book is printed on acid-free paper.

03   04   05   06   10 9 8 7 6 5 4 3 2 1

Acquisitions editor:	Rachel Livsey
Production editor:	Sanford Robinson
Editorial Assistant:	Phyllis Cappello
Cover designer:	Michael Dubowe
Production artist:	Lisa Miller

Contents

Preface

Readers may find it useful at the outset to learn what this book *is* and what it *is not*.

What the book is: This volume has been designed as a guide for graduate students who wish to understand

- The characteristics of a wide variety of qualitative and quantitative research methods.
- Conditions under which a particular research method is most appropriate.
- Twenty different ways that qualitative and quantitative methods can be blended in the written proposals that graduate students prepare to describe their thesis or dissertation research plans.
- How to disseminate the results of the research to readers well beyond the faculty members who supervised the students' work.

What the book is not: This volume does not offer

- Detailed steps to take for conducting research from beginning to end. There are already numerous books which serve as effective guides to that step-by-step process, including the following that are listed among the references at the end of this volume (Cone & Foster, 1993; Glatthorn, 1998; Madsen, 1991; Rudestam & Newton, 1992; Sternberg, 1981; Thomas & Brubaker, 2000, 2001).
- A prescription of *the correct way* to combine qualitative and quantitative methods. Instead, the book describes a wide range of methods—including their advantages and limitations—and numerous samples of thesis and dissertation proposals that blend qualitative

and quantitative approaches in different patterns. Then, from among those options, students can select the combination of methods that appears to suit their needs.

In closing these prefatory remarks, I wish to express my appreciation to Rachel Livsey, the Corwin Press editor who first suggested that I write such a book as this one and who guided it along the path to publication. I would also like to thank Sanford Robinson, the editor who ensured that the book's production process advanced so smoothly.

Finally, the contributions of the following reviewers of the initial draft of this book are gratefully acknowledged:

John W. Creswell
Professor of Educational Psychology
Director of Office of Qualitative and
    Mixed Methods Research
University of Nebraska-Lincoln
Lincoln, NE

Norvell Norhtcutt
Sr. Lecturer
University of Texas at Austin
Austin, TX

Dr. Roxana M. DellaVecchia
Assistant Dean
Towson University
Towson, MD

Cynthia A. Tananis
Assistant Professor
University of Pittsburgh
Pittsburgh, PA

—R. Murray Thomas

About the Author

R. Murray Thomas (PhD, Stanford University) is an emeritus professor at the University of California, Santa Barbara, where he taught educational psychology and headed the program in international education for 30 years before retiring. Prior to coming to the University of California, he had served as a high school teacher in Honolulu and as a professor at San Francisco State University, the State University of New York (Brockport), and Pajajaran University in West Java, Indonesia. His professional publications exceed 340, including 48 books that he authored, coauthored, or edited.

1

The Qualitative and the Quantitative

If graduate students are to blend qualitative and quantitative research methods in their theses and dissertations, they can profit at the outset from considering three questions: How are the terms *qualitative* and *quantitative* best defined? What are examples of qualitative and quantitative methods? How can the two methods be compatibly combined?

This chapter opens with alternative answers to the three questions, then continues with (a) an illustrative research method and (b) an illustrative dissertation proposal that blends qualitative and quantitative approaches.

Qualitative and Quantitative Defined

The simplest way to distinguish between qualitative and quantitative may be to say that qualitative methods involve a researcher describing *kinds* of characteristics of people and events without comparing events in terms of measurements or amounts. Quantitative methods, on the other hand, focus attention on measurements and *amounts* (more and less, larger and smaller, often and seldom, similar and different) of the characteristics displayed by the people and events that the researcher studies.

However, researchers who are concerned with such matters are often not content with such a simple distinction (they might say "simplistic distinction") between the two approaches. Hence, they portray *qualitative* and *quantitative* in other ways and often in far greater detail. By way of illustration, consider the following definitions of *qualitative methods*.

1. Qualitative research is multimethod in focus, involving an interpretive, naturalistic approach to its subject matter. This means that qualitative researchers study things in their natural settings, attempting to make sense of, or interpret phenomena in terms of the meanings people bring to them. Qualitative research involves the studied use and collection of a

variety of empirical materials—case study, personal experience, intro-spective, life story, interview, observational, historical, interactional, and visual texts—that describe routine and problematic moments and meanings in people's lives. (Denzin & Lincoln, 1994, p. 2)

2. Qualitative researchers seek to make sense of personal stories and the ways in which they interact. . . . *Qualitative inquiry* is an umbrella term for various philosophical orientations to interpretive research. For ex-ample, qualitative researchers might call their work ethnography, case study, phenomenology, educational criticism, . . . human ethnology, ecological psychology, holistic ethnography, cognitive anthropology, ethnography of communication, symbolic interactionism, . . . microeth-nography, ethnomethodology, postmodern ethnography. . . [or] partici-patory research. (Glesne & Peshkin, 1992, pp. 1)

Next, note the way quantitative methods have been characterized by two sets of writers.

1. Quantitative research uses numbers and statistical methods. It tends to be based on numerical measurements of specific aspects of phenomena; it abstracts from particular instances to seek general description or to test causal hypotheses; it seeks measurements and analyses that are easily replicable by other researchers. (King, Keohane, & Verba, 1994. pp. 3-4)

2. Quantitative researchers seek explanations and predictions that will gen-eralize to other persons and places. Careful sampling strategies and ex-perimental designs are aspects of quantitative methods aimed at produce generalizable results. In quantitative research, the researcher's role is to observe and measure, and care is taken to keep the researchers from "contaminating" the data through personal involvement with the re-search subjects. Researchers "objectivity" is of utmost concern. (Glesne & Peshkin, 1992, p. 6)

Thus, it is apparent that researchers are not all of the same mind in de-fining qualitative and quantitative methods. And definitions become even more confusing when authors differ markedly in what they intend by the term *method*. Some writers, when speaking of *method*, focus on one facet of research activity while others focus on quite a different facet. As an illustration, the expression *participatory method* concerns the roles that researchers can assume when conducting a study. For example, an investigator who is examining students' behavior in a college chemistry laboratory can observe the group either from the perspective of an out-sider (a visitor with a notebook or video camera) or—by enrolling in the class and participating with fellow students in the lab work—from the vantage point of an insider. In contrast to such a researcher-role per-spective, the phrases *content-analysis method* and *interview method* concern techniques used for gathering information (analyzing printed documents in the case of content analysis and talking with informants in the case of interviews). A still different perspective is reflected in the method referred to as *grounded theory*. That term is used to indicate that the researcher does not bring a preconceived theory (such as Piaget's model of cognitive development or Bandura's theory of social cognition) to the interpretation of collected information (such as recorded observations of nursery-school children's play or physicians' answers to questionnaire items about diagnosing Alzheimer's disorder). Instead, grounded-theory investigators extract theory out of the collected information itself.

So it is that the professional literature contains a multitude of research methods that bear a multitude of labels and focus on diverse aspects of the research process. Part I of this volume is designed to explain the nature of many of those methods, including (a) the procedures involved in putting each method into practice and (b) each method's strengths and limitations.

Qualitative and Quantitative Examples

As a preparation for the detailed descriptions of methods in Part I, the following brief sketches of eight sample studies illustrate something of the diversity of both qualitative and quantitative approaches. Examples in the first set are mainly qualitative. Examples in the second set are chiefly quantitative.

Four Qualitative Studies

Chronicle. Title: *A History of Kent Center—1783-2000.* This description of the development of a small Midwestern town is based on the content analysis of library materials (newspapers, town-meeting records) and on interviews with long-time residents.

Explanatory biography. Title: *Elizabeth Carswell, Inventive Educator.* In tracing the career pattern of a noteworthy high-school English teacher, the researcher attempts to explain both (a) the forces that fashioned Mrs. Carswell's life-course pattern and (b) the influence she exerted on the lives of students. The data have been gathered primarily through face-to-face interviews with Mrs. Carswell and with her former students, colleagues, friends, and relatives as well as through the analysis of a collection of letters she exchanged with friends and former students over the years.

Ethnography. Title: *Child Rearing in a Present-Day Hopi Community.* A doctoral candidate spends a three-month summer vacation living in a Hopi-reservation community in the Southwestern United States in order to study (a) how four Hopi families treat children of different age levels, (b) the Hopi adults' reasoning that guides their child-rearing practices, (c) problems parents encounter in raising their children, (d) how parents cope with the problems, and (e) what effect such child-rearing methods appear to have on children's behavior. The researcher gathers information by means of observing events in the four families' daily lives and by interviewing parents, children, and other members of the community.

Liberal-feminist study. Title: *Bias in the Workplace: Promotion Practices in Two Corporations.* The author identifies discrepancies between men and women in how well their career records warrant their promotion to positions of greater responsibility and greater reward in the local branches of two large international corporations. Data for the research have been collected by means of (a) content analysis of records of the educational backgrounds and work experiences of a sample of the corporations' employees and (b) interviews with both men and women employees, including several officials who hold critical decision-making positions. The author concludes that men have been given preferential treatment over women in promotion policies. *Liberal-feminist theory* has provided the perspective for interpreting the data. According to Rosemarie Putnam Tong (1998), proponents of the liberal-feminism movement contend that few, if any, claims about differences between the sexes are supported by fact, except perhaps claims about physical strength. Thus, any observed differences between the genders in intelligence, logical reasoning, initiative, resoluteness, and leadership are the result of (a) legal and customary restrictions placed on females' rights and opportunities and (b) the society's practice of convincing children that such a division of roles and rights is reasonable and fair. Consequently, according to the theory, proper and fair female development would be fostered by the members of society honoring, by word and deed, the equality of females and males in legal and customary rights, in intelligence, in leadership qualities, in emotional stability, and the like.

Four Quantitative Studies

Telephone survey. Title: *Predicting Statewide Election Outcomes: A South Carolina Case.* Prior to a November election, a company specializing in public opinion polls conducts a sequence of three pre-election telephone surveys (six weeks, three weeks, and one week prior to the election) involving a statewide sample of registered voters. The telephone interviews are designed to reveal which candidates the voters prefer and which ballot initiatives voters intend to support on election day. The detailed results of the surveys are then provided to a graduate student who helped design and conduct the study. The student produces an analysis of the collected data in the form of a doctoral dissertation.

Experiment. Title: *Criticizing Others' Products: The Effects of Negative-Comparison Advertising.* Recent decades have witnessed a growing incidence of companies maligning competitors' products in newspaper and magazine ads and in television commercials. In an effort to determine the effect on consumers of such advertising, as compared to advertising that focuses entirely on a company's own products, a student conducts the following experiment. Two groups of participants (college students, Rotary Club members) are furnished a sixteen-page brochure designed to simulate a series of magazine advertisements. Each pair of pages features full-page advertisements praising the same product—with each product being a fictitious brand so that participants will not judge an advertisement on the basis of their existing preference for a well-known brand. The products featured in the eight pairs of ads appear in this sequence: automobile, breakfast food, diet soft drink, long-distance phone service, vacation resort, television receiver, pain-relief medicine, and laundry soap. In each pair, the ad on one page praises the qualities of a particular brand of product without mentioning any competing brands. The ad on the opposite page not only mentions the names of brands manufactured by other companies, but also claims that those competing brands are inferior to the one sold by the company that created the advertisement. In other words, one version of the ad (*positive style*) is limited to praising the sponsoring company's product, whereas the other version (*negative-comparison style*) not only extols the qualities of the sponsor's brand but denigrates competitors' products.

Participants in the experiment are asked to view each pair of ads and, for each pair, answer the following questions: Which ad—the one on the left or the one on the right—would more likely convince people to buy the recommended product? Why do you think that the ad you chose would be the more convincing one?

The researcher then interprets the collected responses in a way that answers the trio of questions that the experiment has been designed to clarify: What effect does negative-comparison advertising, as compared to positive advertising, have on potential customers' product preferences? What reasons do consumers offer for preferring one type of advertisement over the other type? Do subgroups (college students versus business people, females versus males) respond differently to positive and negative-comparative styles of advertising?

Correlational study. Title: *Factors Associated with Teenage Delinquency.* The researcher collects information about a series of factors in the lives of 27 teenage boys who were assigned by the court to a juvenile detention facility and of 32 teenage boys who have never been arrested. The factors include each boy's (a) school attendance record, (b) grade-point average, (c) extracurricular activities, (d) health record (including height and weight), (e) typical friends/companions (including the incidence of friends' arrests and truancy). Additional factors are parents' (f) marital status, (g) occupations, and (h) education levels. Each factor is converted into a numerical scale or set of categories, and group statistics ([1] group average and extent of variation within the group for the scaled variables and [2] percentages for the categorized variables) are calculated for the delinquent group and for the nondelinquent group. Then correlations are calculated between each factor and the youths' delinquent/nondelinquent status. With the resulting figures in hand, the researcher decides whether there is a significant difference between delinquents and nondelinquents on the eight factors.

Quantitative content analysis. Title: *Ethnic Representations in American History Textbooks.* As a thesis project, a student calculates the amount of attention given to different ethnic groups in three high-school American-history textbooks. The data-collection task consists of counting (a) the number of times each ethnic group is mentioned, (b) the amount of space dedicated to the discussion of each group, and (c) how often the mention of each group casts the group in a positive, negative, or neutral light. The student employs computer software that is designed for content analysis in order to ease the burden of surveying the textbooks' contents and to better ensure that the computation of amounts is accurate.

The Demise of a Controversy

In the not-too-distant past, the literature on research methods included debates between individuals who favored qualitative approaches over quantitative or vice versa. As Stewart and Shields have noted, on each side of this controversy there have been people who demeaned the beliefs of those on the other side by implying that such folks were dolts.

> Debates about quantitative and qualitative methodologies tend to be cast as a contest between innovative, socially responsible methods versus obstinately conservative and narrow-minded methods [an opinion of advocates of qualitative approaches], or precise, sophisticated techniques versus mere "common sense" [an opinion of supporters of quantitative approaches]. (Stewart & Shields, 2001, p. 307)

However, most authors today apparently see qualitative and quantitative approaches as complementary rather than antagonistic.

> 1. Quantitative methods are, in general, supported by the positivist or scientific paradigm, which leads us to regard the world as made up of observable, measurable facts. In contrast, qualitative methods are generally supported by the interpretivist paradigm, which portrays a world in which reality is socially constructed, complex, and ever changing. . . . Because the positivist and the intepretivist paradigms rest on different assumptions about the nature of the world, they require different in-

struments and procedures to find the type of data desired. This does not mean, however, that the positivist never uses interviews nor that the intepretivist never uses a survey. They may, but such methods are supplementary, not dominant. (Glesne & Peshkin, 1992, pp. 8-9.)

2. The two traditions—[quantitative and qualitative]—appear quite different; indeed they sometimes seem to be at war. Our view is that these differences are mainly ones of style and specific technique. . . . Most research does not fit clearly into one category—qualitative or quantitative—or the other. The best often combines features of each. In the same research project, some data may be collected that is amenable to statistical analysis, while other equally significant information is not. . . . Neither quantitative nor qualitative research is superior to the other; . . . we do not regard quantitative research to be any more scientific than qualitative research. (King, Keohane, & Verba, 1994, pp. 5, 7)

3. [Both qualitative and quantitative methods] can be used effectively in the same research project. However, most projects and researchers place their emphasis on one form or another, partly out of conviction, but also because of training and the nature of the problems studied. (Strauss & Corbin, 1990, p. 18)

The perspective I espouse throughout this book is in keeping with the rationale offered by these authors, who often adopt the philosopher's label *pragmatism* to identify a mixed-methodology perspective (Tashakkori & Teddlie, 1998, pp. 11-13). Consequently, the significant issue is not whether one method is overall superior to another but, rather, whether the method a researcher employs can yield convincing answers to the questions that the investigation is intended to settle.

Typical pragmatists support their position by asserting that qualitative and quantitative approaches are alike in the fundamental values on which they are founded, including "belief in the value-ladenness of inquiry, belief in the theory-ladenness of facts, belief that reality is multiple and constructed, [and] belief in the fallibility of knowledge" (Tashakkori & Teddlie, 1998, p. 13).

I am convinced that each research method is suited to answering certain types of questions but not appropriate to answering other types. Furthermore, the best answer frequently results from using a combination of qualitative and quantitative methods. And that's what this book is about. Part I describes many qualitative and quantitative methods. Then Part II illustrates diverse ways of blending multiple methods to answer diverse kinds of research questions.

To help students identify how they might disseminate the results of their research to a wider audience of readers than those who find the thesis or dissertation at the local university library, Chapter 13 in Part II describes a variety of ways to publish the results.

To help students identify how they might disseminate the results of their research to a wider audience of readers than those who find the thesis or dissertation at the local university library, Chapter 13 in Part II describes a variety of ways to publish the results.

An Example of How Methods Can Be Described

The purpose of the following example is to demonstrate the way the methods in Part I are depicted. Each portrayal in Part I follows the same sequence of topics—the particular method's (a) typical label, (b) description, (c) typical procedure in applying the method, (d) its advantages, (e) its limitations, and (f) further sources of information about the method.

Here is an illustration of such a presentation pattern, using grounded-theory method as the example.

Title. Grounded Theory

Description. The term *grounded theory* and explanations of grounded theory's characteristics have been with us hardly more than three decades. The term was introduced in 1967 by Glaser and Strauss in *The Discovery of Grounded Theory.* In that volume, the authors contrasted (a) creating theory during the process of gathering information (using the collected evidence as the soil from which theory is generated) with (b) bringing to the research project a theory that was the result of "armchair speculation" about how and why social phenomena occur as they do. In support of their grounded-theory recommendation, Glaser and Strauss contended that an interpretive model should "fit the situation being researched, and work when put into use" (1967, p. 3). The likelihood of achieving such an outcome was greater, they said, if theory is created during the data-collection process rather than is preconceived and used to guide data collection. In brief, grounded theory, as a research method, consists of discovering theory from data (Glaser & Strauss, 1967, p. 3).

Typical procedure. Although the expression *grounded theory* is of recent vintage, it's clear that attentive people have, for a great many centuries, been deriving theory from their observations of life's events. However, the exact fashion in which the process might be conducted is a matter particularly brought to social scientists' attention during the past 30 years or so. But it's also the case that those who write about grounded theory fail to agree on how such theory is best produced. As Dey noted:

> Disagreements flare up, not only over what the methodology of grounded theory is in principle, but also over how to it put into practice. Indeed, some critics dispute the claims of other researchers to have used grounded the-

ory—not unlike, it may seem to an outsider, the way exponents of various cults bicker over the right interpretation of a religion. . . . [When I was asked about which variety of grounded theory I was going to discuss in my book, I replied that] there were probably as many versions of grounded theory as there were 'grounded theorists.' (Dey, 1999, p. 2)

Despite this lack of consensus about details, there appears to be a set of practices widely agreed upon by those who subscribe to a grounded-theory approach. According to Cresswell (1998),

- The aim of grounded theory is to generate or discover a theory.
- The researcher has to set aside theoretical ideas to allow a "substantive" theory to emerge.
- Theory focuses on how individuals interact in relation to the phenomenon under study.
- Theory asserts a plausible relation between concepts and sets of concepts.
- Theory is derived from data acquired through fieldwork interviews, observations, and documents.
- Data analysis is systematic and begins as soon as data become available.
- Data analysis proceeds through identifying categories and connecting them.
- Further data collection (or sampling) is based on emerging concepts.
- These concepts are developed through constant comparison with additional data.
- Data collection can stop when new conceptualizations emerge.
- Data analyses proceeds from "open" coding (identifying categories, properties, and dimensions) through axial coding (examining conditions, strategies, and consequences) to selective coding around an emerging story line.
- The resulting theory can be reported in a narrative framework or as a set of propositions. (Dey, 1999, pp. 1-2)

One form that grounded theory can assume is that of a *grounded typology*. The term *theory*, in a very general sense, can refer to (a) an identified set of components that account for how some phenomenon occurs and (b) a description of how those components interact in order to produce the phenomenon. The terms *typology* and *taxonomy* refer to (a) the system of categories into which phenomena can be located and (b) how those categories are related to each other. A *grounded typology* is a classification system that a researcher derives by means of analyzing collected information rather than by adopting someone else's typology. For example, an anthropologist who wishes to catalog the personalities of distressed individuals in a large city's homeless population may either utilize an established typology—such as the American Psychiatric Association's *Diagnostic and Statistical Manual of Mental Disorders: IV*—or may create her own grounded typology by analyzing her recorded observations of 50 individuals from that population.

Advantages. Proponents of grounded-theory methodology find the approach's chief strength in its ability to provide an interpretation of events that suits the particular conditions of those events, rather than the researcher imposing a theoretical perspective on the data that fails to accommodate the events' conditions. As Strauss and Corbin (1990, p. 23) put it,

> If theory is faithful to the everyday reality of the substantive areas and carefully induced from diverse data, then it should fit that substantive area.

A second advantage claimed for grounded theory is that it results in an interpretation meaningful to both the researcher and the people the researcher studies. Because the resultant theory represents the reality of the particular incidents studied, the theory should "make sense both to the persons who were studied and to those practicing in that area," (Strauss & Corbin, 1990, p. 23)

Furthermore, when grounded theory is well done, and its data "comprehensive and the interpretations conceptual and broad, then the theory should be abstract enough and include sufficient variation to make it applicable to a variety of contexts related to that phenomenon" (Strauss & Corbin, 1990, p. 23).

Limitations. Perhaps the greatest barrier to the use of grounded theory is a researcher's lack of the skills required to put it into effective practice. According to Strauss and Corbin, those skills include the capacity

> to step back and critically analyze situations, to recognize and avoid bias, to obtain valid and reliable data, and to think abstractly. To do these, a qualitative researcher requires theoretical and social sensitivity, the ability to maintain analytical distance while at the same time drawing upon past experience and theoretical knowledge to interpret what is seen, astute powers of observation, and good interactional skills. (Strauss & Corbin, 1990, p. 18)

Further resources. The following items among the references at the end of this book furnish additional information about the nature and application of grounded theory: Cresswell, 1998; Dey, 1999; Glaser, 1978, 1992; Glaser & Strauss, 1967; Strauss & Corbin, 1990.

With the foregoing sample description of a research method in hand, we turn now to a sample of a blended-methods dissertation proposal.

An Illustrative Dissertation Proposal

As noted earlier, Part II of this book offers brief descriptions of 20 thesis and dissertation proposals that blend qualitative and quantitative methods in various patterns. The term *proposal* refers to the written plan that a graduate student typically presents to the faculty member—or members—responsible for directing and evaluating the student's thesis or dissertation.

The dual purpose of the examples in Part II is to illustrate (a) diverse ways in which qualitative and quantitative methods can be combined and (b) varied forms that project proposals can assume. The following condensed version of a sample proposal is included at this juncture to illustrate a typical form of the plans that will be met in Part II. Following the description of the proposal, the qualitative/quantitative features of the proposal's research methods are summarized under the label *The qualitative/quantitative blend.*

Dissertation title. Suitable Consequences for Lawbreakers

Research questions. In cases involving various kinds of lawbreaking, (a) what do people suggest as suitable consequences to be experienced by the individuals found guilty of violating the law and (b) what reasons do people offer for recommending such consequences?

The project's intended significance. This study is intended to offer a modest contribution to the available literature about (a) the consequences that people believe several kinds of lawbreakers deserve to face and (b) the forms of reasoning that people offer in support of those consequences. The study's results may be of particular interest to lawyers who deal with juries and to criminologists, social workers, and clinical psychologists whose professions involve understanding the operation of the criminal-justice system.

Research procedure. Written descriptions of eight cases of rule-breaking or lawbreaking will be presented to each of 100 individuals who are asked—for each case—to recommend the consequences (punishment or treatment) that the offenders should face and to explain why such a recommendation is appropriate. The cases appear on a questionnaire (opinionnaire) designed to reveal the 100 participants' opinions about the appropriate treatment of lawbreakers

- whose violations are of different degrees of seriousness (ranging from minor breaches of rules to homicide),

- who are of different age levels (ranging from the early teens to old age), and
- who apparently differed in their motives or intentions (self protection, revenge, malevolence).

In four of the cases, the offenders are females. In the other four, the offenders are males.

Participants in the study. The respondents who fill out the opinionnaire will consist of approximately 50 junior-high-school students (divided more or less equally by gender) and approximately 50 university students (divided more or less equally by gender). The opinionnaire will be administered either by the present writer or by a teacher during a class period or a group meeting.

Data interpretation and presentation. The outcome of the study will be reported as both a set of statistical summaries and a collection of individual participants' verbatim responses.

Statistical summaries: The researcher will prepare statistical summaries by first assigning respondents' answers to categories representing (a) consequences, (b) seriousness of violations, (c) lawbreakers' age levels, (d) lawbreakers' genders, (e) lawbreakers' estimated motives, (f) the study-participants' school levels (junior high versus university), (g) the study-participants' genders, and (h) the rationales participants offer in support of their recommendations. For the variables *age, gender,* and *school level,* the types of categories needed for recording information are obvious. Then, as a system of categories for recording *the seriousness of violations,* a typology will be adopted from a source in the professional literature (see Thomas, 1995, *Classifying Reactions to Wrongdoing—Taxonomies of (1) Misdeeds, (2) Sanctions, and (3) Aims of Sanctions).* The three remaining classification typologies *(consequences, estimated motives, supporting rationales)* will be derived by the present writer analyzing the collected opinionnaire responses, thereby creating three grounded typologies.

The statistical summaries will be cast in a series of tables that include the frequencies of each variable and the percentages that those frequencies represent out of the total number of respondents.

The purpose of the summaries is to furnish an overview of the most/least popular consequences and of supporting rationales as they relate to (a) lawbreakers' ages, genders, and motives and (b) participants' school levels and genders.

Individuals' response patterns. Whereas statistical summaries are useful for revealing general group trends in decisions about lawbreakers, summaries fail to convey individuals' ways of reasoning—ways that can be expected to vary somewhat from one participant to another. In order to illustrate diverse ways that individual participants arrived at their judgments of the eight cases, the dissertation will include one or two chapters that present verbatim examples of what a variety of participants wrote. The examples will be selected to represent a diversity of arguments that respondents adduced in support of their recommended consequences for the lawbreakers.

The qualitative-quantitative blend. The most obvious quantitative aspect of the *Proposed Consequences* proposal is the set of statistical summaries. The most obvious qualitative feature is the collection of participants' rationales that they offered in support of their recommendations. Although grounded typologies have been used in the past for both qualitative and quantitative studies, during recent years grounded typologies—and grounded theories in general—appear to have been associated more often with qualitative approaches.

Conclusion

The fivefold purpose of this chapter has been to (a) review definitions of *qualitative research* and *quantitative research*, (b) consider examples of qualitative and quantitative methods, (c) demonstrate the form in which research methods are presented in Part I, and (d) illustrate the manner of describing the blended research proposals that comprise Part II.

Part I

A Catalogue of Methods— Qualitative and Quantitative

Part I offers brief descriptions of a wide range of research methods so that readers can recognize the features of individual methods which can be combined in various patterns to produce the sorts of blended qualitative/quantitative research designs found in Part II.

How, then, are the chapters of Part I organized to accomplish such a purpose? As suggested in Chapter 1, each researcher's statements about methods are from that individual's particular vantage point. For instance, the investigator may be speaking of methodology in terms of

- broadly encompassing approaches to accumulating knowledge (qualitative, quantitative, blended qualitative/quantitative) or
- the time period encompassed by an investigation (historical versus contemporary) or
- ways of collecting information (interviews, tests, observations) or
- the relationship of the researcher to the people who are the objects of study (etic perspective versus emic perspective) or
- ways of selecting the participants in a study (random sampling, convenience sampling) or
- ways of organizing collected information (narrative, typological, statistical, graphic) or
- ways of interpreting the collected information (explanatory, predictive, evaluative, hermeneutic) or
- some other perspective.

The chapters in Part I describe methods from several of these viewpoints so that readers can gain a multifaceted conception of research methodology. For example, Chapters 2, 3, and 4 combine time periods (historical versus contemporary) with broad research approaches (qualitative versus quantitative). Specifically, Chapter 2 describes popular types of historical studies (chronicle, biography, autobiography). Chapters 3 and 4 focus on projects that concern the status of events at the time the research is conducted. Chapter 3 emphasizes contemporary qualitative descriptions (ethnography, personal experience), whereas Chapter 4 stresses contemporary quantitative approaches (surveys, correlation studies, experiments).

Chapter 5 features a still different aspect of methodology—the techniques used for collecting the information required by the methods of Chapters 2, 3, and 4. Those techniques include content analyses, observations, questionnaires, interviews, and tests.

Chapter 6 concerns the relationship between the researcher and the researched, focusing particularly on how the researcher's chosen role can influence the progress and outcome of a study.

Part I closes with Chapter 7, which offers a lengthy discussion of methods of interpreting the results of research projects. The chapter focuses particularly on issues of (a) what conclusions can be legitimately drawn about the compiled data and (b) how broadly conclusions of a particular study can appropriately be applied to people, places, times, and events other than those that have been directly investigated.

Throughout Part I, the intertwining of the chapters is continually apparent. Methods focusing on the time dimension (historical versus contemporary in Chapters 2, 3, and 4) are inexorably interwoven with data-collection techniques (Chapter 5), with the relationship between the researcher and the people and places being studied (Chapter 6), and with modes of interpreting a study's results (Chapter 7). Therefore, within any given chapter, readers can expect occasional reference to other chapters in Part I that bear on the current topic of discussion.

2
Historical Perspectives

The expression *historical method*, in its most obvious sense, refers to the means of identifying how some phenomenon has changed or has remained the same with the passing of time. In this context, *time* means years, decades, or centuries rather than days, weeks, or months.

Perhaps the most evident way that one historical study differs from all others is in its scope, with *scope* defined as (a) the time period encompassed, (b) the type of contribution the study is intended to make, and (c) the kinds of events on which the study focuses. Scope is often implied in a work's title, then explained in more detail by the questions the study is expected to answer. For example, consider the following three titles and sets of guide questions.

Title. A Shawnee County Chronicle—1600-2000
Guide questions. Who were living in the Shawnee County region in 1600?
What was their way of life (occupations, housing, food, clothing, ceremonies)?
What sorts of outsiders moved into the region at different times between 1600 and 2000? What were their styles of life?
What changes occurred in occupations, land use, and life styles over the years?
At different periods of time, how did the existing residents of the county respond to the new arrivals?
What conflicts among the county's inhabitants arose over the decades, and how were the conflicts resolved?

Title. The Rise and Decline of Mining in the Rapid River Watershed
Guide questions. What areas are included in the Rapid River watershed?
When and how did gold and silver mining start?
What important events contributed to the growth of the mining industry, population expansion, and the form that the communities assumed?
At the height of mining in the watershed, what was the size and composition of the population and of institutions serving the population (government, businesses, schools, churches, entertainment establishments)?

Who were the most important contributors to the development of the area?

When did the mining industry begin to decline, and what were the main reasons for its decline?

How does the present condition of the Rapid River mining industry and of the population compare with their condition at the height of the industry's prosperity?

What does the future hold for life in the Rapid River watershed?

Title. *Transitions in Family Status: A Study of Five Generations of McGuires.*

Guide questions. What criteria are suitable for judging the level of an individual's and a family's social status?

Who were Sean and Maggie McGuire? From what backgrounds did they come when they settled in San Francisco in the late nineteenth century? What was their social status as judged by the criteria adopted in this research project?

Who were the descendents of Sean and Maggie McGuire over the next four generations?

What were the descendents' positions in terms of the criteria used in this study for determining individuals' and families' social status?

What implications do the results of this research project hold for future investigations of social status?

With these examples of historical perspectives in mind, we turn now to seven versions of historical methodology—chronicle, explanatory history, life-course study, evaluative history, combination history, biography, and autobiography.

Chronicles

Description. A *chronicle*, as the term is intended here, is a narrative tracing a sequence of events in the life of a community, institution, geographical region, nation, or the like over a period of years. A chronicle in its pure form is limited to telling what happened to whom, where, how, and when, without the author speculating about what caused events to occur as they did or judging whether individuals or events were desirable or undesirable, good or bad. *A Chronicle of Shawnee County* is an example of such a history.

Typical procedure. The following are two common approaches to composing a chronicle.

The first method consists of a researcher gathering a host of information about the chosen scope or topic, arranging the information in chronological order, and selecting those portions of the data that will be described in the account. This selection process can be guided either by the historian's intuitive impression of which people and events are most worth including or by the author's searching through the material to find one or more themes to feature in the account. The chosen themes can be cast as questions that direct decisions about what to include in the final product and about how to organize the narrative.

The second method involves the researcher bringing prepared themes to the task of searching for information. As in the above approach, the themes can be cast as questions that focus attention on the kinds of information needed. Thus, a researcher hunts through material from a particular historical period and extracts only those events that appear useful for answering the theme questions. For instance, in the case of *A Chronicle of Shawnee County*, the author takes notes solely about matters relevant to the study's five guide questions.

Advantages. The most obvious value of chronicles is that they preserve the memory of past events that otherwise would be lost to future generations.

Limitations. Perhaps the greatest threat to the accuracy of historical accounts is the restricted quantity and quality of information available to a researcher. In other words, the historian is forced to work with an incomplete collection of primary data. A variety of factors over the past have contributed to the loss or distortion of historical records. Throughout the centuries, valuable books and letters have been destroyed by fire and flood. In wartime, armies intentionally demolish the libraries and archives of the vanquished peoples. The victors in revolutions and political elections replace the defeated forces' accounts of events with their own version of what took place. Manuscripts, letters, books, and newspapers are lost through the neglect or ignorance of people who fail to recognize the potential future importance of those materials. In addition, many significant social developments may never have been cast in written form for any of several reasons—the particular society had only a spoken form of language, or the development occurred within a segment of the population that was illiterate, or those people who might have recorded the events did not consider them worth writing about. Consequently, no documentation of such developments became available.

A second limitation of chronicles results from the fact that no historical study is an "objective" account of reality. Instead, every chronicle is heavy laden with the author's subjective judgments. The scope of the topic studied, the questions that guide the choice of events and people to include, the methods of collecting information, and the way the final narrative is organized—all involve subjective judgments. Therefore, historians may be accused of distorting the picture of the past because they bring to their work a bias (religious, philosophical, theoretical, ethnic, political, social-class) that predisposes them to favor certain source materials and to discount others.

In view of these risks to the authenticity and balance of accounts of the past, conscientious historians adopt several safeguards to promote the accuracy of their work. One way is to obtain multiple reports of a particular event or document in order to determine how closely different versions agree. For instance, the minutes of a city-council meeting can be compared with a newspaper report of the incident or against interviews with people who participated in the meeting. Where there are contradictions between accounts of an episode, the researcher may choose to present each account for readers to judge for themselves and, perhaps, offer arguments in support of each version; or the author may adduce a line of logic that favors one account over another.

A third limitation of chronicles is that readers often are not satisfied with only a retelling of events. They want the author to suggest what the events mean, such as (a) why episodes occurred as they did, (b) how events might have happened another way if conditions had been different, (c) who was affected by the episodes, or (d) what the recounted events portend for the future.

Further resources. More detailed guidance in preparing chronicles is offered in Broomsedge (2002) and Larocca (2002).

Explanatory Histories

Description. In an explanatory history, the author is especially interested in the causes of events. Thus, the question of why things happened in a particular way is the historian's central concern, and that concern guides the choice of episodes, of people, and of significant environmental circumstances to include.

Typical procedure. Like chronicles, explanatory histories usually consist of selected episodes and eras presented in chronological sequence. However, unlike the authors of pure chronicles, explanatory historians' choice what to offer in their narrative is guided by of a theory of cause. The theory represents the researcher's estimate of how one event or combination of events determined—entirely or at least partially—what happened later. For example, what has been referred to as the *great-person theory* proposes that important events are chiefly the result of a particular individual's actions. If that person had not assumed the role that he or she played in life, history would have turned out quite differently. In contrast to the great-person interpretation, an *influential-times theory* holds that significant events result, not from a particular individual's actions, but, rather, from the confluence of a combination of multiple factors. So, if a particular person (political leader, inventor, scholar, industrialist) had not been present at the time, some other person would have assumed that same role, and events would have occurred in much the same way. A third theoretical position combines both the great-person and influential-times perspectives and explains history as the interaction between influential individuals and the societal and physical conditions of the era.

In addition to the great-person and influential-times concepts, there are a great many other theories of cause that can determine the contents and form that an explanatory history assumes. For example, *conflict theory* explains historical outcomes as the result of competition between two or more contending individuals or groups. *Social-exchange theory* interprets events in terms of conventional ways individuals and groups respond to how they are treated by others. *Social-evolution theory* views history as a progression of increasingly mature forms of social organization.

There appear to be three principal sources of the theories that historians employ. One source is the historiography literature—descriptions of techniques and theories of historical research. A second source is a historical account that someone else has written. A third source is the collection of episodes the author intends to describe and explain. This third approach qualifies as *grounded theory*, in the sense of the researcher creating a method of interpretation by analyzing a sequence of historical events, then estimating which earlier events were responsible for the later ones and how such a causal process operated.

At the beginning of this chapter, *The Rise and Decline of Mining in the Rapid River Watershed* is an explanatory history and illustrates the kinds of questions that the historian hopes to answer. Some of the questions—as in the case of chronicles—ask only for a description of events.

- At the height of mining in the watershed, what was the size and composition of the population and of institutions serving the population (government, businesses, schools, churches, entertainment establishments)?

However, other questions obligate the historian to explain the causes of events.

- When did the mining industry begin to decline, and what were the main reasons for its decline?

Advantages. The chief advantage of explanatory histories is that they provide what many readers highly value—not just a description of happenings but also a way to account for why episodes occurred as they did.

Limitations. Like chronicles, the accuracy of explanatory histories is threatened by a lack of complete information from the past. Furthermore, the author's theory of cause limits which events—from among all those in the available records—will be described. Each theory also delimits the sorts of causal connections the author proposes among the recounted events. In other words, an explanatory history is inevitably an edited, biased view of the past.

Further resources. The following references include useful information about writing explanatory history: Arthur, Bridenthal, Kelly-Gadol, & Lerner, 1976; Bentley, 1997; *Broomsedge Chronicles Writing Samples,* 2002; McCaw, 2000; Stuchtey & Wende, 2000.

Life-Course Studies

Description. One explanatory method that has attracted attention in recent decades is based on a life-course approach to human development that attempts to answer the question: How is a person's development influenced by the condition of the surrounding society at each juncture of the individual's lifespan? In effect, life-course methodology focuses on the result of a biologically evolving individual's interacting with social contexts that are sometimes stable and other times transitory.

Two assumptions underlying life-course methodology concern (a) societal stability and change and (b) the time and place in which an individual is located when social conditions are stable and when they are in flux. The first assumption holds that each individual is born into, and raised within, a society that moves through phases of stability and change that can significantly influence a person's development (Elder, 1996; Elder, Modell, & Parke, 1993). The second assumption is that each person is located in a particular time and place in relation to the society's phases. Hence, "the influence of a historical event on the life course depends on the stage at which individuals experience the event" (Elder, 1996, p. 52)

Among the significant macro-societal features that can vary with the passing of time are ones related to

public order and safety (peace vs. war, riots, civil disobedience, strikes, crime)

politics (system of governance—democratic, autocratic, socialistic)

economics (prosperity vs. depression, capitalism vs. state socialism, job market, credit availability, workforce productivity, income levels)

social-class structure (stability of classes, types and degrees of differences among classes, ease of mobility from one class to another)

ethnic composition (numbers and sizes of recognized ethnic divisions, extent of amicable vs. antagonistic relations among divisions, likenesses and differences among divisions [physical appearance, customs, usual roles in the society])

transportation and communication media (wagon, train, automobile, bus, airplane, books, newspapers, telephones, television, computer networks)

The relationship between when children arrive in the world and the timing of societal eras is portrayed in Figure 2-1 with five age cohorts—children born in 1920, 1940, 1960, 1980, and 1995 (Thomas, 2001).

Figure 2-1

Relationship of Societal Conditions and Birth Cohorts

Indicative Societal Events & Trends		Decades	Birth Cohorts
			One Two Three Four Five
U.S. women win voting rights	Ku Klux Klan power increases	1920	
Popularity of autos grows	Probusiness U.S. government		
Stock market crash	Great economic depression	1930	
Alcohol prohibition repealed	High unemployment rate		
Roosevelt's New Deal	Labor unions grow strong		
U.S. enters World War II	High wartime employment	1940	
Wartime economic prosperity	Wartime family separation		
GI-Bill: veterans enter college	Postwar labor strikes	1950	
United Nations formed	Postwar baby boom		
McCarthy communist scare	School racial integration		
Civil rights demonstrations	Youths rebel against authority	1960	
Vietnam War	Illicit drug-use increases		
Anti-Vietnam War protests	Sexual freedom	1970	
Feminist movement	Postmodernism introduced		
Affirmative-action programs	Rising divorce rate		
High interest rates	Increased teenage pregnancies	1980	
Credit cards: easy credit	Gay rights movement		
High inflation	AIDS infections increase	1990	
Low inflation	Computer networks		
Low interest rates	1/3 of U.S. children in		
Low unemployment	one-parent families	2000	

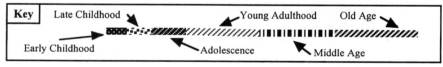

Key	Late Childhood	Young Adulthood	Old Age
Early Childhood		Adolescence	Middle Age

Source: R. M. Thomas. (2001). *Recent Theories of Human Development*. Thousand Oaks, CA: Sage. By permission of the publisher.

Consider, first, American children born in 1920 (Cohort One). World War I ended just two years before members of the 1920 cohort were born. Later that year, American women were accorded the right to vote in all public elections. In the economic sphere, the U.S. government adopted probusiness policies, issued injunctions against striking workers, raised tariffs on imported goods, and limited immigrants to 164,000 annually, with immigration quotas favoring European nations. The stock market flourished under conditions of financial prosperity, of few controls on investment practices, and of easy credit. The popularity of automobiles, radios, and movies grew rapidly, thereby offering children of Cohort One mobility and access to entertainment that children from no previous cohort had enjoyed. As the decade advanced, the Ku Klux Klan (with its anti-Negro, anti-Jewish, anti-Catholic program) grew in membership and power. Racial discrimination was widespread. Then, in 1929 the stock market crashed, helping launch the Great Depression—a disaster from which the nation would not entirely recover until industrial production rose with the advent of World War II at the end of the 1930s. To cope with the depression throughout the 1930s, President Franklin Roosevelt introduced a variety of social reconstruction measures under the label New Deal. Controls were placed on banks and on the stock market. A federal social-security program was inaugurated to ensure that people would have an income in their old age. During the 1930s, membership in labor unions grew rapidly, accompanied by a new level of political activity on the part of workers. The decade closed with Europe at war and the U.S. populace divided in their opinions about whether the U.S. should actively support Britain and France in the fight against Germany and Italy.

Now to Cohort Two. The question of the U.S. entering the war was settled in December, 1941, when Japanese planes attacked military installations in Hawaii. Thus, many children born in 1940 would be raised during early childhood by their mothers and grandparents, because their fathers were away in the armed forces during World War II. For a substantial number of children, this early separation from their fathers would contribute to a difficult child-father relationship after the father returned home (Stolz, 1968). During the 1960s, members of Cohort Two were between ages 20 and 30, participating in the changed youth culture of that decade. For some youths—but certainly not all, and probably not the majority—this would mean rebelling against authorities, joining civil rights and antiwar demonstrations, using illicit drugs, and frequently changing sex partners.

In the 1960s, Cohort Two members would become the parents of Cohort Three children and often provide a different family context than they themselves had experienced as children during and after World War II. Unlike the Cohort Two child, some Cohort Three children could more often see their family's and neighborhood's "normal way of life" as featuring marijuana and cocaine, casual sex, and rebellion against traditional authorities. Twenty years later, in the 1980s, members of Cohort Two would be middle-aged, some of them now grandparents. But with the growing incidence of divorce, many would not be with their original conjugal partners.

Members of Cohort Three—now the parents of Cohort Four—would bring the attitudes acquired during their childhood to the task of childrearing, including viewpoints from the growing feminist movement that asserted women's rights to pursue their own careers, either inside or outside of marriage. Cohort Four children would grow up at a time of easy financial credit, with many parents taking advantage of credit cards to indulge their own and their offsprings' desire for material goods in a spirit of, "We deserve to live well." During the middle and latter 1990s, financial interest rates were lower, credit not so easy, inflation low, and employment rates high. The United States labor market now differed significantly from that of the 1940s when manufacturing had been a dominant source of jobs in the United States. By the 1990s, many low-skill factory jobs had moved overseas to countries with low labor costs, so that jobs in the United States were increasingly in service and sales activities, with the better-paying jobs requiring specialized skills, such as those involving computers. In the realm of sexual behavior, children in Cohort Four would newly face choices posed by the popularizing of casual sexual intercourse in the mass-communication media (television, computer networks), the advance of the gay rights movement, and the growing incidence of AIDS (acquired immune deficiency syndrome).

Finally, children born in 1995 would be affected in their late childhood and adolescence by the changes in societal conditions that would appear during the early years of the new millennium. (Thomas, 2001, pp. 97-99)

In summary, not only are societal trends reflected in the lives of children who constitute a given birth cohort, but the lives of individuals from different cohorts are linked in ways that also influence development, particularly when the values and lifestyles of one cohort conflict with those of another, thereby resulting in disagreements between parents and their children as well as among grandparents, parents, and the young.

Typical procedure. One popular approach to conducting a life-course study consists of (a) specifying the individual or group whose development is to be analyzed, (b) designating the time period to be encompassed by the study, (c) identifying influential events and conditions in the broader societal context during that time period, and (d) estimating how those conditions influenced the development of the focal individuals or groups at different times during their life spans.

Advantages. The principal value of life-course studies derives from their focusing attention on how the periodically shifting conditions in the surrounding society affect people's development at different junctures during their life span.

Limitations. Producing a life-course account of people's lives poses a considerable challenge for the researcher, who is obliged to identify which events in the surrounding society exerted significant influence on the people's fate and convincingly links those events in a causal chain to the twists and turns of individuals' lives.

Further resources. Additional information about the conduct of life-course research can be found in Elder, 1996; Elder, Modell, & Parke, 1993; Heckhausen & Schulz, 1999; and Kreppner, 1989.

Evaluative Histories

Description. An evaluative history is one that features judgments of the desirability/undesirability, propriety/impropriety, efficiency/inefficiency, or morality/immorality of events and people's actions. In effect, evaluative histories are accounts of the past whose content and form are heavily influenced by the historian's value judgments. A key purpose of such works is to present a persuasive case in support of the convictions held by the historian about what was good and what was bad during a selected time period or set of past events.

Typical procedure. Evaluative histories, like chronicles and explanatory histories, usually include a large amount of description of people, physical environments, social conditions, and specific episodes (births, marriages, deaths, wars, floods, elections, inventions, publications, and more). The choice of which conditions and episodes should be included in the account is heavily influenced by the author's opinion about what was desirable or undesirable about the period on which the history focuses. Hence, as the historian chooses what to write about, he or she has in mind a set of criteria for distinguishing good from bad, desirable from undesirable, or proper from improper. In many evaluative histories (perhaps in most), those values are not stated outright but must be inferred from the author's appraisals, as in these examples:

> "Through the practice of apartheid, the European colonists violated the Africans' right to freedom and self-determination."
>
> "The teenager was then expelled, because school personnel, quite understandably, could not tolerate the foul talk and lack of respect for authority that the youth displayed."
>
> "The foolish adoption of a rule forbidding the telling of ethnic jokes increased the strained relations between employees and the company's top officials."

I am convinced that the task of composing a well-crafted evaluative history is performed more efficiently if the author, at the beginning, has consciously determined what set of values will be espoused in the history rather than if the author depends solely on intuitive appraisals during the process of writing. Not only is the precision of writing the history improved by establishing an intentional set of values to guide the appraisal of historical events; but if the author explains those values early in the historical account, readers can be aware at the outset of the evaluative vantage point from which the history has been written.

Among the example of histories described at the beginning of this chapter, the one titled *Transitions in Family Status: A Study of Five Generations of McGuires* is an evaluative type. As in chronicles and explanatory histories, some of the guide questions call for factual description.

- Who were Sean and Maggie McGuire? From what backgrounds did they come when they settled in San Francisco in the late nineteenth century? Who were the descendents of Sean and Maggie McGuire over the next four generations?

Other questions call for an appraisal guided by a set of values.

- What was Sean and Maggie McGuire's social status? What were the social positions of their descendents?

The author of this history obviously intends to tell readers the set of values used for estimating social status.

- What criteria are suitable for judging the level of an individual's and a family's social status?

Advantages. Readers are frequently interested in judging the desirability and propriety of people and events of the past. An evaluative history focuses attention on such matters and offers the historian's judgments—ones that readers can ponder and accept or reject.

Limitations. Evaluative histories suffer from the same potential shortcomings that limit the accuracy of chronicles, that is, the elusiveness of trustworthy records of the past. In addition, an evaluative history is crucially affected by the author's values that determine which events and what sort of interpretation the author includes.

Combination Histories

It seems obvious that historical accounts are usually not limited to a factual recital of occurrences (a pure chronicle), an estimate of causes of events (a dominantly explanatory history), or the assessment of events (a decidedly evaluative history). Most histories are some combination of factual descriptions, attempts to identify causes, and appraisals of events and people's actions. Thus, what really distinguishes studies that are identified as chronicles, explanatory histories, or evaluative histories is the degree of emphasis that authors place on factual descriptions, estimated causes, and judgments of desirability. The more that a historical account mixes these three components in equal measure, the more they qualify as *combination histories,* as that term is intended here.

It is apparent that combination histories are subject to the advantages and limitations of all three of the constituent types—chronicles, causal explanations, and evaluations.

Biographies

Description. A biography is a record of another person's life. The record is usually in written form, but it can also be audiorecorded or videorecorded. Or it may be composed of a combination of media, such as a written record accompanied by photographs and perhaps audiorecorded or videorecorded excerpts from the biographee's life. A biography can be in the form of a chronicle, consisting solely of a description of episodes in an individual's, or it can include the author's interpretation (estimates of cause, evaluations of people and events). Various sorts of interpretation may be offered, such as (a) suggested themes, interests, or problems that figured prominently in the person's life, (b) judgments about how other people affected the biographee's development, (c) appraisals of the person's decisions at key junctures of her or his life, and (d) speculation about how the biographee was affected by the physical and social environments that she or he inhabited.

Preparing an interpretive biography involves the study of documents that describe critical incidents and defining moments in an individual's life—including such documents as autobiographies, biographies, letters, diaries, oral and personal histories, newspapers, and obituaries (Denzin, 1989). In addition, preparing a biography of someone who has lived in recent times typically involves interviewing people who knew the biographee personally or who were well acquainted with the subject's habits and reputation.

Purposes and procedure. Biographies can be designed to serve such functions as:

- Preserving a record of the personal development and the contributions of a unique or prominent person.
- Correcting previous accounts by presenting a revised portrayal of an individual who earlier had been depicted as a different sort of person.
- Through the medium of one person's life, teaching readers lessons about wise and unwise ways of living.
- Tracing backstage and onstage actions of the biographee, with particular attention to ways in which that individual reconciled or failed to reconcile conflicts in his or her life, thereby illustrating how contradictions affected the individual's fate and events of the times (Pfitzer, 1991).

With one or more such themes in mind, the researcher hunts for incidents in the biographee's life that support and elucidate those themes, then writes a narrative that conveys this version of the individual's life in an interesting and persuasive manner.

Advantages. Perhaps the most important advantage of biographies is their ability to depict the unique character of a person's life—a life which, in its details and pattern of development, is unlike anyone else's. Biographies can inform readers of persistent themes, consistencies, and inconsistencies in the subjects' lives by illuminating the historical, cultural contexts in which those personalities evolve. Readers may also derive lessons about life that are inferred from the behavior revealed in the biographer's account.

Limitations. Because interpretive biography involves researchers drawing inferences about the intentions, goals, beliefs, values, and feelings of the people they write about, there is the danger that those inferences may be in error. It's not unusual for a biographer to miss finding all of the evidence bearing on a conclusion or interpretation. Consequently, the author may be criticized for being too subjective, for basing interpretation on inadequate sources, or—out of ulterior motive— adopting a biased perspective that results in an account that is unduly favorable to the subject (too "soft") or unreasonably critical (too "harsh"). If the author is hasty, thereby drawing conclusions from an incomplete search for evidence, critics may charge that he or she has produced "blitzkrieg biography," a lightning-fast work of a misleading nature.

Further resources. References offering guidance in writing biographies include Atkinson,1998; Kridel, 1998; Denzin, 1989; Magarey, Guerin, & Hamilton, 1992; Parke, 1996; and Young-Bruehl, 1998.

Autobiographies

Description. An autobiography is an person's story of his or her own life prepared entirely by that person (*traditional autobiography*) or created with the assistance of someone else who has the time, patience, and expertise to create a well-crafted narrative (*assisted autobiography*).

The typical intent of autobiography is to provide readers an insider's view of a life by describing how events are interpreted by the person who has lived those events and who is the product of their influence. Consequently, autobiographies are intentionally subjective—designed to reveal the motives, ambitions, values, joys, and sorrows that help explain the author's life.

Theses and dissertations rarely assume the form of autobiography, because the content of a graduate student's own life, or the manner of describing that life, is usually not seen by faculty advisers as sufficiently interesting or instructive to serve as the focus of scholarly attention. However, in the postmodern atmosphere of some university departments in recent decades, autobiographical theses and dissertations are not merely tolerated by are warmly welcomed.

Assisted autobiographies, in which a graduate student serves as the mediator who organizes the life material and writes the narrative, are more often considered acceptable by faculty members as proper objects of research than are traditional autobiographies. Such assisted narratives are perhaps best labeled *authorized biographies*—built on information supplied entirely by the person whose life story is told and endorsed by that person as an authentic description of his or her life.

Typical procedure. There are several ways that assisted autobiographies may be prepared. One way consists of the graduate student bringing a preconceived organizational plan that contains a series of topics or questions which define the intended contents of the final narrative. The task of the person whose life story is being told is to furnish answers to the questions, in either oral or written form. Answering the questions may also include providing letters, diaries, newspaper clippings, photographs, and memorabilia from which the thesis or dissertation writer can draw information.

Another way is for the graduate student to bring no preconceived questions or organizational plan to the task. Instead, the person whose life is being depicted is asked to talk or write at great length about her of his life history, describing incidents and people that come to mind as significant influences. The student-collaborator then searches through this mass of raw material to identify themes, decision points, and links of cause-and-effect which characterize the subject's life; and finally casts the result of the search as a narrative that traces the themes and influences throughout the subject's life.

Advantages. Autobiographies are valued for their ability to portray an person's life from the person's own perspective, revealing motives, beliefs, emotional reactions, and interpretations of events that might not be discovered by an outsider functioning entirely as a biographer.

Limitations. The accuracy of autobiographies depends on both the clarity of people's memories and their willingness to reveal information they feel might prove embarrassing. Autobiographies, in effect, give their subjects the opportunity to be self-serving—to concoct a partially fictional account that portrays them as more adventuresome, influential, noble, creative, oppressed, exploited, or self-sacrificing than is deserved. Consequently, the vision of reality conveyed in an autobiography may, either intentionally or unwittingly, be somewhat at odds with the truth.

Further resources. Examples of autobiographies and descriptions of how they can be prepared are found in Anderson, 1997; Andrews, 1993; Eakin, 1991); Reed-Danahay, 1997; and Stone, 1981.

Conclusion

The purpose of this chapter has been to offer brief descriptions of several popular research methods that depend on the collection and analysis of information from the past. Those methods have included historical approaches (chronicles, explanatory histories, life-course studies, evaluative histories, combined types), biographies, and autobiographies. Although such methods are chiefly qualitative, they may also include minor amounts of quantitative matter, such as population comparisons, results of public-opinion surveys, school-enrollment figures, and changes in the incidence of various technologies (modes of communication and transportation, industrial-production techniques) over time.

3
Present-Status Perspectives— Qualitative

Whereas the historical methods described in Chapter 2 depend on information collected about the past, the methods in Chapters 3 and 4 depend on information about the present condition of whatever is being studied. Chapter 3 focuses on qualitative perspectives (verbal portrayals of the current status of people and events in terms of *kinds* of characteristics and actions) and Chapter 4 on quantitative perspectives (the current status of people and events in terms of *amounts* and *frequencies* of characteristics and actions).

As suggested in Chapter 1, the expression *qualitative research*, in its most general sense, refers to collecting and interpreting information about some phenomenon without concern for quantities. Qualitative approaches typically involve the analysis of the way a variety of characteristics are patterned, as in the patterning of reciprocal influences among members of an athletic team, of the diverse styles of communication within different families, or of the conflicts among a community's ethnic groups.

Because there is no standard system for classifying qualitative methods, the scheme adopted in this chapter is rather arbitrary, employing three of the more popular terms for identifying qualitative approaches. As the discussion develops, it becomes apparent that there is a good deal of overlapping of the three types—case studies, ethnographies, and experience narratives.

Case Studies

Description. A case study typically consists of a description of an entity and the entity's actions. Frequently, case studies also offer explanations of why the entity acts as it does. Entities that are the focus of case studies can be of various sorts, such as individuals, groups, organizations, or events.

- *Individuals*— A Typical Week in the Life of a High School Principal
  Treating an Autistic Teenager
  Paulo Freire as an Educational Administrator

- *Groups*— A Bell Choir on Tour
  Las Vegas Show Girls
  An Inner-City Street Gang

- *Organizations*— The State Life-Insurance Commission
  Activities of the Funeral Directors' Association
  Politics in a Local Teamsters Union

- *Events*— The New Year's Day Riot
  The 2003 Bay City Election
  Bush Family Reunions

Although case studies usually focus on a single entity, they can assume a comparative form whenever the likenesses and differences between two or more entities are analyzed. A special type of case study is *ethnography*, whose characteristics are described in the next section of this chapter.

Typical Procedure. As with other forms of research, a convenient way to specify the focus of a case study and to select suitable ways to gather information is to identify the questions that the study is expected to answer.

In planning case studies, researchers always have in mind questions or problems they hope to solve. Those questions can range from the general to the specific, as the following pair of examples demonstrates.

General— How does that social-studies class operate? What goes on in that classroom?

Specific— How much freedom do students in the social-studies class have to express their opinions, choose topics they will study, and choose their methods of study?

General— What is life like for Luke Johnson in his role as a candidate for Congress?

Specific— How does Luke Johnson obtain campaign funds, how does he decide where to campaign, what is his position on important political issues, and how much of his speeches and campaign literature does he write by himself?

The kinds of questions a case study is designed to answer serve as useful guides to the methods the researcher can use for collecting evidence. For instance, the question "How does that social-studies class operate?" implies that the most reasonable method for answering it will be for the researcher to spend hours in the classroom observing what goes on. In comparison, specific questions are more helpful for focusing the researcher's attention during observation periods and for suggesting other methods of data collection. Those other methods might include interviews with students and the teacher to learn how the class's topics and methods of study are decided. Or answers to the questions could be compiled by means of questionnaires that students and the teacher fill out.

In summary, the more specific the questions that guide the research, the more help the researcher receives in selecting appropriate data-collection techniques.

Advantages. The greatest advantage of a case study is that it permits a researcher to reveal the way a multiplicity of factors have interacted to produce the unique character of the entity that is the subject of the research. If we can assume that every person, group, organization, or event is unique—unlike any other in its details—then the case study becomes a suitable vehicle for depicting that uniqueness.

Limitations. An important limitation of the case approach is that generalizations or principles drawn from one case can be applied to other cases only at considerable risk of error. This limitation becomes important when people who read research reports are not interested solely in the outcomes of a particular investigation but are interested in how the report of a given case can help them understand other similar people, institutions, or events. Hence, the question: "What knowledge derived from the present example can validly be applied to explaining a broader collection of instances?" The risk of error in assuming that the results in other cases will be identical to the results in the present case can be reduced if the investigator studies more than one entity in order to identify likenesses and differences between entities and thereby recognize how much confidence can be placed in conclusions drawn from the first case studied.

Further resources. Detailed case-study approaches are described in the following references: Nazarea, 1999; Scholz & Tietje, 2002; Stewart & Strathern, 2000; Wallace & Gruber, 1989.

Ethnographies

Description. As suggested earlier in this chapter, ethnography is a special kind of case study in which the researcher, over a period of time, participates in the activities of the people, organization, or event being investigated. Ethnography is the chief method used by cultural anthropologists to understand the structure and inner workings of a group they have chosen to study. Here are two typical ways ethnography has been defined.

Ethnography [is the] descriptive study of a particular human society or the process of making such a study. Contemporary ethnography is based almost entirely on fieldwork and requires the complete immersion of the anthropologist in the culture and everyday life of the people who are the subject of the study. (Ethnography, 1994, p. 582)

Ethnography means, literally, a picture of the "way of life" of some identifiable group of people. Conceivably, those people could be any culture-bearing group, in any time and place. . . . Particular individuals, customs, institutions, or events are of anthropological interest as they relate to a generalized description of the life-way of a socially interacting group. (Wolcott, 1988, p. 188)

The societies on which ethnographies focus include those found within a classroom, a labor union, a social club, a family, a neighborhood, an automobile agency, a business office, a women's organization, a church, a department in a university, and far more.

Whereas most case studies are intended to reveal the individualistic attributes of a particular person, organization, or event, the more common purpose of ethnographies is to identify beliefs and customs shared by members of a social system. In effect, case studies typically emphasize features that make one person or organization different from others, whereas ethnographies more often emphasize the commonalities that unify members of a group.

Typical Procedure.   An ethnographer usually assumes the role of participant-observer, donning the analytical lens of a cultural anthropologist and entering the chosen group for an extended period of time to study how the group functions. For instance, a graduate student assumes the position of a teacher's aide in a kindergarten, thereby able to experience classroom events from a teacher's vantage point and to mingle with the children on the playfield and in the lunchroom. Or a researcher joins a local political party's staff of volunteers, attends meetings, accepts assignments, and talks with coworkers about the group's activities and the members' interactions.

No society—whatever its size—is sufficiently simple to be analyzed completely within a single research project. Thus, as with historical research, it is necessary for an investigator to select the aspects of culture that will be the focus of the particular study. Those aspects can be identified by questions that guide the collection of data. Guide questions can be either selected before the focal group is studied or generated after the researcher has already gained some experience observing the group. Frequently, the guide questions derive from both of these sources—preconceived general queries plus additional questions that surface during the process of observation. Consider, for example, how one of the following questions would influence a researcher's observations of a group differently than would any of the other three questions.

- From what sources and by what methods do members of the group acquire their knowledge and skills? In other words, how have members of the group learned what they know and do?
- What is the power and authority structure within the group? That is, who has power over whom, why, and how is that power exerted?
- In what ways are the group members' activities and welfare dependent on their material culture—tools, equipment, supplies, and apparatus used for shelter, dress, transportation, communication, amusement, protection, and the like?
- What religious beliefs and practices are widespread within the group, and what functions do those beliefs and practices apparently perform in people's lives?

Advantages. Ethnographic research can serve various purposes. It can reveal characteristics shared among members of a group—characteristics that render the group's culture distinctive, thereby helping consumers of the research understand how and why one group differs from another. Ethnographies can also expose the internal operations of a group or organization by identifying the relative influence of different members, tracing routes of communication, suggesting the origins of the group's activities, showing how people achieve their status, and identifying the sanctions applied to ensure that members abide by group standards.

Limitations: Denzin (1997, p. 3) has cautioned researchers not to expect ethnography to portray the "objective truth" about a group or organization. Consequently, he has defined ethnography as "that form of inquiry and writing that produces descriptions and accounts about the ways of life of the writer and those written about." Therefore, even though authors may assert that they have simply recorded "what really happened," their account is inevitably a rendition filtered through their particular mental magnifying glass, resulting in different versions of the same event as seen by different investigators.

As in other kinds of case studies, conclusions drawn from the ethnographic study of one group can be applied to other groups only at considerable peril because of the unique conditions that may determine the pattern of life in each setting. Furthermore, participant-observers can become so intimately immersed in a group that they lose the objectivity of perception that they intended to bring to the study. If, on the other hand, ethnographers fail to engage intimately in the life of the group they study—and thereby derive a flawed impression of the group's modes of interaction—they are apt to convey an inaccurate picture of what life in that environment means to the people who inhabit it.

Further resources. Recent examples of ethnographic approaches are available in Carspecken, 1996; Erickson & Stull, 1998; Fetterman, 1998; Goodall, 2000; Marcus, 1999; Stringer, 1997; Wolcott, 1999.

Experience Narratives

Description: The term *experience narrative,* as intended here, refers to an account of an event—or of several related events—as described by a person who was involved in the described episodes, either as an active participant or as an observer. In other words, experience narratives are stories about influential incidents in a person's own life.

Whereas an autobiography recounts an insider's view of the author's life that extends over a lengthy time period and illuminates various facets of that life, an experience narrative encompasses a more limited time period and focuses on more restricted subject matter.

In recent decades, people's descriptions and interpretations of their own experiences have been increasingly accepted as suitable versions of research by academicians, particularly academicians of a postmodern persuasion.

The purpose of experience narratives (also known as *personal stories*) is to reveal individualistic perceptions of selected life episodes. The emphasis is on differences among people in their experiences and in their ways of viewing their lives, with the account including individuals' own modes of communication—words, gestures, songs, dances, symbols, art works—rather than described solely in a researcher's words. In the experience-narrative approach, the researcher acts chiefly as an organizer or compiler of the narratives. Therefore, studies of this sort are cooperative efforts in which the compiler (the thesis or dissertation author) and the informant (the person whose experience is being reported) are credited with being co-researchers.

Typical Procedure: One familiar approach to conducting experience-narrative research consists of six steps (Thomas & Brubaker, 2000, pp. 110-111):

1. The compiler explains to the informant the realm of life experiences that is the focus of attention, such as the informant's (a) present conception of God, (b) becoming an abused child, (c) most memorable holiday, (d) suffering discrimination, (e) encounters with members of a particular ethnic group, or the like.

2. The compiler describes (a) the informant's expected role and why the informant's narrated experiences are valued and (b) the compiler's own role.

3. The informant speaks freely about the topic as the compiler records the narration verbatim, preferably through the use of an audio or video re-

corder so the account will be accurate. When such equipment is unavailable or the informant objects to its use, the compiler must depend on notes written at that time or as soon as possible after the session.

4. During the narration, the compiler may feel it necessary to offer prompts that keep the informant on the topic and encourage an elaboration of aspects that have been unclear or inadequately developed. For example, when investigating a respondent's conception of God, a compiler may ask, "What do you feel is your relationship to God?" or "Does God ever help you? And if so, how?"

5. In presenting the recorded narrative in the thesis or dissertation, the compiler prefaces the narrative with a description of:
   5.1 The research topic, that is, the aspect of life which has been the focus of the informant's story.
   5.2 Who the informant was and why such an informant is a suitable source of information.
   5.3 The division of labor between the informant and the compiler in the conduct of the research.
   5.4 The context of the narrative session.
   5.5 Conditions that may have influenced the outcome of the session.

Experience-narrative research assumes a comparative form when two or more individuals' accounts are included in the study. In that case, the researcher will likely point out common themes, similarities, and contrasts which appear in the several accounts.

Advantages. Narratives have the potential for demonstrating both the uniqueness of individuals' lives and the similarity among lives that are lived under different circumstances. In regard to uniqueness, narratives enable readers to participate vicariously in other people's thoughts and emotions that are associated with events the readers would never directly experience in their own lives. Furthermore, narratives collected from people living under very different circumstances can show that those individuals may have much in common in the desires, emotions, and responses they display under their dissimilar life conditions.

Limitations. Experience narratives are not effective devices for revealing how characteristics (education, wealth, type of occupation, ethnic background, religious affiliation, disease, and much more) are distributed throughout a population. Nor do narratives provide trustworthy generalizations (such as about causes of events or about solving problems) for understanding and treating people other than those whose personal stories have been compiled.

Further resources. For examples of experience narratives, see Almond, 2002; Chase & Rogers, 2001; Fabian, 2000; Gutiérrez-Jones, 2001; Lesage, 2002; Taylor, 1999.

Conclusion

The aim of this chapter has been to describe three closely related research approaches (case studies, ethnography, experience narratives) that depend chiefly on qualitative decision-making, that is, on the researcher drawing distinctions of *kind* rather than *amount*.

4
Present-Status Perspectives—
Quantitative

As noted in Chapter 3, the historical methods described in Chapter 2 depend on information collected about the past, while the methods in Chapters 3 and 4 depend on information about the present condition of whatever is being studied. In contrast to the qualitative perspectives offered in Chapter 3 (verbal portrayals of the current status of people and events), Chapter 4 describes quantitative research methods (the current status of people and events in terms of amounts and frequencies).

The three types of methods described in the following pages are surveys, correlation analyses, and experiments.

Surveys

Description. Survey methods involve gathering information about the current status of some *target variable* within a particular *collectivity*, then reporting a summary of the findings. The summary includes data in quantitative form.

A *target variable* is a specified characteristic of a group or collectivity. There is an enormous variety of potential target variables. For instance, just within the realm of schooling, surveys are conducted to determine (a) students' knowledge in a subject-matter field, (b) school enrollments, (c) curriculum content, (d) students' study habits, (e) the quality of school buildings, (f) the instructional use of computers, (g) teachers' salaries, (h) classroom discipline regulations, (i) types of learning objectives, (j) methods of selecting school principals, (k) the popularity of different classroom teaching methods, (l) the amount of funds spent per pupil, (m) the length of the school year, (n) the kind and amount of parent participation in school activities, and thousands of additional matters.

A *collectivity* is a group of things of a specified kind that becomes the focus of a survey. Collectivities can be people, objects, places, institutions, events, or time periods—or a combination of more than one of these variables. For example, in a survey of students' mathematical knowledge, the collectivity can consist of individuals (people) in public-school ninth grades (institutions) in Chicago (place) during 2003 (time period).

Typical procedure. Conducting a survey usually involves

- specifying the characteristic (target variable) of interest,
- identifying the collectivity that would display that variable (people, institutions, places, events, and the like),
- deciding how best to gather information from the collectivity,
- gathering the information, and
- summarizing the results in a readily comprehensible form.

A few of the many patterns that such components of surveys can assume are suggested in Table 4-1. The left column lists illustrative target variables. The center column identifies sources of information about the target variables. The right column suggests data-gathering techniques.

Obviously, the few examples in Table 4-1 represent only a miniscule number of topics that are the subject of surveys. Other survey topics could have served equally well as illustrations—such topics as laws, regulations, political systems, gross national products, cultural traditions, people's worldviews and life styles, food habits, occupations, leisure-time pursuits, possessions, artistic endeavors, recreational interests, social status, and far more.

Often the information needed in a research project is not obtained directly from people, institutions, or observed events. Instead, the information is drawn from previously conducted studies that bear on the project's topic. The researcher's task becomes one of (a) collecting multiple reports of research that focuses on the chosen topic, then (b) synthesizing the different studies' results in a manner that yields more comprehensive conclusions about the topic than could be drawn from any one study in the collection. The purpose of such a procedure is to combine reported studies in a way that shows which conclusions validly apply to the entire collection and which apply to no more than one or a few of the studies.

The expression *meta-analysis* identifies a particular form of synthesizing that has become increasingly popular in recent decades. Meta-analysis is based on the following line of reasoning.

> The traditional process of integrating [the conclusions from] a body of research literature is essentially intuitive and the style of reporting narrative. Because the reviewer's methods are often unspecified, it is usually difficult to discern how the original research findings have contributed to the integration. A careful analysis can sometimes reveal that different reviewers use

Table 4-1

Components of Direct-Data Surveys

Target variables	Information Sources	Data-gathering methods
Achievement:		
academic	school records	test scores, grades, awards
athletic	teams' record books, sports commentators	content analysis interviews
financial	income tax returns	content analysis
literary	book sales reports, critics' reviews	content analysis content analysis
theatrical	magazines, newspapers	content analysis
Customs:		
teenagers' clothing	students' appearance, magazines, TV shows	direct observation content analysis
dietary	people's self-reports restaurant managers	questionnaire interview
religious	church leaders	interview
	parishioners	interview
	church documents	content analysis
Opinions about:		
human rights	people	interview, opinionnaire
drinking, smoking	people	interview, opinionnaire
death penalty	people	interview, opinionnaire
social behavior	people	interview, opinionnaire
politicians	people	interview
ethnic relations	students	opinionnaire
Policies about:		
school discipline	faculty handbooks	content analysis
	teachers, principals	interview, questionnaire
college admission	college catalogues	content analysis
voting	election regulations	content analysis

the same research reports in support of contrary conclusions. . . . The most serious problem for reviewers to cope with is the volume of relevant research literature to be integrated. Most reviewers appear to deal with this by choosing only a subset of the studies. Some take the studies they know most intimately. Others take those they value most highly, usually on the basis of methodological quality. Few, however, give any indication of the means by which they selected studies for review. (McGaw, 1985, p. 3322)

The label *meta-analysis* identifies any quantitative integration of empirical research reports. Two varieties of meta-analytic methodology for defining the target variable of relevant studies and calculating the likenesses and differences among studies are those described by Glass, McGaw, and Smith (1981) and by Hunter, Schmidt, and Jackson (1982).

Advantages. Surveys are most useful for revealing the current status of a target variable within a particular entity, such as within a nation, region, neighborhood, religious denomination, ethnic group, political party, business organization, gender group, university, basketball league, and the like. Furthermore, the accuracy of description is enhanced if the status of variables is cast in numerical form (frequencies, percents, correlation coefficients, averages, extent of variability) than if the results are reported by means of such imprecise verbal expressions as *many, majority, a few, some, negligible amounts, often, rarely,* or *significantly more.*

Limitations. Because typical surveys report averages and percentages of the target variable as found within the collectivity, they fail to show the unique way that the target variable fits into the pattern of the individual units within the collectivity. For instance, a statewide survey of the reading skills of sixth-grade pupils—as reflected in standardized silent-reading test scores—will be reported as averages and amounts of variability in school districts and individual schools. The survey may also provide information (by school and by school district), about such things as the average socioeconomic status of pupils' families, the size of a school library's holdings, the average teacher's professional preparation, and the school's per-pupil expenditures.

However, the survey does not portray individual children's life conditions as those conditions affect children's reading skills, such as how adequately a girl's parents supervise her homework assignments, the amount and types of reading matter in her home, who her companions are and how they influence her interests, how she spends her time outside of school, the people she admires and emulates, her physical health, and far more. In short, quantitative surveys fail to describe the qualitative features that make for the uniqueness of each member of the collectivity that the survey is intended to represent.

Further resources. Suggestions about how to conduct surveys are available in the following references: Babbie, 1990; Barnett, 1991: Braverman & Slater, 1996; Fink & Kosecoff, 1998; Weisberg, Krasnick, & Bowen, 1996).

Correlation Analyses

Description. Correlation studies are designed to answer the general question: What happens to one variable when another variable changes? Or the question may be phrased as: To what extent does one variable change as another variable is altered? Such questions can assume any of the following forms when they are asked about two specific variables.

- Are girls generally more artistic than boys?
- How does the frequency and seriousness of injuries in auto accidents change when people are required to use seat belts?
- Do children from one-parent families succeed in school as well as those from two-parent families?
- Does the incidence of petty crime rise when a community's population-density increases?
- To what degree are voters' income levels related to voters' willingness to issue bonds for financing additional community-recreation facilities?
- Do teenagers express greater tolerance for people of varied ethnic backgrounds than do elderly individuals?
- What is the relationship between people's religious affiliations and how well they abide by federal income-tax regulations?

Descriptions of the relationship between variables can range in precision from very general verbal observations to highly specific statistical amounts. Consider these correlation statements that progress from the vague to the exact.

- As the dancer's chances to perform before an audience increased, so did her confidence.
- More boys than girls appeared interested in computer games.
- Following the drill sessions on word analysis, the students' spelling errors decreased by nearly a half.
- Eighty-three percent of rural residents and 16 percent of city dwellers voted for the farm-subsidy plan.
- The Pearson product-moment coefficient derived from comparing students' general-intelligence scores with their extroversion scores was +.27 for seventh-graders and +.38 for eleventh-graders.

Correlations can be either positive or negative. In positive correlations, an increase in one variable parallels an increase in the other, as occurred in the case of the dancer (more audience appearances are associated with more confidence). In negative correlations, an increase in one variable is accompanied by a decrease in the other, as in the spelling-test example (more drill is associated with fewer spelling errors). If, when one variable changes, nothing happens to the other, then the two variables are not correlated at all.

It's obvious that not all correlated things are associated with each other in the same degree. At the highest level of correlation, each change in one variable is accompanied by a comparable amount of change in the other variable. At the lowest level of correlation, change in one variable is associated with no change at all in the other variable. For instance, if blonds on the average have no more friends than do brunettes or redheads, then there is no correlation between hair color and quantity of friends.

Typical procedures. Various statistical procedures are available for expressing relationships, with each procedure designed to suit a particular form of data.

Consider, for example, the most frequently used method for calculating the degree of relationship between two variables—a technique introduced by the British statistician Karl Pearson (1857-1936) and identified by the symbol *r*. (More than 90% of all correlation coefficients reported in the research literature are Pearson *r*'s.) Pearson's *r* is most appropriate for judging the magnitude of relationship between two variables when each variable is in the form of a scale consisting of a series of equal intervals—such intervals as inches, miles, liters, pounds, minutes, dollars, and Centigrade degrees. Therefore, with Pearson's technique, we could measure the extent of correlation between children's heights and ages to answer the question "To what extent does children's growth in height increase exactly at the same rate as their age advances?" Let's assume that we measure a child's height on each birthday between ages 2 and 18. Let's also assume that we discover that the child has consistently grown exactly 2.1875 inches (6.6875 centimeters) per year. We could plot this outcome as a scatter diagram, showing that each additional year (the horizontal axis) was accompanied by an additional 2.1875 inches of height (the vertical axis) (Figure 4-1).

In Pearson's system, degrees of correlation can vary from 0.0 to 1.00. The case plotted in Figure 4-1 is an example of perfect +1.00 correlation. The points, at which the two variables—years and heights—meet, form a perfectly straight diagonal line, because each increase in age is accompanied by an increase in height that is identical at each age level. It is apparent, however, that such a case is extremely unlikely in real life. Not only do the young grow faster during some years than during others, but in later adolescence growth typically slows, so that annual increases do not form a straight diagonal line. Instead, the line bends down gradually in the late teens. Thus, the correlation plotted in Figure 4-2 is more realistic, showing a slower growth rate prior to puberty, then a rapid spurt

Figure 4-1

Pearson Correlation Coefficient +1.00

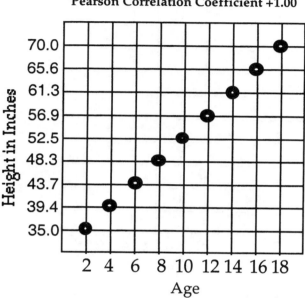

between ages 12 and 14. The Pearson coefficient for the growth pattern in Figure 4-2 is +.98. (If we were actually studying the relationship between age and height from age 2 to 18 or beyond, we would be slightly better served by using a variation of Pearson's formula that is referred to as *curvilinear correlation*, which would accommodate for the slowing of growth in the latter teens.)

Other scales that do not truly consist of same-size segments are often treated as if they had equal units, so that Pearson's method is still used in computing the degree of correlation between two variables. Intelligence tests and achievement tests are examples of measures that do not consist of same-size units, because the test items are not all of equal difficulty.

Consider, now, another situation. Imagine that we have developed a 60-item *Creative Imagination Inventory* that we administer to 20 adults, ages 30 to 60. Our intent is to test the hypothesis that creative imagination declines with advancing age. Therefore, after the participants have completed the inventories and we have examined their answers, we find that those folks' creative imagination scores ranged from a low of 15 to a high of 58. Plotting the points at which each score intersected with the

Figure 4-2

Pearson Correlation Coefficient +.98

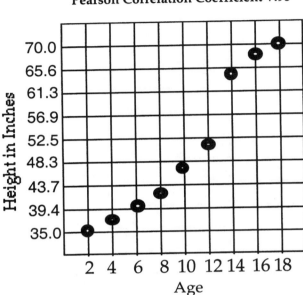

person's age produces the scatter diagram in Figure 4-3. The pattern of dots on the diagram suggests that there is very little relationship, if any at all, between the participants' ages and their scores on the inventory. We apparently can reject our hypothesis that creative imagination typically declines as people grow older.

We can now apply the above method of interpreting correlation coefficients to the following results of three research projects that yielded different magnitudes of relationship.

- Fourth-graders' scores on a standardized reading test and their scores on a mathematics test = +.82 (Slavin, 1984, p. 15)
- School achievement and self-concept = +35   (Follman, 1984, p. 702)
- Family size and Spanish-language achievement of secondary-school applicants in Mexico = -.16   (Palafox, Prawda, & Velez, 1994, p. 173)

The highest level of relationship (+.82) is between fourth-graders' scores on reading and on mathematics (a strong tendency for skilled readers to earn higher math scores than do poor readers). A far lower level of relationship (+35) is found between students' school achievement and their self-concepts (students with higher grades tend to have

Figure 4-3

Person Correlation Coefficient -.11

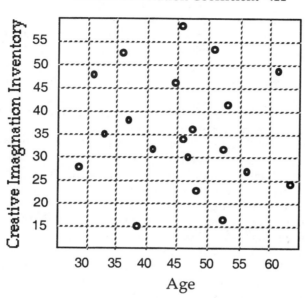

stronger self-concepts than those with lower grades, but there are still numerous exceptions to that tendency). To only a slight extent (-.16) do Mexican high school applicants from smaller families have greater command of the Spanish language than do ones from larger families (the correlation is negative because greater skill in Spanish is accompanied by smaller, rather than larger, family size). However, a coefficient as low as -.16 is so close to no correlation at all (0.0), that knowing the size of a girl's family is almost no help at all for predicting her mastery of Spanish or for predicting her family size from information about her Spanish-language test scores.

In each of these studies, both of the variables were in the form of equal-unit (or nearly-equal unit) scales, so that a Pearson-type computation was warranted. However, other sorts of variables call for other methods of computation. For instance, if two variables are in the form of a series of ranks (such as ranking students by popularity and by extent of their participation in extracurricular activities), Spearman's rank-order procedure—symbolized by the Greek letter ρ (rho)—is appropriate. Spearman coefficients, like Pearson r's, can range from 0 to 1.00 in either a positive or negative direction. Interpreting magnitudes of ρ is much like interpreting magnitudes of r.

Sometimes one of the two variables is in the form of a graduated sequence of quantities (heights, minutes, test scores) and the other in the form of a dichotomy (young/old, boy/girl, bilingual/monolingual). Two computational techniques for determining the association between an equal-unit variable and a dichotomized variable are the *biserial* and *point-biserial* methods. Each of these techniques yields correlation coefficients that are estimates of what the Pearson r would be if each variable formed a normally distributed series rather than one of them being a dichotomy.

When the two variables are both dichotomous, calculating a phi (r_ϕ) coefficient provides an estimate of a Pearson r.

Sometimes one of the variables does not increase at a constant rate. An example is the relationship between peoples' ages (which do advance as a regular rate) and their eye-hand coordination scores (which advance rapidly in childhood, remain rather steady through much of adulthood, and decline in old age). Thus, the relationship between age and eye-hand coordination assumes the form of a curve, thereby warranting the computation of a *curvilinear* correlation coefficient eta (η).

There are also additional ways to calculate the degree of relationship among variables. Which technique is most appropriate for a particular research project depends on the form in which the variables are cast (equal-unit scales, dichotomies, etc.) and the kind of research question being investigated.

Advantages. Using statistical techniques for calculating the degree of relationship between phenomena has the advantage of providing more precise information than do estimates of relationships that are cast in such phrases as *not much of a connection among . . ., a lot of influence on . . . , most of them can be expected to be. . . .,* or *they usually are . . . .*

Until the advent of electronic computers in the latter decades of the twentieth century, calculating correlations was a burdensome, time-consuming task, performed by hand and prone to computational errors. However, with the widespread dissemination of personal computers and their statistical programs, calculating accurate correlations of all sorts is very easy, indeed. Once the raw data are entered into the computer, a variety of statistics—means, standard deviations, percentages, correlations— appear instantaneously at the touch of a key.

Disadvantages. Like any other statistic, the worth of a correlation coefficient is only as good as the data on which it is based. If the test used to measure students' achievement in science is faulty, a correlation computed between students' science-test scores and their command of the

English language will be untrustworthy. If vague criteria are used for placing lawbreakers in categories representing different levels of offense, then coefficients reflecting the relationship between types of offense and recidivism will be invalid. Manipulating data in high-powered computers by means of fancy statistics cannot compensate for bad data. As the oft-used saying goes, "Garbage in, garbage out."

Many of the phenomena that researchers investigate do not lend themselves to precise quantification. Furthermore, most—if not all—of life's events are related to other events in extremely complex ways which are not merely difficult to measure, but perhaps impossible to measure accurately. In such cases, statistical techniques are of no use for estimating the connections among events and variables. Therefore, the best researchers can do is to offer whatever logical and intuitive judgments they can manage, and to recognize that those judgments, at best, are no more than partially accurate estimates of the actual interactions that the events involve.

Further resources. Detailed steps for calculating the types of correlation mentioned in the chapter, along with additional correlation methods suited to the nature of other forms of data, are described by the following authors: Glass & Hopkins, 1996; Hays, 1994; Jaccard & Becker, 1990; Kendall & Gibbons, 1990; Siegel & Castellan, 1988; Sirkin, 1995; and Sprinthall, 1997.

Experiments

Description. An experiment consists of treating objects in a defined way and then evaluating the outcome to determine how the treatment apparently influenced the objects and why the treatment had such an effect. The word *objects* in this context refers to such things as people, animals, plant life, places (mountains, rivers), machines, and more. In the social and behavioral sciences—and in such allied disciplines as education, social work, counseling, and business administration—the objects are people, either individually or in groups.

The purpose of an experiment is to manipulate treatment conditions in a way that will reveal (a) which conditions are responsible for what occurs to objects and (b) how much those conditions have contributed to the observed result. The four major components of experiments (an object, the object's initial condition, the treatment, and the object's condition following the treatment) are implied in the research questions that experiments are designed to answer.

- What influence will drug *XYX* have on the behavior of children who have been diagnosed as suffering from attention-deficit disorder?

- How does a series of videotaped dramas about youths' sex behavior influence high school students' expressed attitudes toward their own and their schoolmates' sexual activity?
- Do college students gain a better understanding of theoretical physics if they are required to conduct physics laboratory experiments rather than if they only attend lectures and read the physic class's textbook?
- What difference, if any, is there between teenagers (ages 12-17) and adults (ages 25-40) in speed and accuracy when they are first learning to search the Internet with the aid of a guidebook?

There are numerous types of experiments, with each type accompanied by particular strengths and weaknesses. The following paragraphs briefly describe four popular types: (a) treatment+evaluation, (b) pretest+treatment+posttest, (c) multiple-treatments, and (d) time-series. Additional experimental designs will be found in the resources at the end of this section.

Treatment+evaluation. The simplest experimental design involves (a) applying a treatment to an individual or group, (b) evaluating how well the individual or group performs following the treatment, and (c) estimating how much the treatment contributed to that performance.

For example, a high-school teacher may wish to evaluate the effectiveness of a new American history textbook by directing her students to study the chapter about the Civil War as a homework assignment. After the class members have read the chapter, the teacher gives a test to discover how much the students now know about the chapter's contents. If the students earn high scores on the test, the teacher might conclude that the textbook has been a very effective learning tool. If they earn low scores, she might decide that the book is poorly suited to her class's needs and abilities.

Such treatment-plus-evaluation experiments are often called *ex post facto* or *after the fact* because the researcher has drawn conclusions about the influence of the treatment—the particular textbook assignment—solely on the basis of testing students after they had experienced the treatment.

The chief advantage of the ex post facto model is that it's easy to use. It involves little bother on the part of the experimenter. But the treatment+evaluation design leaves a variety of important questions unanswered about factors that may have contributed to the students' test performance. In particular, the teacher doesn't know how much the students already understood about the Civil War before they read the textbook. It's even possible that some students had a more accurate knowledge of the war before they studied the text, and that the textbook explained things in such a muddled fashion that it confused the readers, causing them to doubt what they already knew. Furthermore, the teacher is unaware of other sources of information—such as the Internet and its World Wide Web—that students may have used during the homework period. And she may wonder whether the class learned more using the new textbook than they would have learned from some other book or from classroom lecture/discussion sessions.

Pretest+treatment+posttest. To furnish a more convincing foundation for estimating the influence of the American history text, the teacher could replace her treatment+evaluation plan with a pretest+treatment+posttest (p+t+p) design. In this case, before assigning students to read the chapter on the Civil War, she would have them take a test (pretest) over the subject-matter treated in the chapter. Subsequently, after the students had completed the reading assignment (treatment), she would test (posttest) their grasp of the chapter's content. In order to estimate how much the textbook had added to the learners' knowledge, she would subtract each student's pretest score from his or her posttest score and conclude that the obtained difference (*change score*) represented the contributions made by the book. In other words, the experimenter's judgment would be based, not on the posttest scores, but on the extent of change from pretest to posttest.

Multiple treatments. Even though the p+t+p design furnishes useful information about students' knowledge before the treatment was administered, it leaves in doubt several other matters. For instance, how effective is reading the new text as compared to reading the old textbook? And would students have learned more from searching the Internet than from reading the textbook?

Thus, to assess the effectiveness of two or more methods, the pretest+treatment+posttest design could be expanded in the following manner.

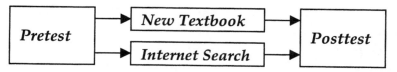

In applying this expanded design, the teacher divides her students into two groups. If we assume that she teaches four sections of American history each day, then two of the classes could be given the textbook assignment and the other two given a set of questions to answer by searching the World Wide Web. All four classes would take the same pretest and posttest. Then the change scores (each student's pretest score subtracted from her or his posttest score) would be summed across all students in the reading group and across all students in the Internet group and the total divided by the number of students in the particular group. The resulting *average change score* for each group would suggest to the experimenter the comparative overall effectiveness of the two treatment methods.

However, the expanded p+t+p design has still not accounted for another factor—reactive effects—that may have influenced the posttest scores. As Ball (1985, p. 4200) has explained,

> Reactive effects in measurement occur when the behavior elicited by a measurement procedure is not characteristic of the behavior that would have occurred in the absence of the measurement procedure.

In the history-class experiment, the questions in the pretest may alert students to knowledge about the Civil War in a manner that will affect their posttest performance. In other words, students may derive some information about the Civil War from the pretest. Consequently, the posttest scores could be the result of the pretest and treatment combined, leaving the researcher in doubt about how much the reading assignment or the Internet search influenced students' knowledge. Therefore, in order to separate the potential reactive effect of the pretest from the treatment, the teacher could add a new component to the p+t+p design. She could assign half of the textbook-reading group to take the pretest (Subgroup A) while the other half does not take the pretest (Subgroup B). The same would be done with the Internet-searching group (Subgroup C and Subgroup D), thereby producing the following design.

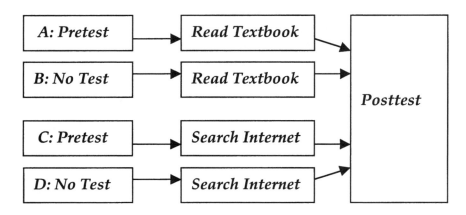

Thus, the advantage of this expanded design is that it enables the investigator to compare the apparent effectiveness of the two treatments (textbook reading versus Internet searching) and also to identify the possible influence of pretesting on the final outcome.

However, expanding the design from two groups to four groups means that the number of students in each group will be cut in half. Consequently, the amount of faith the researcher can place in conclusions drawn from the experiment is reduced. In effect, the degree of the confidence that can be invested in the assessment of a treatment increases with the number of people who participated in the treatment. Consequently, in adopting the four-group model, the teacher will have sacrificed one advantage (larger groups) for another (information about the reactive effect of pretesting).

However, even in the p+t+p expanded design, the experimenter still has not answered another question in which she is interested. How long-lasting is the students' knowledge about the Civil War? Changing the experimental design into a time series can help answer that query.

Time series. Information about how the result of a treatment may either diminish or increase over time can be sought by adding posttests at various periods following the end of the treatment.

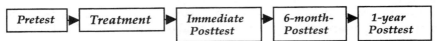

But that advantage is accompanied by several potential problems. If the experiment has been conducted with subjects who are not readily available for a considerable time after the treatment ended, then a time-series design can be difficult to implement, because participants can be lost before the later phases of posttesting take place. In addition, such a design does not furnish information about what factors following the end of the treatment may have caused any decrease or increase in participants' test scores or skills as shown on later posttests. For instance, some students in the American history class may, after the experiment ended, have seen television programs or read books about the Civil War, so that the results of that additional learning could affect those students' scores on later posttests. Hence, the delayed posttest would not be an accurate reflection of what such students had learned during the earlier treatment.

Summary. There is no experimental design that is superior to all others for all research situations. The choice of a design requires that the investigator balance a variety of conditions against each other, such as the availability of participants, how much the experiment costs, the researcher's investment of time and energy, possible undesirable side effects, and the gravity of decisions that will be based on the results of the experiment (how seriously those decisions will affect people's welfare).

Further resources. The experimental designs described in the foregoing paragraphs are only a small number of the existing types. Numerous others that suit particular research conditions are available. The nature of those others, the situations for which they are appropriate, and the steps to be followed in employing those models can be found in Campbell & Stanley, 1966; Glass, McGaw, & Smith, 1981; and Miles & Huberman, 1994.

Conclusion

Surveys, correlation studies, and experiments are effective methods for gathering information about selected characteristics of (a) members of a group and (b) the group as a whole. Surveys reveal the present status of the selected characteristics, correlation studies reveal degrees of relationship among characteristics, and experiments furnish information about apparent causes of changes in characteristics. Furthermore, the three methods provide results in the form of numerical amounts and frequencies that enable researchers to draw precise distinctions between members of a group and between groups as units.

Surveys, correlation studies, and experiments are not effective for depicting the patterning of qualities that make up the lives of individuals, groups, or institutions, nor are the three methods appropriate for portraying the complexities of historical developments.

5

Data-Collection
Processes and Instruments

When people speak of research methods, they often are referring to processes and instruments used for gathering information. Three important processes are content analyses, observations, and interviews. Three important instruments are factual questionnaires, inventories, and tests. The purpose of this chapter is to identify basic characteristics of these data-collection techniques and to illustrate their qualitative and quantitative forms.

Content Analyses

Description. The process of content analysis entails searching through one or more communications to answer questions that the investigator brings to the search. Content analyses are not limited to written or printed documents but extend as well to audio recordings, still photographs, motion-picture films, video recordings, and the like.

The analysis of a communication's contents is guided by a question or set of questions that the researcher hopes to answer. As shown in Table 5-1, the questions can be limited to qualitative features of the communication or can concern quantitative aspects as well.

Research employing content analysis often focuses on a single entity, such as one person's life or one town's history or one school's student-conduct regulations. However, other projects assume a comparative form in which the analysis involves searching for likenesses and differences among two or more sets of communications. For example, in gathering data for a thesis comparing the juvenile-crime systems of Texas and New York, a student may analyze criminal-law codes and juvenile-court cases from each of the states.

Table 5-1

Qualitative and Quantitative Aims of Content Analyses

Qualitative Questions	*Quantitative Questions*
What kinds of promises did the senator make in his campaign speeches?	How many different kinds of promises did the senator make in his campaign speeches?
In the three American history books, what traits are attributed to Indians?	In the American history books, what percentage of space is dedicated to Indians and their way of life?
In the principal's attempt to explain the students' low test scores, what sorts of causes did she propose?	In terms of the relative frequency of different causes of students' low test scores, in what order did the principal rank her proposed causes?
In the six biographies of Theodore Roosevelt that were analyzed, what personality characteristics were ascribed to Roosevelt by the authors?	To what extent did the six authors agree on Roosevelt's personality traits? In other words, what was the degree of correlation among the authors' opinions about Theodore Roosevelt's character?
In 12 movies (6 from the 1930s and 6 from the 1990s) that included at least one black actor, how were blacks portrayed in terms of social status? In what ways were black actors' roles alike and different between the 1930s and 1990s?	In 12 movies (6 from the 1930s and 6 from the 1990s) that included at least one black actor, what percentage of a film's time were black actors in the scenes in the 1930 films compared to the 1990 films?
In the four school districts' budgets, what main categories and sub-categories were included, and which categories appeared in all four districts' budgets?	What were the dollar amounts allocated for each category and sub-category of each school district's budget, and how did the amounts in one district compare with the amounts in the other three districts?
In published interviews (newspaper, news-magazine, TV) with leading Democrats and Republicans regarding their reactions to the president's State of the Union address, what kinds of opinions did the interviewees express?	In Democrats' and Republicans' published reactions to the president's State of the Union address, to what extent did members of each party agree with the president and with other members of their own party?

Typical procedure. One common approach to content analysis involves six steps, illustrated here with a research project about teenage pregnancy.

- The question—or set of questions—that the analysis is supposed to answer is specified.

  What has been the incidence of teenage pregnancy in the United States during different decades over the past half century?

- Likely sources of answers are identified and accessed.

  Government census reports, Internet web sites, books offering statistical summaries of social conditions, academic journals, weekly news magazines.

- Key words and phrases are generated to guide the search of publications and web sites.

  teenage pregnancy, teen pregnancy, teen sexual activity, adolescents' sexual behavior, teen mothers, teens' sex knowledge, birth-control practices, childbearing, moral behavior in adolescence

- The researcher applies the key words and phrases in exploring the sources.

  A book's table of contents and index are scanned to locate pages on which key words or phrases may appear.

  A magazine's or journal's table of contents is inspected to locate articles relating to the key words.

  In a search of the Internet's World Wide Web, the key words and phrases are entered via a search engine (Google, Alta Vista, Teoma, or the like).

- The pertinent pages of books, periodicals, and web sites are skimmed for information pertinent to the guide question.

- Useful information is recorded as handwritten notes (on note cards or tablet paper) or as notes keyed into a computer file (a separate file for each guide question or a separate section within a file) or as a photocopy of the relevant passages.

Advantages. Content analysis is the lone technique suitable for gathering information about what communications contain. Hence, content analysis is the only appropriate method for answering a great host of research questions.

The efficiency of the content-analysis process has been enhanced in recent years with the introduction of (a) large-memory personal computers, (b) scanners that photocopy documents into computers, and (c) optical-character-recognition (OCR) computer software. Thus, a document can be entered into a computer, page by page, in a form that can be edited and searched automatically for key words and phrases. With the aid of the *find* function of a word-processor program, at the touch of a key the computer can locate each instance in a document that such a word as *pregnancy* or a phase such as *teenage childbearing* appears. Consequently, a researcher not only can immediately find each instance of a key word but also can quickly count the number of times the key word appears in the document. In addition, special content-analysis computer software has become available at an increasing rate. As a result, the burden of conducting certain forms of content analysis is being significantly reduced.

Limitations. Compared with other data-collection methods (questionnaire surveys, paper-pencil testing), content analysis is far more time-consuming and laborious in relation to the amount of information obtained. Furthermore, the accuracy and comprehensiveness of the results of an analysis are dependent on how well the analyzed documents represent the researcher's field of interest. For instance, conclusions drawn about the incidence of teenage pregnancy will be faulty if they have been derived from the analysis of biased, flawed, or incomplete source materials.

Further resources. Detailed guidance in the conduct of content analysis—including computer-assisted analysis—is available in the following references: *CLCWeb Library, 2002*; Hodson, 1999; Krippendorf, 1980; Neuendorf, 2001; Popping, 2000; Riffe, Lacy, & Fico, 1998; Roberts, 1997; Thomas, 1998; Titscher, Meyer, Wodak, & Vetter, 2000; West, 2000.

Observations

Description. Gathering information by means of observation involves watching and/or listening to events, then recording what occurred. Observation can be either direct or mediated. In direct observation, the researcher immediately sees and hears what is happening. Such is the case when the observer is (a) in a courtroom watching a witness testify, (b) at a football game when a naked streaker runs onto the field, (c) on the street when a police officer consoles a woman whose son has been injured in an auto accident, or (a) in a kindergarten when the teacher intervenes in a children's quarrel about who deserves to ride the tricycle first. Observation is mediated when the researcher hears or sees a reproduction (audiotape or videotape) of an earlier event.

Typical procedure. As in the case of content analysis, observation can suitably be directed by the question or set of questions the researcher is attempting to answer. Those questions can represent either a qualitative or a quantitative perspective, as suggested in Table 5-2.

Table 5-2

Qualitative and Quantitative Aims of Observations

Qualitative Questions	*Quantitative Questions*
Which "filler words" (ones that convey no meaning, such as *uh, you know, like, man*) did the youth use in the interview?	What was the extent of agreement between the two observers (inter-rater reliability) regarding the kinds and frequency of filler words in the youth's conversation?
At which bits of dialogue and actors' gestures did the audience laugh?	How long did the audience's laughter last and how loud was the laughter at different times in the drama?
In the debate, what kinds of critical comments did each candidate make about each of his opponents?	What percent of each candidate's speech was dedicated to criticisms of his opponents and what percent dedicated to descriptions of his own record and proposals?
During free-play period in the nursery school, with which children did Jeanie play? Did Jeanie seek the other children's company, or did they seek her out?	How much time did Jeanie spend with each of the children she played with during the nursery school's free-play period?

The act of observing can vary in the degree to which it is guided. In other words, the question that directs the observer's attention can range from the very general (What goes on in a college seminar?) to the very specific (What percentage of the time in this seminar does the professor speak and what percentage of the time does each student speak?). An important fact about the human perception process is that a person can purposely attend to only one thing at a time (except for activities that have become habitual and automatic, like the acts involved in driving a car). This fact is reflected in the old saw "You see what you look for." Thus, the very general directive "Observe what goes on in a college seminar" serves only a browsing or "messing-around" function. It may be useful in orienting an observer to the general nature of a seminar and it may become the source of more specific features of the seminar that warrant attention, but such a vague question is a very inefficient guide to gathering data. Thus, a basic rule of thumb proposes that the more specific the guide question, the more efficient the observation. Consider, for example, how differently an observer's attention in a seminar (one professor, 18 students) will be directed by one of the following questions than by another of them.

- What ideas are introduced by the professor and what ideas are introduced by students?
- Which students speak and how often?
- What disagreements appear among participants, and which participants do those disagreements involve?
- What physical mannerisms are displayed by the professor. Which mannerisms likely enhance the presentation of ideas and which likely function as distractions?
- How are the seminar members (professor and students) attired? That is, what variety of clothing, hairstyles, and personal adornments is seen among the participants?
- What postures are observed among the seminar members? What changes in posture appear during the period, and do those changes seem related to the nature of the discussion at the moment?
- How many males and how many females are in the seminar? Does the participation of the males differ from that of the females in terms of (a) amount of time students speak and (b) the introduction of new ideas?

In summary, the more specific the questions that direct observation, the more focused the observer's attention will be, and the more accurate the report of the observation.

Advantages and limitations. Direct observation has the advantages of (a) providing information from spontaneous, unplanned, unexpected events, (b) not requiring any special equipment (audio-recorder, video-recorder), and (c) being amenable to difficult contexts (noisy, crowded settings). However, an immediate, accurate record of what occurred is often difficult for the observer to produce. For instance, written notes taken at the time of an episode can distract the observer momentarily from the event, the notes may be incomplete, participants in the episode may be perturbed by the note-taking, and the note-taking may need to be postponed until a later time when details of the event may have been forgotten.

Mediated observation has the advantage of furnishing an authentic auditory and/or visual record of what occurred, a record that the researcher can review time and again to help ensure that important aspects of the incident are not overlooked or their nature mistaken. As the testimony of witnesses in court cases amply demonstrates, people who have observed the same event can often differ in their reports of what actually occurred. Therefore, one of the chief concerns in using observation as a source of evidence in research studies is to maximize the accuracy of observers' reports. Audiotapes and videotapes of events can help foster the reliability of those reports. However, a researcher's using recording equipment may intimidate an event's participants and thereby alter the incident from the pattern it would naturally have assumed. Furthermore, the need for researchers to operate the equipment (change tapes, move to a more convenient location) can distract them from noticing significant features of the event.

Further resources. Guidance in observation techniques is available in Daniels, Doolin, Beaumont, & Beaumont, 2001; Dewalt & Dewalt, 2002; Frank & Bird, 2000; Janesick, 1998; Kirk & Miller, 1986; Patten, 2001.

Interviews

Description. Interviews usually involve a researcher orally asking questions for individuals to answer orally. However, with the advent of the Internet, interviews can also be conducted in written form, with the researcher sending typed questions via a computer network to respondents who answer in typed form. Interviews traditionally have been conducted face-to-face and one-to-one, with the researcher speaking directly with one interviewee at a time. But in recent decades, telephone interviews have become increasingly common. Whenever the telephone also provides simultaneous video transmission so the researcher and respondent see each other on a television screen as they talk, the interview more closely simulates the face-to-face variety.

Typical procedures. When planning an interview, researchers can profit from deciding which of several strategies best fits their needs. Four popular strategies bear the labels *loose-question, tight-question, converging-question,* and *response-guided.*

Loose-question approach. The purpose of a loose- or broad-question strategy is to elicit respondents' interpretation of a very general query. Consider, for instance, an interview designed to discover the diversity of definitions and emotions that teenagers attach to expressions that are common in teen culture. Therefore, the interviewer casts questions in a fashion that allows respondents unrestricted freedom to tell what a word or phrase means to them.

- If somebody asked you what *rap music* is like, what would you say?
- What does the word *drugs* mean to you?
- In your opinion, what is meant by the phrase *parents in control?*
- How would you explain the meaning of the word *discipline?* And how do you feel about *discipline?*

In adopting a loose strategy, an interviewer resists respondents' attempts to have questions rephrased in greater detail, since the intent of the approach is to expose the diversity of interviewees' interpretations.

Tight-question approach.   Whereas a loose strategy features open-ended questions, a tight strategy is designed to discover respondents' preferences among a limited number of options.   Thus, tight questions require interviewees to select from among a restricted set of answers—*yes/no* or *like/dislike* or some other multiple-choice option.

- For which candidate do you intend to vote in the upcoming election? Cassidy, Gonzalez, Johnson, or Schrint?
- Do you approve of affirmative-action policies that furnish special college-admission opportunities for students from disadvantaged ethnic groups?
- Which of these beverages do you drink at least once a week? Milk? Beer? Some sort of cola? Orange juice? Whisky?

Sometimes an interviewer follows-up a multiple-choice question with a request for the respondent to offer a rationale in support of the choice —that is, to explain why the individual prefers that option over the others.

- Why do you think Gonzalez is a better choice for the senate than the other candidates?
- Why do you believe affirmative-action policies should be continued?

Converging-question approach.   The converging or funnel strategy is designed to incorporate advantages of both the loose and tight methods. The interviewer first asks broad, open-ended questions to learn what is uppermost in the respondent's mind in relation to the topic at hand. Then, following the respondent's reply, the interviewer asks one or more sharply pointed questions. By way of illustration, consider this sequence of queries designed for interviewing youths who had spent a period of time in juvenile hall (a facility for detaining juveniles who have broken the law).

What do you think of juvenile hall? I mean, what was life like at the hall?
What did you think of the kids there?
Did you make friends with any of the kids?
When you were with those friends, what did you usually talk about?
Did they talk about using drugs?

Response-guided approach.   In a response-guided strategy, the interviewer begins with a prepared question, then spontaneously creates follow-up queries that are logical extensions of the answer the interviewee has given to the opening question. This approach enables the researcher to investigate in detail the respondent's opinion about issues related to the initial question. The procedure is rather like a fencing match in which an opponent's way of parrying the swordsman's thrust influences the swordsman's next move. An example is this segment of an interview from a study focusing on the relationship between physical fitness and the recreational pursuits of men ages 40 to 50.

> *Interviewer*—Do you engage in any sports?
> *Subject*—Golf. That's pretty much it.
> *Interviewer*—How often do you play?
> *Subject*—I try to get out once a week. Some weeks in the summer I get out a couple of times.
> *Interviewer*—Do you use a cart or walk?
> *Subject*—Where I play, you can either ride a cart or walk.
> *Interviewer*—And which do you do?
> *Subject*—I walk . . . and I carry my clubs, no caddie.
> *Interviewer*—For 18 holes?
> *Subject*—Usually nine. Eighteen takes more time than I can spare.

Interviewing—like content analysis and observation—can be designed to yield either qualitative or quantitative information and to provide information about both knowledge or and attitudes. Table 5-3 offers examples of both qualitative and quantitative questions.

Table 5-3

Qualitative and Quantitative Aims of Interviews

Qualitative Questions	*Quantitative Questions*
What kinds of promises did the senator make during his four campaigns for office as reported from interviews?	How many kinds of promises did the senator make during each campaign, and what proportion of promises were the same from one campaign to another?
What beliefs did teachers express regarding the school district's new rules about teachers' extracurricular responsibilities?	What percent of the teachers' comments about extracurricular duties were in support of the rules and what percent were critical?
What explanation did the stock broker offer for the recent ups and downs of the stock market?	To what degree did the six stock brokers concur on the causes of the recent dramatic rise and fall of stock prices?
What reasons did voters offer for preferring Lucelli over Porteus in the coming election?	What percent of the interviewees said they would vote for Lucelli and what percent for Porteus?

Advantages. Much of the information collected by means of interviews could be collected on printed questionnaires. However, interviewing provides the researcher with greater flexibility and personal control than do questionnaires. For instance, a respondent who finds the phrasing of an interview question unclear can ask for the interviewer to explain the question—a kind of help rarely available with questionnaires. Furthermore, interviewees can more easily elaborate on their answers than can respondents who complete questionnaires. And the one-on-one personal relationship that an interview provides is usually more effective in eliciting respondents' sincere participation in a research project than is the impersonal relationship implied by questionnaires that are distributed to a group or sent through the mail.

In comparison to direct observation, interviews are more efficient for collecting information about people's knowledge, personal backgrounds, and opinions.

Limitations. Interviews take lots of time, since they require that the researcher meet separately with each respondent, and part of the conversation may be of no value to the research project. Furthermore, an interview may be an ineffective way to gather trustworthy information whenever the questions touch on matters that interviewees find personally sensitive.

Further resources. Among the references at the end of this book, the following offer aid with the conduct of interviews: Aubel, 1994; Brady, 1976; Cannell, 1977; Douglas, 1985; Fowler, 1990; Guenzel, 1983; Seidman, 1997.

Factual Questionnaires

Description. The word *questionnaire* is typically used in a very general sense to mean any printed set of questions that participants in a survey are asked to answer, either (a) by checking one choice from among several possible answers listed beneath a question or (b) by writing out an answer. Questionnaires have been used for collecting two principal types of information that respondents are equipped to furnish—facts and opinions. *Facts*, as intended here, are items of information about which questionnaire respondents have knowledge. *Opinions* are expressions of attitudes or preferences. However, in this chapter the meaning of *questionnaires* is limited to printed forms on which respondents are asked for the sorts of factual information implied by the questions in Table 5-4. In the next section of the chapter, the term *inventories* refers to printed forms on which respondents are asked to express attitudes, opinions, and preferences.

Table 5-4

Qualitative and Quantitative Aims of Questionnaires

Qualitative Questions	*Quantitative Questions*
What has been Mrs. Lettie Johnson's educational background and record of work experience in regard to types of jobs performed and the length of service in each job?	Among the 27 applicants for the computer-programmer position, in what order should individuals be ranked in terms of amount of programming experience?
What language or languages are spoken in the home of sixth-grader Elena Martinez, whose family immigrated to the United States five years ago?	In how many homes of the school's sixth graders is Spanish spoken: (a) all of the time, (b) part of the time, (c) never?

Typical procedure. One method of creating and administering questionnaires involves eight steps that can be illustrated with a study of high school students' out-of-school activities.

1. *Research focus.* The researcher states the central question—or questions—that the project is to answer.

   In what activities do high school students engage when they are not in school, and why those activities?

2. *Constituent subquestions.* Specific questions whose answers contribute to answering the central question are identified.

   What activities do students pursue on different days and at different times of day or night and during different times of the year?
   How much time do students dedicate to different activities during a typical month?
   How did they get started in the activities they now pursue?
   What value do they seem to see in the different sorts of activities?
   What activities did they pursue in the past that they no longer pursue, or that they pursue less frequently, and why?

3. *Questionnaire format.* The questionnaire's structure is selected in view of the respondents' likely (a) level of reading and writing skills, (b) knowledge of the information sought on the questionnaire, and (c) willingness to report such information in the form that the questionnaire requires.

   To encourage students to be truthful and forthright in answering the questions, they will not be asked to include their names on the questionnaire. The questionnaire directions and items will be worded in a manner that could be understood by anyone who reads and writes as skillfully as an average six-grade student. Thus, even the less adept high school students should be able to understand the contents of the questionnaire and record their answers.

The questionnaire will be divided into two parts—an open-ended-question section and a multiple-choice-question section. The items in the two parts are designed to elicit answers to the project's specific subquestions. The first section will contain such questions as: "In the evening after dinner, how do you usually spend your time?" The purpose of the open-ended questions is to discover what activities are more prominent in a student's mind. The multiple-choice questions will be in the following form:

> Write an **X** on the line in front of each thing you do at least once a week:
> ___ Play videogames
> ___ Go to a movie
> ___ Play ball (such as basketball, football, volleyball, baseball, softball)
> ___ Do homework
> ___ Go to a party
> ___ Hang out with friends
> ___ Other things (Write those things in this line.)_____

The multiple-choice section is intended to identify activities that may not have been uppermost in students' minds (and thus overlooked in the open-ended-question section) but in which they nevertheless engage.

4. *Manner of administration.* The way the questionnaire will be administered to respondents is determined.

   Students will fill out the questionnaire in their English class.

5. *Tryout.* The initial form of the instrument is tried out with a sample of respondents to identify weaknesses in the questionnaire and in the manner of administering it.

   The instrument, in its initial form, will be completed by 10 students, who will be interviewed after they finish the questionnaire to reveal difficulties they may have had in understanding the items and answering them.

6. *Revision.* The results of the tryout are used for improving the clarity of the instrument and the way of administering it.

   On the basis of the 10 students' experience, the questionnaire's directions, format, and wording of items will be improved.

7. *Selection of recipients.* The people who will be asked to complete the questionnaire are identified.

The students who will participate in this survey are all those enrolled in English classes at St. Ives High School.

8. *Administration.* The questionnaire is distributed to recipients, who are asked to fill it out and return it to the researcher.

The questionnaires will be administered to students during a single English-class period under the supervision of the class's usual teacher, who will then forward the completed questionnaires to the researcher.

Advantages. An important strength of questionnaires is that they enable a researcher to collect a large quantity of data in a relatively short period of time. In addition, the researcher need not be present at the time the information is provided, and data can be collected from people in distant places if the questionnaires are sent by regular mail or over the Internet. Furthermore, a wide variety of information can be gathered from respondents, particularly if the questions are multiple-choice types that allow people to express their opinions by merely marking one or more items in a list of options.

When multiple-choice items are used, it is an easy task to classify answers and calculate their frequencies. Classifying answers to open-ended questions is more difficult and more prone to disagreements between the people who do the classifying.

Limitations. A significant disadvantage of questionnaire surveys is that, if the researcher is not present to supervise the participants as they complete the questionnaire, participants can easily avoid filling out the form and returning it to the researcher. Thus, the smaller the percentage of questionnaires returned to the author, the less confidence the author can place in how well the returned questionnaires reflect in a balanced manner the kinds of people the survey is intended to represent. Consequently, researchers are obliged to adopt ways to encourage a high rate of return of properly completed instruments. Those ways can include (a) designing questionnaires that are relatively short, easy to understand, and easy to complete, (b) following up the initial distribution of questionnaires with appeals to participants to fill out and return the forms within a reasonable period of time, and (c) offering incentives (money, prizes, privileges) for returning questionnaires.

Unlike interviews, questionnaires rarely provide an opportunity for participants to receive clarification of confusing items, nor do questionnaires offer a convenient way for respondents to elaborate their answers and explain conditions that affect their opinions.

Further resources. Books focusing on the design and administration of questionnaires include those by Berdie, Anderson, & Niebuhr, 1986; Cox, 1996; Foddy, 1993; Labaw, 1981; Oppenheim, 1992.

Inventories

Description. As noted earlier, the word *inventory*, as used here, means a printed document on which participants in a research project are asked to report their attitudes or preferences—their likes and dislikes, their approvals and disapprovals. And, like factual questionnaires, the task of designing inventories can be guided by questions the research project is intended to answer, as shown in Table 5-5.

Table 5-5

Qualitative and Quantitative Aims of Inventories

Qualitative Questions	*Quantitative Questions*
Among the 36 occupations on the Vocational Interest Inventory, which five did Mavis find most appealing, and why?	For each of the 36 occupations on the Vocational Interest Inventory, how many of the 113 job applicants chose that occupation as one of their three favorites?
What personality profile resulted from Rolando's pattern of answers on the *Self-Perception Survey Form*?	What was the most common personality trait among the 43 mental-health-clinic clients who filled out the *Self-Perception Survey Form*?
On the Musical-Taste Inventory, how did the pattern of Mark's preferences compare with Chelsea's pattern?	Among the 132 people who completed the Musical-Taste Inventory, what was the order—from most-liked to least-liked—in which the 20 musical selections were rated?

Procedures, advantages, and limitations. The same methods of creating factual questionnaires are used to devise inventories. And the strengths and weaknesses of inventories are also the same as those of factual questionnaires.

Further resources. In addition to the resources listed for factual questionnaires, the following books are useful as guides to creating and administering inventories: Aiken, 1997; Angleitner & Wiggins, 1986; Byrne, 1996; Graham, 1984; Loevinger, 1998.

Tests

Description. The term *test* in the present context means a set of printed questions designed to discover how well a test-taker commands the information and skills of a particular domain of knowledge. Traditionally, such a test has been in the form of pages of paper containing questions to answer and problems to solve, with test-takers writing their answers on the test sheets or on separate answer forms. However, at an increasing rate, test items are presented to participants on a computer screen, to be answered by the participant's either selecting answers from among several proffered options or else typing out a few words or sentences as answers or solutions.

Like the other processes and instruments reviewed in this chapter, tests can be used to furnish either qualitative or quantitative information, as suggested in Table 5-6. For each question in Table 5-6, a kind of test item that would be appropriate for answering that particular question is identified in the parentheses at the end of the question.

Table 5-6

Qualitative and Quantitative Aims of Tests

Qualitative Questions	*Quantitative Questions*
How accurately did Carlyle solve problems that involved each of the four geometry theorems studied so far this semester? (short answer)	How many of the 32 students in the class accurately solved problems involving the four geometry theorems? (short answer)
How well did Alicia discriminate among the assigned functions of the three divisions of the national government—legislative, administrative, and jucicial? (multiple-choice or matching)	What percentage of students accurately identified functions assigned to the three divisions of government? (multiple-choice, matching)
How logical was the reasoning Marcos offered in explaining causes of ethnic prejudice among high school students? (essay)	What percent of class members offered "fear of people who are different" as a factor contributing to ethnic prejudice? (essay)
Which grammar and punctuation skills has Alejandra mastered, and which does she still need to improve? (completion, essay, multiple choice)	In the order of their frequency, which grammar and punctuation skills has the class as a whole failed to master? (completion, essay, multiple-choice)

Typical procedures. One popular method of developing an achievement test for use in a research project can be demonstrated with the example of testing middle-school students' command of the knowledge and skills they studied in a social-studies unit on geography. The method involves the researcher's:

- Inspecting the entire collection of vocabulary terms and map-reading skills that were studied, then selecting from that collection a subset of terms and skills that will sample students' knowledge in of the geography lessons a balanced manner.

  Such terms as: continent, peninsula, island, tectonic plates, mercator projection, relief map, political map, mileage scale, and atmospheric pressure.

  Such skills as: (a) interpreting the symbols in a map's legend, (b) identifying time zones, (c) estimating the road-travel distance between cities in kilometers, (d) identifying the highest and lowest elevations, (e) telling the longitude and latitude positions of five cities, and (f) interpreting population-density indicators.

- Deciding on the types of test items to use for evaluating the students' knowledge and skills.

  Test items are located in two sections. The first section focuses on vocabulary terms and the second on map interpretation. The researcher wants to learn how well students *recognize* correct meanings for vocabulary terms. Recognition can be assessed with four-option multiple-choice items, such as:

  Directions: On the line in front of each numbered item, write the letter of the best answer from among the four possible answers under the item.

  ____ 1. A peninsula is:
    (a) a piece of land surrounded on all sides by water.
    (b) a very small continent near a large continent.
    (c) a strip of land almost entirely surrounded by water.
    (d) the same as an isthmus.

  The map interpretation section contains a map that students are to mark to reveal how well they interpret the map elements.

  Directions: The sentences below tell you what to write on the map.
    1. On the largest bay on the map, write the name of the **time zone** in which that bay is located.
    2. Write a **T** on the tallest mountain.
    3. On the road between Clay City and Centerville, write the distance in kilometers between the two cities.
    4. Write the letter **L** beside the airport closest to latitude 55 degrees.

- Trying out the initial version of the test with a sample of 10 students who will not be participating in the final, official testing. The 10 students will be asked to take the test and then explain out any difficulties they had in understanding the test directions or any test items.

- Improving the test in order to eliminate weaknesses identified during the tryout.

Advantages and limitations. Test results can be used for various purposes, including (a) to assign letter grades to students, (b) to determine who is entitled to be promoted to a higher grader or to graduate, (c) to rate an educational program's efficiency, (d) or to reveal the pattern of strengths and weaknesses in a student's store of knowledge. As a means of improving students' learning, the last of these purposes—that of diagnosing individuals' strengths and shortcomings—is the most constructive, since a diagnosis can suggest what the teacher and student need to do to enhance the student's skills and knowledge.

The most popular types of test items have been true-false, multiple-choice, matching, completion (fill in a blank in the sentence), short answer, and essay. Each type has its own strengths and weaknesses. For instance, true-false items are easy for the test constructor to create, and true-false questions can cover many bits of knowledge in a short space and brief time. However, they are highly susceptible to guessing and to misinterpretation on the part of test takers. Multiple-choice items are well adapted to discovering test takers' ability to select the most appropriate answer from among several alternatives. Hence, multiple-choice and matching items are useful for discovering how well participants distinguish among (a) definitions of terms, (b) inventors and their inventions, (c) cities and their locations, (d) the dates of important events, and far more. However, multiple-choice questions are not effective for assessing people's skills at organizing and presenting ideas, which are skills more adequately evaluated by means of essay tests or interviews. On the other hand, essay tests require writing ability and they cannot sample as much of participants' knowledge in as short a time as can multiple-choice, matching, or completion items.

Further resources. Assistance with the construction of achievement tests is available in Gronlund, 1998; Hambleton & Zaal, 1991; McArthur, 1987; Roid & Haladyna, 1982.

Conclusion

The aim of this chapter has been to illustrate ways that content analyses, observations, interviews, factual questionnaires, inventories, and tests—as research processes and instruments—can be viewed from qualitative and quantitative vantage points.

6

Researcher Role Perspectives

Until recent decades, a typical ambition of most researchers was to discover the *objective truth* about events—truth unaffected by the investigator's personal interests, beliefs, and values. But today, most researchers would likely agree that subjectivity inevitably influences their work in several important ways, including

- the choice of the questions they hope to answer,
- the sources from which they gather their information,
- the techniques they use to collect that information,
- how data are classified and interpreted, and
- researchers' personal relationships with the people and events they investigate.

Interest in the last of these matters has led to the creation of methods that focus on how the results of an investigation are affected by the role an investigator adopts in relation to the things being studied. Those methods have born such labels as *participatory research* and *action research*.

Participatory methodology—in its most basic form—concerns the difference between an *outsider's view* and an *insider's view*. For example, in the case of a stage drama, the members of the audience have an outsider's view, whereas members of the drama troupe—actors, director, stage hands—have an insider's view. Among anthropologists, the terms *etic* and *emic* are often used to identify this outside/inside distinction. A person using an etic method stands aloof from the observed events, seeing things (hopefully with an "objective" eye) that happen without any intimate engagement in the event. A person using an emic method is one of the actual participants in the observed event.

However, this simple etic/emic distinction fails to reveal the variety of relationship options available to an investigator. Hence, rather than the options being portrayed as two opposite approaches, the options are better depicted as positions along a scale that ranges from (a) the perspective most remotely removed from the studied event to (b) the perspective most intimately engaged in the event. For example, imagine a project in which the investigator wishes to analyze the leadership and followership relations among the seven members of a church committee that is responsible for generating increased church income. The researcher plans to collect the needed information by observing committee members during their deliberations. Consider, then, the following descriptions of five ways that the observation could be conducted. The descriptions begin with the method most removed from direct contact with committee members (Method A) and ends with the method that most intimately engages the researcher with the members (Method E).

- Method A: Unobtrusive videocameras are installed at two locations near the ceiling of the committee's meeting room, and a microphone is placed in a vase of flowers in the center of the desk around which the committee members conduct their deliberations. The committee members are the only people in the room. Each committee meeting is recorded on a videotape that the researcher can analyze at a later date.

- Method B: In the meeting room, the researcher sits silently 12 feet from the committee from where she observes the members' comments, gestures, facial expressions, and postures during committee sessions—but she does not write notes about the deliberations during the session. A small tape recorder beneath a cloth in the center of the table records what the committee members say, so the researcher will have a verbatim record of members' remarks to analyze later.

- Method C: The researcher sits close to the group and writes notes about committee members' comments and actions as the session progresses. A visible audiotape recorder in the middle of the table records what members say.

- Method D: The researcher sits at the table along with the committee members and writes notes about what they say and do. Occasionally she asks a question to clarify some point she failed to grasp. She controls the operation of an audiotape recorder located in the center of the table.

- Method E: The researcher is a member of the church committee and thereby assumes an active role in the discussion. She jots down occasional notes. Each committee session is recorded on two videocameras operated by two of the researcher's friends, who periodically move about the room to get a clear view of whichever participant is speaking at the moment.

In participatory methodology, not only are various choices of roles available to the researcher—with each choice representing a different degree of personal engagement in the episode—but in the most advanced version of the method, the subjects of the research assume part of the researcher's task of designing and conducting the study. An example of such an advanced version is the approach that W. F. Whyte (1991) refers to as *participatory action research.* He argues for "the scientific and practical values of participatory action research and [advocates] its incorporation into the tool kit of the social sciences" (Whyte, Greenwood, & Lazes, 1991, p. 19).

> In participatory action research (PAR), some of the people in the organization or community under study participate actively with the professional researcher throughout the research process from the initial design to the final presentation of results and discussion of their action implications. PAR thus contrasts sharply with the conventional model of pure research, in which members of organizations and communities are treated as passive subjects, with some of them participating only to the extent of authorizing the project, being its subjects, and receiving the results. PAR is *applied* research, but it also contrasts sharply with the most common type of applied research, in which researchers serve as professional experts, designing the project, gathering the data, interpreting the findings, and recommending action to the client organization. Like the conventional model of pure research, this [common form of applied research] also is an elitist model of research relationships. In PAR, some of the members of the organization we study are actively engaged in the quest for information and ideas to guide their future actions. (Whyte, Greenwood, & Lazes, 1991, p. 20)

Most of Whyte's studies have been designed to improve the efficiency of business operations, whereas Mary Brydon-Miller espouses a form of participatory action research intended to promote a critical-social-science agenda of righting society's wrongs by

- [focusing] on communities and populations that have traditionally been exploited or oppressed.
- [addressing] both the specific concerns of the community and the fundamental causes of the oppression with the goal of achieving positive social change.
- [producing] research, education, and action to which all participants contribute their unique skills and knowledge and through which all participants learn and are transformed. (Brydon-Miller, 1991, p. 80)

Because participatory action research intentionally engages the people who are studied in formulating and conducting the investigation, the original researcher intentionally creates a very flexible initial plan, then alters the plan on the basis of suggestions from the subjects of study. As a result, the final research design and its application are the product of negotiations between the researcher and the researched.

Tolman and Brydon-Miller (1991, p. 5) describe participatory methods as "primarily qualitative, using various forms of interview, ethnographic, and social action strategies to generate data that are systematically analyzed in the forms in which they are produced."

The strengths and weaknesses of participatory methods depend on such variables as the degree of engagement of the researcher with the studied subjects and the competencies of both the researcher and the people being studied.

Degree of Engagement

The more remote the connection between observers and their subjects, the less likely the observers will influence the incidents they witness. Remoteness increases the probability that people in the episode will act in their typical fashion. Thus, the observed events will be an accurate sample of those individuals' usual behavior. However, in being remote, the observer is apt to miss subtle aspects of events or to misinterpret what occurs. This is where intimacy makes an important contribution. The closer the observer's relationship with the subjects, the more likely the observer will see, hear, and feel inconspicuous but significant features of an event and will have the background knowledge required for deriving an insightful interpretation of what those features mean. But too much intimacy—too close an emotional identification of the observer with the observed—can damage the objectivity that is valued in typical scientific investigations. Hence, researchers' hearts may unduly influence their heads, so the report of their observations may reflect what they wish the world were like rather than what the world really is like.

As Wolcott, an anthropologist, has suggested,

> [The resesearcher]—ordinarily an outsider to the group being studied—tries hard to know more about the cultural system he or she is studying than any individual who is a natural participant in it, at once advantaged by the outsider's broad and analytical perspective but, by reason of that same detachment, unlikely ever totally to comprehend the insider's point of view. The [investigator] walks a fine line. With too much distance and perspective, one is labeled aloof, remote, insensitive, superficial; with too much familiarity, empathy, and identification, one is suspected of having "gone native." (Wolcott, 1988, pp. 188-189)

Competencies of Participants

Whenever an investigator invites subjects to help design and conduct a research project, the success of the venture depends heavily on which skills and knowledge that each—researcher and subjects—can contribute to the various tasks in the research process. In other words, it is counterproductive for the researcher to seek participants' opinions about matters foreign to their experience, just as it is counterproductive for the researcher to decide how to deal with matters about which he or she has little or no knowledge. For example, imagine that a graduate student plans to study (a) the problems faced by Latin American immigrants to the United States in adjusting to their new way of life, (b) the solutions they attempt, and (c) the success of different solutions in different social environments. Therefore, in selecting the aspects of the research to which immigrants will be asked to contribute, the student can profitably be guided by such questions as

- In which parts of the planning and conduct of the research may the immigrants have greater skill or knowledge than I?
- How do I decide which of the immigrants might have the required skill or knowledge and be willing to share it with me?
- How can I best enlist such individuals' cooperation and define the role that I want them to assume, without their exceeding the level of privilege and responsibility in the research project that is intended in my request?

In this hypothetical project, aspects of the study to which immigrants might usefully contribute could include (a) in which language interviews with different immigrants might best be conducted (English, Spanish, an American-Indian dialect?); (b) ways of stating interview questions to make clear what kind of information is being sought, so that the interviewee is not offended by the content or phrasing of the question; and (c) characteristics of interviewers (gender, ethnic identity, social-class status) that would likely affect participants' willingness to respond to questions in an honest, detailed fashion.

Further resources. Additional information about participatory methods and examples of their application can be found in: Hurst, 1995; Sohng, 1995; Stutzman, 2001; Tolman & Brydon-Miller, 2000; Whyte, 1991.

7

Interpretation Methods

For convenience of discussion, the typical research project can be seen as consisting of two phases—the descriptive and the interpretive. In the descriptive phase, the researcher is responsible for accurately depicting the events and people that are the objects of the study. In the interpretive phase, the researcher proposes meanings that go beyond the description itself.

Kinds of Meaning

The sort of meaning being proposed can often be inferred from questions that the research is designed to answer, as illustrated by the examples in Table 7-1, where various kinds of meaning are identified in the left column and illustrative questions focusing on each kind are listed in the right column. In each example, the dominant perspective—qualitative or quantitative—adopted for answering the question is suggested in parentheses at the end.

The kinds of meaning proposed in Table 7-1 are not mutually exclusive. Instead, they often overlap. For instance, *meaning* in the sense of explaining why events occur as they do (causation) overlaps *meaning* in the sense of estimating future outcomes (prediction), because predictions are typically founded on the predictor's assumption about which factors are expected to combine to produce future events. In a similar fashion, *meaning* in terms of drawing comparisons overlaps *meaning* as evaluation whenever one of the things being compared is judged to be better than the others.

The list of meanings in Table 7-1 clearly does not exhaust the variety of interpretations that can be drawn from—or assigned to—descriptive evidence. Additional kinds of interpretation can focus on (a) traits of individuals or groups, (b) consequences that follow an event, (c) people's motives and emotional reactions, (d) the validity of evidence, and more.

Table 7-1

Kinds of Meaning

Kinds of Meaning	Questions Whose Answers Provide Meaning in Terms of the Kinds Listed in the Left Column
Causation:	Which forces combined to produce the defeat of William Johnson in the gubernatorial election? (qualitative)
	How much of the variance in second-graders' academic performance can be accounted for by the dominant language spoken in their homes? (quantitative)
Comparison:	In what ways were the mother's treatment of her sons similar to and different from her treatment of her daughters? (qualitative)
	From the viewpoint of a team's scoring efficiency, what are the most important differences among three football teams—the Mustangs, the Owls, and the Pirates? (qualitative/quantitative)
Prediction:	If the school board authorizes higher test-score standards for high-school graduation, what reactions can be expected from parents, students, and teachers? (qualitative)
	In view of trends in the county's population growth over the past two decades, what size population might be expected ten years from now? (quantitative)
Evaluation:	How effective was Eleanor Roosevelt as the wife of the president of the United States during the Second World War? (qualitative)
	How close did the city government come to reaching its budget goal? (quantitative)
Generalization:	How likely is it that the moral values displayed by the "flappers" in Scott Fitzgerald's novels were the same values held by the majority of young American women in the 1920s? (qualitative)
	How much confidence can I place in the belief that the pattern of math scores found in the sample of 125 high-school seniors that I tested is the same as the pattern of scores that would have resulted if all 11,000 of the city's seniors had been tested? (quantitative)

Table 7-1 (continued)

Kinds of Meaning

Kinds of Meaning	Questions Whose Answers Provide Meaning in Terms of the Kinds Listed in the Left Column
Function:	What role did the Army Corps of Engineers play in the Gulf War? (qualitative) What percentage of the school district's funds last year derived from property taxes? (quantitative)
Context:	In relation to the public acceptability of slavery, how did the political/cultural atmosphere in Virginia in 1800 compare with the political/cultural atmosphere in 2000? (qualitative) How did the increasingly widespread distribution of credit cards over the last half of the twentieth century affect (a) people's attitudes toward spending and (b) per-capita indebtedness? (qualitative/quantitative)
Process:	What sequence of events led to the high school faculty adopting stricter discipline rules? (qualitative) On the basis of what evidence did the college's athletic teams advance from Division-III to Division-I in the National Collegiate Athletic Association system? (quantitative)
Personal Effect:	How was Florence Nightingale's life affected by the Crimean War? (qualitative) What influence did Henry Ford's developing the Model-T have on Ford's personal income? (quantitative)
Hypothesis Testing:	How well does the evidence about Morton Levingwell's classroom teaching support the charge that he was encouraging his students to embrace a gay lifestyle? (qualitative) How accurate is the high school principal's estimate that preventing students from leaving the campus at lunchtime will result in reduced absences from afternoon classes? (quantitative)
Symbolism:	What is the psychological significance of the street gang's displaying a sketch of a jackal on its logo? (qualitative).

There are numerous patterns of thought in which people can engage as they fashion an interpretation, and those patterns can differ from one type of meaning to another. This point is illustrated in the following pages with examples of different approaches to interpretation for five of the types of meaning listed in Table 7-1: causation, comparison, generalization, context, and symbolism.

Causation

When we approach interpretation from the vantage point of *cause* (*causation, causality*), we find ourselves grappling with very complex matters. Perhaps the most popular conception of *cause* is reflected in the question "Why did that event happen as it did?" Hence, *cause*, in this sense, is an account of (a) the factor—or factors—that produce an event and (b) how those factors interact. However, this notion of cause is only one among various conceptions proposed by philosophers over the centuries. Beginning with Aristotle 2,300 years ago, scholars have offered a diversity of *cause* definitions identified by such labels as *material cause, formal cause, efficient cause, final cause, proximate cause, remote cause, intrinsic cause,* and others. But for the purpose of this chapter, it is unnecessary to investigate the complexities of those definitions. I am limiting the versions of cause to the one that focuses on the matter of which factors account for an event.

One useful perspective for identifying apparent causal factors is that of correlation, as signified by the question "When one thing changes, what happens to other things?" When the temperature changes from +13 degrees Centigrade to –13 degrees, what happens to water in a pan? When boys grow in height from 41 inches to 67 inches, what happens to their weight? When adults drink five shots of whiskey rather than none before driving their cars, what happens to the auto-accident rate? When parents divorce, what happens to their children's feelings of security? When 12-year-old girls, in contrast to boys, take a reading-skills test, what happens to test scores?

The fact that people recognize different degrees of correlation between variables is demonstrated in everyday life by such comments as:

- "When the clouds get that dark, you can almost always expect rain."
- "Knowing a woman's religion tells you nothing about how honest she is."
- "About half the time I can guess a man's occupation from the way he dresses."

Although recognizing a correlation between things is a necessary step in accounting for the cause of an event, identifying a correlation is not sufficient to explain cause. This point can be illustrated with an old anecdote about the relationship between storks and human births in Holland. Observers in the Netherlands had noticed a positive correlation between the quantity of storks in a community and the incidence of babies born—the more storks present, the more infants born. This information might be used to support the legendary storks-bring-babies explanation that has been given to young children who ask where babies come from. But alternative interpretations of the stork/baby correlation are possible, such as storks prefer quiet village life to noisy, polluted city life, so they inhabit villages more often than cities. And villagers raise larger families than do city dwellers, for a variety of reasons. Thus, the fact that there is a positive correlation between the number of storks and number of babies in communities is not adequate for explaining the incidence of human births.

> Thus, it is critical that researchers recognize the difference between *casual, incidental* correlations and *causal, determining* correlations. For example, in a small town in Kansas they tell of an astute observer who, while spending both winter and summer hours lounging in front of the general store, noted a positive correlation between the softness of the pavement on Main Street and the speed at which milk soured. The softer the pavement, the faster milk curdled. Hence, he proposed that the town council install firmer paving (replace asphalt with concrete) to retard the souring of milk. (Thomas & Brubaker, 2000, p. 125)

What is actually required for a persuasive interpretation of cause is both (a) evidence of correlation between two variables, or among several variables (multiple correlation), and (b) a convincing line of reasoning to demonstrate that an event (the effect) could not have occurred if it had not been for the presence of a particular previous event (factor, variable) or of a combination of previous or concurrent events (multiple causes).

The line of logic that a researcher adduces in support of an interpretation of cause derives from qualitative decision-making that is often supported by quantitative correlation evidence.

An important consideration in judging the likely causal relationship between variables is the magnitude of their correlation. That magnitude can be expressed in more or less precise terms. Here are three examples of less precise descriptions.

- Generally, women exhibit their emotions more openly than men do.
- There's a tendency for kids who do well in math to be good at playing such games as Monopoly.
- The larger a high school's budget for interscholastic athletics, the somewhat better win-loss record that school's teams will have.

The following are more precise descriptions of those same relationships.

- On the 50-point *Emotional Expression Scale*, the average score for women was 43 and for men was 25.
- The correlation between kids' math-test scores and their rankings as successful Monopoly players was +.76.
- The correlation between schools' athletic-department expenditures and those schools' win-loss records in football and baseball was +.57.

It seems obvious that more precise ways of describing degrees of relationship among variables are preferable to less precise ways.

Thus, merely demonstrating a positive or negative relationship is not sufficient to support a claim of cause. What is also required is a persuasive line of logic showing that one variable was at least partially the result of one or more of the other correlated variables. Frequently, the supporting argument is designed to show that one factor (the cause) preceded the other (the effect) and that the two could not have occurred in reverse order. Furthermore, developing a convincing rationale that links two or more variables in a causal relationship often entails describing how such a relationship is mediated by a chain of variables—a relationship involving a sequence of linkages extending from previous causes to immediate ones.

Summary. The task of accounting for the causes of events involves two steps: (a) presenting convincing evidence that two or more phenomena are correlated and (b) offering a persuasive line of reasoning that the correlation was not just incidental or casual but, instead, was causal, that is, one variable (the outcome or effect) could not have occurred if one or more of its correlates (the causes) had not occurred before—or concurrently with—the outcome variable.

Observing high quantitative correlations among variables is useful in guiding a search for causal factors behind such a phenomenon as emotional expression, because the variables that are strongly correlated with emotional expression may themselves be causal factors or at least may guide the researcher to other closely related variables that do, indeed, influence the way emotions are revealed. But low correlations—particularly ones that approach 0.0 —are useless as guides in our hunt for causes.

Comparison

The act of comparing things consists of identifying how the chosen things are *similar to* and *different from* each other. Some comparisons focus only on similarities, others only on differences (contrasts), and still others on both likenesses and differences.

One thought process that people can adopt for deriving comparative interpretations consists of five steps: (a) choosing the category of objects (people, places, events, historical period, etc.) to be compared, (b) identifying which two or more types of objects within that category are to be compared, (c) selecting the characteristics of the objects on which the comparison will focus, (d) collecting and presenting descriptive information about the status of each object, and (e) offering conclusions about how the objects are alike and/or different. These steps can be demonstrated with a hypothetical research project.

Category of objects to be compared. The researcher in our illustrative case has chosen to compare high school students. The selection at this step is founded primarily on qualitative considerations—a choice of which *kinds* of objects to study rather than which *amounts* of objects.

Types of objects within the category. There are many types of high school students that could be studied, either as individuals or as groups (girls versus boys, freshmen versus seniors, the tall versus the short, Chinese-Americans versus Jewish-Americans, and far more). In our example, the researcher wishes to compare high school students in terms of both gender and religious affiliation—(a) boys versus girls and (b) Protestants versus Catholics versus Jews versus Muslims versus "another religion" versus nonbelievers. At this step the decision is again qualitative—choosing which kinds of people to compare.

Characteristics of such subjects. There is a seemingly infinite list of students' characteristics that might be investigated, such as their English-language writing skills, their heights and weights, their use of drugs and alcohol, favorite movies, study habits, parents' occupations, mental health, vocational ambitions, sexual activities, and thousands of others. In our hypothetical project, the characteristic (variable) of interest is the set of moral values on which students base their judgments of wrongdoing. Once more, the decision is based on qualities—on kinds of characteristics, not on amounts or frequencies.

It is clear that these first three steps (choosing a category, the types in the category, and characteristics of those types) are usually taken at the beginning of the project. By making the three choices at the outset, the researcher is foretelling the sort of interpretation that he or she expects to draw. That intention can then be expressed in one or more questions that guide the last two steps—(d) collecting evidence and (d) judging what the evidence means. The guide questions in our illustrative study could be:

> On what moral values do high school students base their judgments of what constitutes wrongdoing in people's behavior? To what extent are the moral values expressed by high school girls the same as those expressed by high school boys? To what extent are the values expressed by students who affiliate themselves with one religion similar to and different from the values expressed by students who affiliate themselves with other religions (Protestantism, Catholicism, Judaism, Islam, "another religion," and no religion)?

Collecting and presenting descriptive information. This stage of the process involves selecting the method of gathering information, applying that method, and describing the results of the collection process. Imagine that our fictitious researcher decides to conduct a questionnaire survey in which 400 or so high school students tell (a) what consequences they believe should be assigned to the main characters in eight cases of apparent wrongdoing and (b) the students' reasons for considering such consequences appropriate.

After the completed questionnaires have been collected, the researcher organizes a description of students' answers by translating each reason into the apparent moral value on which that reason has been based. The following are examples of kinds of values that could result from this procedure.

Respect for the law. People should obey formally constituted laws.

Responsibility. People should fulfill those obligations which, by custom, are considered to be duties in keeping with the individual's stage of life or roles that he or she assumes in society.

Contractual integrity. People who have freely agreed to perform an action should faithfully carry out that commitment.

Evenhanded justice. Laws and regulations should be applied equally to everyone.

Concern for human life. Everyone should protect others from physical and emotional harm.

Social amity and cohesion. Everyone should try to maintain pleasant relations with others and to foster the group solidarity that supports the established social order.

This process of analysis produces, for each student, a list of the values reflected in that student's questionnaire answers.

Interpretation in terms of comparisons. The investigator is now prepared to answer the original research questions that called for comparisons between individuals or among groups.

Comparing individuals. Assume, now, that the author wishes to compare the moral values of two girls, Chelsea and Dawn. One qualitative method could involve preparing two parallel lists, one displaying Chelsea's values and the other Dawn's values. We could then scan the two lists to see how well the girls agreed. And we would be assisted in drawing conclusions if the researcher separated the agreed-upon values from the non-agreed-upon ones. For instance, imagine that each letter in the following lists represents a particular value, similar to the six examples given above.

The Girls Agreed		The Girls Disagreed	
Chelsea	*Dawn*	*Chelsea*	*Dawn*
C	C	A	E
D	D	B	G
K	K	F	J
			H
			I
			L

This method of presenting the data enables us to draw a qualitative comparison by showing likenesses (which kinds of values the girls held in common) and differences (which kinds of values were unique to each girl).

The researcher can also quantify the comparison by reporting the extent of agreement/disagreement as percentages. Because the girls concurred in only three of the 12 values in the two lists, they had 25% agreement and 75% disagreement. Thus, the qualitative method of inspecting the two lists enables us to identify the *kinds* of values on which the girls agreed, whereas the quantitative method of calculating percentages enables us to judge the overall *magnitude* of the girl's accord.

Comparing groups. Whereas a comparison between individuals can be either qualitative or quantitative, comparisons of groups always involve some form of quantification, be it either crude or refined. The comment that "High school girls are more compassionate than high school boys" is quantitatively crude. A report that a +.82 correlation was found between girls' and boys' ranking of values is quantitatively refined. In effect, comparisons expressed in numbers are typically more precise than comparisons expressed in such terms as *many, sometimes, usually, few, rarely, most,* or *partly.*

Generalization—The Problem of Sampling

The final results of a research project usually assume the form of conclusions the researcher has drawn about the things that were studied. Here are five examples of such conclusions.

- On the reading-skills test, the fourth graders as a group achieved an average score of 57, with individuals' scores ranging between scores 23 and 97.
- Evidence from newspaper accounts during the first two decades of the twentieth century suggested that the two principal underlying causes of World War I were (1) German militarists' desire to expand their control over ever-larger territories and (2) advances in warfare technology (artillery, battleships, tanks, submarines, airplanes).
- The consistent application of the sensory-conditioning routine resulted in a 47% reduction in the frequency of the autistic child's head-banging and in a significant improvement in his paying attention to the therapist's requests.
- The pre-election telephone survey showed 83% of Democrats and 53% of Republicans in favor of the homestead-alteration bill.
- In the study of recidivism among treated alcoholics, 38% of the 83 participants in the program had reverted to habitual drinking within five years.

Sometimes researchers are content to limit their conclusions to the people or events that were directly investigated. However, often they are not satisfied with thus restricting the application of their results. Instead, they wish to extend or generalize their conclusions to encompass a larger pool of people or events. In other words, they assume that the people or events they directly studied were only a portion (a sample) of a greater collectivity (population). Kinds of extensions that researchers may envisage are illustrated in Table 7-2, where the things that were directly investigated are listed in the left column, and the broader groups to which researchers wish to apply the conclusions are listed in the right column.

Table 7-2

Extending Conclusions from Samples to Populations

Conclusions drawn about:	*are applied to:*
—127 4th-graders' reading-test scores	all 6,012 of the city's 4th-graders.
—causes of World War I	judging the causes of World War II.
—one autistic child's response to a treatment	estimating all other autistic children's responses to that treatment.
—the national-election voting plans of 2,000 respondents in a telephone poll	all voters nationwide.
—recidivism rates among 83 treated alcoholics	all of a state's treated alcoholics.

When researchers thus attempt to apply a project's results beyond the things that were actually studied, they incur an obligation to demonstrate why such an extension is warranted. Their demonstration can be founded on either qualitative reasoning or quantitative reasoning—or on some combination of the two.

Qualitative reasoning. The typical qualitative argument is based on the assumption that:

(a) if the pattern of causal factors that were responsible for the results in the group that was directly studied (the sample)

(b) is the same pattern found in another group (a population or a different group), then

(c) the conclusions reached in studying the sample will apply to the other group as well.

By way of illustration, imagine that, in an appraisal of the effectiveness of a program intended to deter teenagers from smoking, the researchers concluded that four of the principal causes of youths' acquiring the smoking habit were (1) their parents smoked, (2) their companions smoked, (3) widespread cigarette advertising portrayed smokers as handsome, exciting people engaged in adventures admired by teenagers, and (4) youths did not sufficiently realize the adverse consequences of smoking for both the smokers themselves and others around them. The anti-smoking program had been designed to correct those four assumed causes and also to provide young people alternative ways to fulfill their needs and desires. In order to apply the results of the study to a larger population of young people, the program's sponsors could argue that their methods of correcting the four causes—methods they had found effective in numerous cases—would also be appropriate for youths who had not participated in their program but whose lives displayed the same pattern of causes as the program's subjects.

In summary, a qualitative argument that the results of a research project can validly be generalized beyond the confines of that project is an argument that derives from the theory of causation on which the project was founded. Such an argument could be presented in attempts to generalize the conclusions of any of our earlier examples (reading tests, World War I, autistic child, voting behavior, and alcoholism).

Quantitative reasoning. The typical quantitative rationale is based on the assumption that

(a) a sample of a population will contain the same pattern of significant characteristics as does the population if the members (people, events, objects) of the sample have been drawn from the population at random (with *random* meaning that each member has had an equal chance to be chosen, and choosing one member has not influenced which other members will be chosen), so that

(b) a study of the patterning of selected characteristics of the sample will accurately represent the patterning of those characteristics in the population, so that

(c) conclusions drawn from studying the sample will validly apply to the population as well, and

(d) there are quantitative (statistical) procedures that can help us decide how much confidence we can place in generalizing from the sample to the population.

Whether those quantitative procedures will be appropriate for a given research project depends on such conditions as the sample size and how the sample was drawn.

Sample size. As common sense may suggest, the larger the number of people in the sample, the more faith we can place in the notion that the sample does, indeed, accurately reflect the pattern of characteristics in the population. For instance, if we apply the results of studying 500 high-school students' religious beliefs (the sample) to all 9,000 of the county's high-school students (the population), we can be more confident that such an application is warranted than if we had only 15 students in the sample.

Ways of drawing samples. Two ways to draw a sample of a population bear the labels *random* and *convenience*.

A simple way to select a random sample of a population that is not very large is to write the name each member of the population on a slip of paper, place the slips in a large bowl, mix them up, and draw one slip at a time until the number that will compose the sample have been drawn. We might try such a method for studying college students' opinions about selling beer on campus, a project in which we wish to interview a sample of 50 students in an 11,000-student college and then interpret our conclusions from the 50 interviews as representing the pattern of opinions that would result if we interviewed the entire population of 11,000. But writing 11,000 names on slips of paper would be unduly laborious, so we could achieve the same result by using a table of random numbers (as generated by our computer) as our guide to choosing our 50 interviewees. That is, we would match the first 50 random numbers in the table with the identification numbers that had been assigned to the 11,000 students when they registered in college. Or, when populations are even larger, a different variation of random sampling (multi-stage or cluster sampling) would be the most practical system to adopt (Thomas, 1998, p. 217).

Even though random sampling fosters confidence in the belief that the sample accurately represents the characteristics of a population, random sampling is accompanied by difficulties in (a) drawing a sample from a large population (such as from all college seniors throughout the nation, all of a state's registered voters, all of a region's fast-food restaurants) and (b) gathering data from the members of the sample. Consequently, the over-whelming majority of research studies are conducted on *convenience* or *available* samples. A convenience sample consists of those members of a population (people, events, objects, locations) that are readily available to the researcher, such as:

- 32 sixth graders at Lincoln School in Denver, Colorado, who have written stories about their ambitions for the future
- 26 pedestrians on State Street in Santa Barbara, California, who are willing to be interviewed about the city government's architectural plan for downtown
- 18 members of an extended family on a Hopi reservation with whom an anthropologist spends the summer
- 127 delegates at a Rotary convention who fill out a questionnaire about the charities they support

Nearly every thesis and dissertation is based on data from an available sample.

Statistical procedures. When researchers defend their extending research conclusions beyond the people and events they directly studied, they often use a statistical-estimation process to show how probable it is that the results they obtained in studying a sample are a fair estimate of the results they would have obtained if they had studied the entire population which the sample is supposed to represent. They accomplish this by calculating the margin of error likely involved in generalizing beyond their data. For each kind of statistic they have reported for their sample—percentage, average, variability, correlation—there is a way to calculate a *standard error*—an estimate of how probable the sample figure matches the imagined population figure. In public-opinion poles, standard errors are typically reported in some such fashion as: "Fifty-seven percent of voters (plus or minus an error of 3.7%) believe the increased sewer tax was fair."

However, the acceptability of computing a standard error, and which method will be appropriate, depends on important assumptions about (a) the way the sample was drawn and (b) the form of the population to which conclusions are extended.

(a) If the sample was not drawn randomly or systematically—or nearly so—then the customary statistical treatments are not acceptable. Therefore, if we are using a convenience sample for our project, we are not warranted in calculating standard errors to defend our applying our results beyond our actual data. So the best we can do is to offer a qualitative line of logic in which we argue that the factors that account for the results in our sample (our theory of cause) are equally true for the people or events to which we hope to extend our interpretation.

(b) For certain statistical treatments (such as computing a Pearson *r*, mean, standard deviation), an important assumption underlying the computation of probable error is that the significant characteristics of the population from which the sample came are distributed in the form of a normal curve, that is, a bell-shaped curve in which the most frequent scores (people, events) are bunched around the middle (mean), and the remaining scores gradually diminish in a symmetrical manner above and below the mean. When this assumption can be made with confidence, then parametric (population) statistics are appropriate. When the pattern of score distribution in the population likely takes some other form than that of the normal bell curve, then nonparametric statistics are suitable (rank-order correlation, contingency coefficient, and such).

Summary. Researchers who contend that the conclusions drawn from their project can be applied equally well to people or events that were not directly investigated are obligated to explain why such an extension is reasonable. When the studied sample has been randomly or systematically drawn from the population to which conclusions are to be generalized, then researchers are aided in their argument by statistical procedures that furnish an estimate of the degree of error that such generalizing may involve. However, authors who have used a convenience or available sample cannot depend on statistics for estimating the appropriateness of extending their conclusions beyond the phenomena they have studied. Instead, they are compelled to offer a line of logic—an argument based chiefly on qualitative reasoning—to advance their claim.

Context

The centuries-old word *hermeneutics* was originally used to mean biblical exegesis—the activity in which preachers and religious scholars engage when they take a passage of scripture from a Bible and elaborate on what they imagine it meant at the time it was first written and, perhaps, on what it might mean in people's lives today. In recent decades—and particularly since the 1960s—the term *hermeneutics* has been adopted by researchers in the humanities, social sciences, and behavioral sciences. However, even a sketchy inspection of the literature bearing on hermeneutics reveals that there is considerable lack of agreement about its nature.

Wilhelm Dilthey (1833-1911), the German philosopher most often credited with launching the modern-day hermeneutics movement, defined hermeneutics as "understanding social phenomena in terms of the motives of the participants and the meanings [that such motives] give to institutions and events" (Macsporran, 1982, p. 47). Less clear than Dilthey's statement is Bubner's assertion that "For hermeneutics, understanding means a fundamental apprehension of truth which takes place in intersubjective processes of communication and in the mediation through history" (Bubner in Mannien & Tuomela, 1976, p. 69). Equally elusive seems the meaning Giddens intended when writing that hermeneutics involves "grasping frames of meaning contextually as elements of the practice of particular forms of life—and not only consistencies with frames, but also inconsistencies and disputed or contested meanings" (Macsporran, 1982, p. 48).

In effect, the various meanings assigned to *hermeneutics* range from:

(a) *the very limited* (such as estimating the motives of people in social situations or estimating the intended meaning of a document's content in the context in which the document was first created) to

(b) *the very broad* (the entire art and science of interpretation in all of its versions).

But it's my impression that researchers use the term *hermeneutics* most frequently to mean interpreting (a) how the context in which a communication originated (document, oration, comment, gesture) influenced the communication's meaning at that time and place, and (b) how that same communication should be understood today. Contextual interpretation can, therefore, be appropriate for answering various kinds of research questions, including:

- What sorts of people did Jefferson intend by the word "men" when he wrote "all men are created equal"?

- Exactly what activities did the teenagers have in mind when they said they were "hanging out"?
- For the Japanese, what is the significance of their bowing when they greet someone?
- What features of the social context in India and in the international world in the 1940s made Ghandi's peaceful-resistance movement so successful?
- In Shakespeare's time, how convincing would the audience have found Hamlet's fear of committing suicide?

The task the researcher faces in fashioning a persuasive contextual interpretation typically involves (a) assembling evidence about word meanings and social/political conditions at the time and place of the event that is being explained, (b) showing how those conditions were similar to and different from conditions today, and (c) suggesting how such similarities and differences may influence how well people today understand those earlier times and distant places.

Symbolism

Offering an explanation in terms of symbolism consists of attributing meanings to phenomena (events, people, objects, discourses, behaviors) that are not the literal or apparent meanings typically associated with those phenomena. Or, in some cases, a symbol is so unfamiliar that viewers or listeners are unable to attach any meaning at all to the symbol's sight or sound. Therefore, if readers of research reports are to understand what was intended by such a symbol, the researcher is obliged to include an interpretation.

There are at least two roles symbol interpretation may play in research studies: (a) as the explanation of an entire ritual or belief-system that is the object of a study and (b) as the clarification of occasional expressions embedded in a study.

Ritual or belief-system. The following are examples of complex rituals that carry symbolic meanings which are not obvious to the casual observer and, therefore, need to be explained in detail by the authors who write about such events.

- A college fraternity's initiation ceremony
- Faculty meetings in a public school
- Mass in the Roman Catholic Church
- A potlatch in a Kwakiutl Indian community
- Prayer sessions in a mosque
- Committee assignments in a state legislature
- A Javanese wedding
- Social-interaction relationships on a navy ship

If readers are not already acquainted with the lore surrounding such events, then it is not sufficient for the thesis or dissertation author to describe only the events as they took place. An interpretation that clarifies the symbolic significance of what was seen and heard is also required.

Simple visual images often imply complex meanings. Each of the following icons serves to encapsulate, in the minds of the informed, the complex belief system of the organization or philosophical persuasion with which the icon is associated,

Whenever such a symbol appears in the data of a research project, the author is obligated to identify not only the group or set of convictions implied by the logo, but also to explain what meaning that symbol is intended to convey in the author's project.

An embedded expression. Frequently, brief verbal passages or graphic images that appear in research data require a researcher's interpretation. Such is the case when an analogy or aphorism has been used by an author to suggest, in a concise form, the essence of an event or the nature of a person or a group. For instance, imagine that a doctoral candidate, while preparing a dissertation on adolescents' friendship patterns, reads a research study whose author concludes that "the data support the birds-of-a-feather hypothesis." When the doctoral student refers to that study in his dissertation, he should interpret the symbolism's meaning and its source for readers who are unacquainted with the adage "Birds of a feather flock together" (an aphorism traced back at least as far as Miguel Cervantes's seventeenth century *Don Quijote*).

Here are five more embedded expressions whose symbolic meanings depend on readers understanding particular aspects of Western European or North American culture.

- The senator's financial maneuvers proved to be his Achilles heel.
- In the salary negotiations, it was the representative of the teachers union who dropped the ball.
- The woman on trial appeared to be a modern-day Lady Mcbeth.
- The school principal would have been wise to heed Teddy Roosevelt's advice about speaking and carrying a stick.
- The psychologist made the same mistake as had the boy who cried wolf.

Verifying symbolism interpretation. When attributing meanings to symbols, researchers are responsible for ensuring that their interpretations are accurate. This may be a simple task when the symbols are familiar ones within the researcher's own culture, but the job of verification is more demanding when symbols from other eras or other places are involved. Consider, for instance, a dissertation project focusing on styles of oratory in present-day South Pacific Islands politics. The dissertation's author, in a copy of a Samoan politician's speech that she had collected, encountered the phrase "The legislation I am sponsoring should help prevent future cases of Tufugauli's ears." Two methods the researcher could use for assigning an accurate meaning to the politician's phrase would be (a) to ask a knowledgeable Samoan for an explanation (preferably, to ask more than one knowledgeable Samoan in order to check for consistency) and (b) to search for historical accounts, written in English, that might clarify the intended meaning of Tufugauli's ears. One such account could be Schultz's *Proverbial Expressions of the Samoans* (Schultz, 1965), which offers this explanation.

> The expression "Tufugauli's ears go wandering about" (*Ua tafao taliga o le Tufugauli*), is a warning to beware of traitors. King Sun, the ruler of the islands of Atafu-mea, was famous for the way he oppressed his subjects. One day, as some girls discussed their deplorable state and cursed their ruler, they were overheard by a boy named Tufugauli, who was feigning sleep in a corner of the house where they chatted. Later the boy reported the event to his relative, King Sun, who was infuriated and thereupon severely punished the people of the village. Since everyone except Tufugauli had suffered King Sun's wrath, the people realized that the boy had been the informer. It was then that the girls commented, "Tufugauli's ears go wandering about." (Schultz, 1965, p. 23)

The politician's allusion to the proverb could therefore be interpreted to mean that his proposed legislation would help prevent the types of eavesdropping on private communications that had led to a recent scandal over the unauthorized wiretapping of phones in the community.

Conclusion

The aim of this chapter has been to demonstrate that (a) there are numerous ways to interpret the results of a research project and (b) different ways can consist of different blends of qualitative and quantitative perspectives. The kinds of interpretation mentioned in the chapter have included those focusing on causation, comparison, prediction, evaluation, generalization, function, context, process, personal effect, theory testing, symbolism, consequences, emotional reactions, motives, true-versus-false conclusions, and the trustworthiness of evidence.

Part II

A Variety of Thesis and Dissertation Proposals

The relationship between the contents of Part I and the contents of Part II can be illustrated with a culinary example. The multiple research methods described in Part I are like the ingredients used for preparing a meal —chicken breasts, potatoes, carrots, lettuce, salt, sugar, milk, strawberries, walnuts, orange juice, and such. And the 20 thesis and dissertation proposals in Part II are like the meals created by means of blending the food ingredients in various ways. In effect, each thesis and dissertation plan in Part II represents a different mix of qualitative and quantitative research methods from Part I.

There is no single, universally agreed-upon form in which thesis and dissertations proposals should be cast. The organization and content of an acceptable proposal usually depends on such considerations as the

- preferences of the student's faculty advisers who must approve the plan—particularly the advisers' preferences regarding the amount of detail the proposal should contain, the sections into which the proposal should be divided, and the intended research methodology,
- focus of the study as defined by the questions the project is designed to answer,
- types of research methods the student intends to use,
- availability of the sources of the data that must be collected, and
- studens' own preferences and ingenuity.

To illustrate different forms that proposals may assume, the examples in Part II are intentionally cast in various styles. Different faculty advisers and different students will find some of the styles more acceptable than others.

The 20 proposals in Part II are distributed among five chapters, each focusing on a different type of contribution to knowledge.

- Chapter 8: Solving Immediate Problems
- Chapter 9: Establishing Foundations for Planning
- Chapter 10: Applying and Testing Theories
- Chapter 11: Contributing to Research Methodology
- Chapter 12: Replicating Others' Research

Throughout Part II, every proposal is presented in the same general fashion, with the proposal itself preceded by a *salient features* preface which alerts readers to aspects of the student's plan that warrant attention. Those aspects include the proposal's particular blend of qualitative/quantitative methods and any characteristic of the plan that distinguishes it from others in the collection.

The 20 proposals, in effect, serve as a cafeteria of components from which students may wish to select ideas that can be incorporated into their own thesis or dissertation plans.

8

Solving Immediate Problems

The aim of conducting research is frequently to discover how best to cope with a practical problem. The thesis and dissertation proposals described in this chapter demonstrate six ways that qualitative and quantitative methods can be blended in research that derives from such an aim.

Evaluating Ways of Teaching Science

Salient features. The central focus of this thesis proposal is an experiment in which two methods of science instruction are compared. The quantitative results of the comparison are in the form of students' test scores. Qualitative judgments are involved in the teacher's selecting the items to include on the tests. Qualitative aspects are also found in the post-experiment interviews conducted with selected students to reveal their perceptions of the two methods of instruction they experienced during the experiment. This case also illustrates a compromise between an ideal experimental design and a design that is practicable in a typical school context.

Thesis title: A Comparison of Two Methods of Teaching General Science to Middle-School Students

Introduction: Among science teachers, one traditional instructional method combines lecturing with textbook-reading assignments and group discussions. In recent years, as an alternative to traditional methods, computerized self-instructional programs have been developed that enable a student, through use of a personal computer, to study school subjects at his or her own learning pace. In my role as a teacher of general science in a middle school, I have wondered which approach—the traditional or the computerized—is more effective for teaching about

101

such aspects of science as genetics, atomic theory, cell structure, and symbiosis. The purpose of this thesis is to investigate the comparative effectiveness of my traditional method and a computer approach.

The following description of the project is presented in nine sections: (1) project objectives, (2) experimental design, (3) project participants, (4) treatment content, (5) test construction, (6) administering the treatments, (7) analyzing the quantitative results, (8) conducting follow-up interviews, and (9) project limitations and applications.

Project objectives. The project is designed to answer four questions about teaching science at the middle-school level.

1. For students in general, what is the effectiveness of a computerized self-instructional method as compared to the effectiveness of a method that combines illustrated lectures with textbook readings and group discussions?
2. Does one of those two instructional approaches produce greater variability among students in their learning science than the other approach? In other words, does one method, when compared to the other method, result in a greater knowledge gap between the most successful and least successful students?
3. For particular students, is a computerized self-instructional method more effective than a lecture/textbook/discussion method?
4. What factors in students' lives apparently influence how well they learn (a) science in general and (b) specific aspects of science?

Experimental design. The project is in the form of a two-phase experiment, whose structure is illustrated in the following diagram. As the diagram shows, the design is a pretest/treatment/posttest type. The experiment will extend over six weeks. Phase One will last three weeks (five class periods per week), as will Phase Two. On the first day of each phase, all students will take the same pretest that focuses on the subject-matter of the treatment phase (genetics in Phase One, atomic theory in Phase Two). The pretest is intended to reveal what each student knew about the subject-matter at the beginning of the experiment. On the last day of each phase, all students will take the same posttest that samples the content of the lessons the students had studied during 13 class periods of the treatment. The posttest is intended to show what each student knew about the subject-matter at the end of the treatment.

The labels *Group A* and *Group B* refer to the students who will take part in the experiment. During Phase One, students in Group A will study genetics by means of a lecture/textbook/discussion method, while students in Group B will study genetics by means of a computer program. During Phase Two the groups will be switched, with Group A assigned to computers and Group B assigned to lectures, textbook assignments, and discussion sessions. This switching procedure should provide information about how well individual students succeed under the computer approach as compared to how they fare under the lecture/textbook/discussion approach.

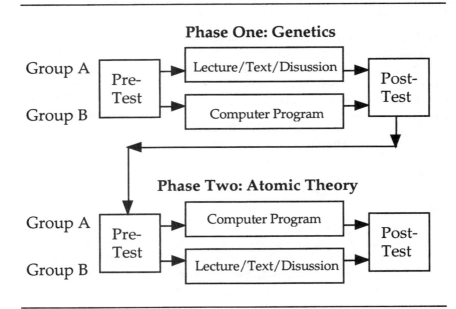

Phase One: Genetics

Group A — Pre-Test → Lecture/Text/Disussion → Post-Test

Group B — Computer Program

Phase Two: Atomic Theory

Group A — Pre-Test → Computer Program → Post-Test

Group B — Lecture/Text/Disussion

Project participants. At the middle school in which I teach, I am assigned four classes of general science, with an average of 30 students per class. I plan to use these students as the subjects of this experiment. Because all four classes are heterogeneous in terms of students' academic achievement (that is, students of the same achievement level are not grouped together in the same class), the average level of accomplishment is typically quite similar from one class to another. Therefore, I plan to place two classes in Group A and the remaining two in Group B, bringing the total number of students in each group to around 60. This means that Group A and Group B will likely be similar in their usual level of academic success.

Treatment content. I chose genetics and atomic theory as the topics for the experiment for two reasons.

First, both topics are at a similar level of difficulty in terms of abstract thinking skills. Therefore, I would expect that understanding the concepts in the Phase One treatment would be about as demanding as understanding the concepts in Phase Two.

Second, both the computerized lessons and the textbook have been produced by the same company, so the contents of the textbook chapters on genetics and atomic theory are essentially the same as the lessons on those topics in the self-instructional computer program. Therefore, the two treatments (computer program versus lectures/textbook/discussions) are quite comparable in terms of their subject-matter.

Test construction. Achievement tests focusing on the content of the textbook chapters and computer programs are included in the instructor's manual that accompanies the textbook and computer package. However, those tests fail to meet the needs of this experiment because (1) there is only one form of each test, (2) there are too many true-false items (true-false types do a poor job of evaluating students' knowledge and skills), and (3) no items adequately measure students' scientific-reasoning skills. Therefore, it will be necessary for me to create my own tests. As shown in the research-design diagram, I will need two tests covering genetics (pre- and posttest) and two covering atomic theory. I plan to adopt the following pair of principles as guides in developing the tests:

1. Each test should be in two equivalent forms. One form will be used as the pretest and the other as the equivalent posttest. The items on the pretest will focus on the same concepts and information as those on the posttest but will be phrased differently so that students, when taking the posttest, cannot simply recall correct answers from the pretest.
2. The items should include both objective types (multiple-choice, fill-in-the-blanks) and essay types. Multiple-choice items are well suited to quickly assessing students' ability to distinguish between correct and incorrect facts, definitions, and applications of concepts. Fill-in (completion) items can efficiently measure recall (not just recognition) of concepts. Essay items can reveal students' ability to organize a persuasive line of reasoning that is based on an accurate command of facts and concepts.

Administering the treatments. My classes usually are held in the general-science classroom. That is where the lecture/textbook/discussion treatment will take place. However, because that classroom lacks enough computers to accommodate 30 students at the same time, the computerized-program treatment will take place in one of the middle school's computer laboratories, where each student will be assigned a personal computer to use throughout each class period. I will serve as the instructor for all four classes.

I foresee a problem of individual students' having different learning speeds during the computer treatment, since some of them are quicker and more diligent workers than their classmates. Consequently, some students will have completed the computer program well before the end of the three weeks. In order that such class members will not be forced to waste time after finishing the basic unit, I will need to provide them supplementary computer programs which enable them to extend their knowledge of science beyond the material in the experiment.

Analyzing the quantitative results. The quantitative results of the experiment will be in the form of each student's scores on the two pretests and two posttests. The first step in the analysis consists of subtracting each student's Phase One pretest score from his or her posttest score and doing the same for Phase Two. The purpose of this step is to arrive at a *change score* for each student from Phase One and also a *change score* from Phase Two. The change score represents how much the student apparently profited from the three-week treatment, that is, how much the student learned beyond what she or he knew at the outset of the study.

The second step in the analysis involves calculating the average change score (mean) and the extent of variability of change scores (standard deviation) for each group (A and B) under each treatment condition (computer and lecture/text/discussion). The four averages resulting from this computation furnishes the information needed to answer to the first of the research questions: "For students in general, what is the effectiveness of a computerized self-instructional method as compared to the effectiveness of a lecture/textbook/discussion method?"

The four standard deviations provide the information needed to answer the second question: "Does one of those two instructional approaches produce greater variability among students in their learning science than does the other approach?"

Comparing each student's change score from Phase One with that student's change score from Phase Two furnishes information useful in answering the third question: "For individual students, is a computerized self-instructional method more effective than a lecture/textbook/discussion method?"

Conducting follow-up interviews: The fourth research question is: "What factors in students' lives apparently influence how well they learn (a) science in general and (b) particular aspects of science?"

I am assuming that those influential factors are not only complex but likely differ from one student to another. Therefore, in an attempt to identify at least a few such factors, I plan to interview selected students to learn how they perceive the study of science in general and how they viewed the methods and subject-matter of the experiment. I imagine that the extent of variation among students in the factors influencing their performance can be most readily revealed by interviewing three kinds of students: (1) ones with high change-scores in both Phase One and Phase Two, (2) ones with low change-scores in both Phase One and Phase Two, (3) ones whose change-scores differed significantly between Phase One and Phase Two.

Therefore, after the quantitative analysis has been performed, I intend to inspect individual students' change-score patterns so as to locate class members who fit the three types that I wish to interview. I believe the factors that could be most readily revealed through such interviews would concern students' *interest* in science topics (particularly in genetics and atomic theory), their *perception of the difficulty* of understanding genetics and atomic theory, and their *preference* of learning method (the individualized computer study approach versus the lecture/textbook/discussion approach). During the interviews, I not only plan to pose questions focusing on these three matters, but I will encourage students to express any other opinions they have about the study of science and about how our class can be made more appealing and valuable to them.

The interviews will be recorded on audiotape so they can later be analyzed and so that illustrative quotations can be extracted for inclusion in the final research report.

Project limitations and applications. The structure of this project represents a compromise between the ideal and the practicable. For example, I would be more confident that members of Group A and Group B were equal in learning potential if the students could have been originally paired in terms of science aptitude and achievement, then one of the pair assigned to Group A and the other to Group B. Or, as an alternative, students might have been assigned to their group through a random-selection process. However, neither of these options is feasible in a typical school, such as the one in which I teach. Therefore, I cannot be absolutely confident that the two groups at the beginning of the experiment were equal in all important ways that would affect their test scores.

Ideally, this experiment would include a much larger number of students who studied additional science topics at different grade levels in more schools than just my own. Then we could be more confident that the results of such an expanded investigation would serve as a guide in how to teach science under various conditions. In short, great caution is warranted in how the outcomes of my study are applied.

The results can be used with greatest confidence in my own middle school for guiding decisions about how to teach general science so that the instructional methods are best suited to each student's characteristics. However, beyond my own school, the outcomes of the experiment may also suggest potential applications for curriculum planners and science teachers in other settings that involve other students, other teachers, other science topics, other materials (textbooks, computer programs), and other evaluation techniques. Consequently, additional experiments of a similar type might profitably be conducted to confirm, revise, or qualify the outcomes reported in this thesis.

Effective Political Ads

Salient features: In this plan, qualitative judgments are reflected in people's expressions of preference for various kinds of political advertisements that appear on television and in mailed brochures. Qualitative decisions are also involved in the experimenter's creating a system for classifying the reasons people offer in support of their preferences. Quantitative methods are used for reporting the numbers of people who prefer different advertisements and the numbers who cite particular reasons for their choices.

Another noteworthy feature of this proposal is the author's including *dummy tables* (tables without data filled in) to make clear at the outset the form in which quantitative results will be displayed.

Dissertation title. *Appealing Characteristics of Political Advertisements*

Background setting. The approach of a public election is always accompanied by a rapid increase of political advertisements on television, on the radio, in newspapers, and in the mail. The inventors of those advertisements try various sorts of appeal in their effort to attract votes for their favorite candidates and favorite ballot initiatives. Some ads employ humor, others appeal to voters' fears, still others attack the ostensible faults of a candidate's opponents, and so on. Therefore, a question that interests both political activists and political scientists is: What kinds of advertising are most successful with what kinds of voters under what circumstances? The purpose of this dissertation project is to contribute to the available knowledge about that question.

Data-collection process. Information about voters' opinions of political ads will be collected by asking a sample of potential voters to judge the appeal of a series of advertisements and to explain the reasoning that supports their judgments.

The form of the advertisements. Two sets of political advertisements will be created. The first set consists of eight one-minute television ads (on videotape) that simulate types of ads that have appeared in actual election campaigns. In the advertisements (labeled Ad-A through Ad-I), the names of candidates for office will be fictitious, so that viewers will not bring preconceived opinions of actual candidates to the task of appraising the ads. Viewers are to tell how compelling they find each ad and to explain why they hold such a view.

The second set is composed of eight printed brochures, with each brochure consisting of a pair of facing pages. Four of the pairs focus on candidates for political offices, while the remaining four concern ballot initiatives (environmental pollution, campaign finance, school bonds, tax reform). In each pair, the ad on the left page employs a different appeal to voters than does the ad on the right page. Voters are asked to choose which ad in each pair they find more persuasive and to explain why they prefer that one.

Variables that differentiate one advertisement from another include:

A candidate's or presenter's physical attractiveness
A presenter's gender
The visual setting (opulent, humble)
Humorous versus serious
Emphasis on a candidate's position versus an attack on an opponent
Real-life versus animated-cartoon characters
Rapid-fire speaking versus slow speaking
The inclusion of a candidate's family versus picturing the candidate alone
Testimonials by notable entertainment figures (actors, athletes, musicians) versus testimonials by prominent political figures
Full-color brochure versus black-and-white brochure

Two samples of potential voters. The subjects in this study will be (1) students in two university introduction-to-political-science classes (a total of about 150 students) and (2) elderly people in a retirement facility (an estimated 40 or 50 individuals). These two types of voters were chosen chiefly because they are available to the present researcher, they represent contrasting generations of voters, and the people can be gathered as a group to participate in the study (the students are obliged to participate as members of the university class, and many of the retirees are glad to pass the time in interesting activities with their peers).

Administering the videotaped and printed advertisements. For the university students, the videotapes and brochures will be administered during two class periods. For the retirees, the videotapes will be shown on one evening and the brochures on another evening.

During the first political-science-class period, each student will be provided a printed *response form* with a short section for personal-identification information (age, gender) and a long section in which students are to record their answers to a pair of questions about each of the eight one-minute advertisements that they will view: "Would you be inclined to vote for this candidate? If yes, then why? If no, then why not?" The class session will begin by the experimenter explaining the general purpose of the study. Then the first videotape will be shown on the classroom television monitors. When the brief ad is finished, the video-tape machine will be stopped while students write their responses to the two survey questions. In the same manner, the seven remaining ads will be displayed and students will write their responses.

During the first half of another university-class period, the brochure portion of the study will be administered. Students will be furnished a packet containing (1) copies of the eight two-page printed brochures and (2) an answer booklet in which students record their choices between the two options in each of the eight pairs of advertisements. Students will also be asked to write their reasons for preferring one of the options over the other.

The same procedure for administering the videotape and brochure ap-proaches will be followed at the retirement facility as that used with the university classes.

Data compilation and analysis. The information from the students' and retirees' videotape and brochure record forms will be reported in a manner that provides answers to the following sets of questions:

1. How many participants stated that they would likely vote for each of the eight candidates represented in the videotapes? How did the per-centage of students compare with the percentage of retirees who would vote for the candidates? How did the percentage of males compare with the percentage of females who would vote for the candidates?

Table 1 shows the form in which the frequencies of yes/no responses to the videotape data will be displayed.

2. How many participants chose each of the options offered in the eight pairs of brochure advertisements in which the ad on the left page dif-fered in style from the ad on the right page? How did the percentage of students compare with the percentage of retirees who preferred a par-ticular option? How did the percentage of males compare with the per-centage of females who preferred a particular option?

Table 2 shows the form in which the frequencies of left/right choices among the brochure-ad styles will be organized.

3. For each of the videotaped ads, what reasons did participants offer in support of their decisions about candidate in the videotape? How did the reasons offered by students compare with the reasons offered by re-tirees? How did the reasons offered by males compare with the reasons offered by females?

Eight tables in the form of Table 3 below will be created to show the frequency of the reasons participants offered in relation to each of the videotaped ads. To prepare each table, I plan (1) to read all of the reasons on every respondent's answer sheet and (2) to identify the *types of reasons*

Table 1

Would You Vote for the Candidate in the Advertisement?

	Students				Retirees				Students+Retireees					
	Male		Female		Male		Female		Male		Female		M+F	
	Y	N	Y	N	Y	N	Y	N	Y	N	Y	N	Y	N
Ad-A														
Ad-B														
Ad-C														
Ad-D														
Ad-E														
Ad-F														
Ad-G														
Ad-H														
Ad-I														

Y=Yes   N=No   M+F=Males plus Females

under which all of the respondents' answers could be placed. In other words, I will create a grounded typology out of the reasons expressed on the answer sheets. Once the typology is complete, I will once again read every respondent's answers for a given videotaped ad and place a tally mark beside the type of reason that each answer reflects. Through such a process I can (1) devise a classification system for the reasons given in support of participants' decisions in each of the eight cases of videotaped ads and (2) prepare a series of eight tables that show the frequency with which each type of reason was offered by the participants in the study. All eight of the resulting tables will take the form of the dummy table shown in Table 3 below.

4. For each pair of brochure ads, what reasons did participants offer in support of their decisions about which of the two ads they preferred? How did the reasons offered by students compare with the reasons offered by retirees? How did the reasons offered by males compare with the reasons offered by females?

Table 2

Which Advertisement—the Left or the Right—Do You Prefer?

	Students				Retirees				Students+Retireees					
	Male		Female		Male		Female		Male		Female		M+F	
	L	R	L	R	L	R	L	R	L	R	L	R	L	R
Pr-A														
Pr-B														
Pr-C														
Pr-D														
Pr-E														
Pr-F														
Pr-G														
Pr-H														
Pr-I														

Pr=Pair of Ads   L=Left Page   R=Right Page   M+F=Males plus Females

The same procedure used to create a system for classifying reasons about the videotaped ads will be used to devise a typology for the brochure ads. Consequently, the frequency of every type of reason for each of the eight brochure-ad comparisons can be shown in eight tables of the same kind as the partial dummy table illustrated in Table 3.

Table 3

Reasons Offered in Support of Decisions about TV Ad-A

Types of Reasons	Students		Retirees		Students+Retireees		
	Male	Fem	Male	Fem	Male	Fem	M+F
Type X							
Type Y							
Type Z							
Type N							

In the reasons tables, the numbers showing the frequencies of each type of reason will be entered in the presently empty cells. Then the percentages of students-versus-retirees and of males-versus-females who offered each type of reason can be computed from the numbers in each table.

The interpretation and application of the results. The job of interpreting the survey results will consist of three main steps. First, the questions posed in the above data-compilation section will be answered on the basis of the filled-in tables. Second, I will speculate about likely causes for any statistically significant differences revealed between students and retirees and between males and females. Third, I will select quotations from participants' reasons for their decisions so as to illustrate the variety viewpoints and patterns of reasoning that individuals expressed in their judgments; and I will speculate about the likely causes for the differences among the people who expressed those opinions.

As a practical application of the study's results, I plan to offer a series of suggestions that creators of political advertisements might profitably follow in preparing ads.

A Functional English-Usage Curriculum

Salient features. The author of this proposal plans to analyze high-school students' written work in order to identify the kinds of errors students committed and the frequency of each type of error. A course-of-study for teaching writing will then be created, focusing attention on correcting the most common mistakes students make in their writing. The author will depend on qualitative content analysis for identifying technical and stylistic shortcomings in students' writing. Qualitative judgments will also be involved in devising a curriculum aimed at correcting students' writing deficiencies. Quantitative data are obtained by the author's calculating the frequency of different kinds of errors and then using those data as guides to which kinds of writing defects warrant the greatest emphasis in the curriculum.

This proposal also illustrates how a pilot study can be used to enhance a research plan.

Dissertation title. *Developing an English-Language Writing Curriculum from a Survey of High-School Students' Writing Errors*

Research objectives. The two central purposes of this dissertation are (a) to identify the most common writing errors that high-school students commit and (b) to develop a six-week writing course based on the results of the error search.

The intended contribution. My review of textbooks and instructors' manuals for teaching writing skills supports the observation that many of the concepts that students are expected to memorize and the skills they are expected to master are of little or no practical use in improving the kinds of writing they will be doing most of their lives. Furthermore, even textbooks that do emphasize the sorts of skills students need in order to write well are not organized in a manner that would appeal to most high-school students. (See Appendix A for the materials that were reviewed in the literature survey.)

Therefore, what seems needed in the field of English composition is a course plan—a curriculum—that emphasizes the correction of students' most common errors. To fulfill such a need, this dissertation plan proposes a survey of students' writing errors that can serve as the foundation for a functional English-usage curriculum.

The research design. The project requires information about the types and frequency of high-school students' writing deficiencies. A procedure for obtaining that information is as follows.

Types and frequencies of errors. Around 425 writing products from high school students will be collected. The products will include both nonfiction and fiction that students have written in social-studies, science, and English classes. I will analyze the papers to identify technical errors and style deficiencies. Technical errors are breaches of conventional rules of English-language composition, as found in spelling, grammar, syntax, or punctuation. The word *style* refers to characteristics of writing that influence (A) how clearly readers can understand the author's meanings and (B) how satisfied or pleased readers are with the manner in which the author has expressed those meanings. Judging the technical aspects of a writing product is easier and more objective than judging the style aspects. In other words, personal taste influences the evaluation of an essay's or short story's style more than does the evaluation of the paper's technical accuracy.

The creation of a classification scheme. As the initial preparation for devising a system for analyzing students' writing products, I have already conducted a pilot study of 40 students' papers, including book reports, essays, brief term papers, and short stories. My purpose was to begin developing a system for classifying technical errors and style deficiencies. The following outline shows the types of errors I found.

1. Technical errors
   1.1 Syntax
       1.1.1 Subject missing
       1.1.2 Verb missing or incomplete
       1.1.3 Comma splice
       1.1.4 Begins with *and, but, then*
       1.1.5 Strung together with *and* or *then*
   1.2 Grammar
       1.2.1 Verb-noun agreement errors
       1.2.2 Verb-tense shift
       1.2.3 Other verb errors
       1.2.4 Pronoun errors
       1.2.5 Distant pronoun referent
       1.2.6 Prepositions missing
   1.3 Spelling
       1.3.1 Misspelled words
       1.3.2 Unintelligible words
   1.4 Punctuation
       1.4.1 Sentence-ending punctuation error or missing
       1.4.2 Commas missing
       1.4.3 Commas incorrectly inserted
       1.4.4 Quotation marks used incorrectly
       1.4.5 Apostrophes for contractions missing or incorrect
       1.4.6 Apostrophes for possession missing or incorrect
   1.5 Capitalization
       1.5.1 Missing at beginning of sentence
       1.5.2 Proper-noun capital missing within sentence
       1.5.3 Capital used when it should not have been used
2. Style deficiencies
   2.1 Organization
       2.1.1 Sequence of ideas confusing
       2.1.2 Uninteresting beginning
       2.1.3 The ending falls flat or is illogical
       2.1.4 Extraneous, distracting segments should be eliminated
   2.2 Word choice
       2.2.1 Repeats the same word too frequently, needs synonyms
       2.2.2 Words insufficiently precise to describe events clearly
       2.2.3 Includes crude words that do not fit the spirit of the topic
   2.3 Economy
       2.3.1 Length of essay or story too short to explain the topic sufficiently
             or to satisfy the reader's curiosity
       2.2.2 The writing product is too long, too repetitive, or with too many
             digressions in order to cover the topic efficiently

This initial version of the writing-error typology will be refined and expanded during the process of analyzing the 425 papers that will comprise the data base for the project.

The source of papers. The 425 papers to be analyzed will be obtained from social-studies, science, and English teachers in two high schools. I will borrow the papers, photocopy each one, and return the originals to the teachers. The names of the students who wrote the papers will be kept secret.

The process of evaluating the writings. The procedure for judging the 425 papers involves four steps.

First, I have already prepared a scoring booklet for use in judging the quality of writing from the perspective of the classification system described above. The booklet tells how to judge a student's writing in terms of each characteristic in the classification system; the explanation of each item is illustrated with examples drawn from students' papers. A three-page score sheet will be filled in for each paper judged. (See Appendix B for the booklet and score sheet.)

Second, a friend of mine (another doctoral candidate) who is a fluent writer will join me in evaluating the same 25 papers, with each of us working independently. The purpose of this stage of the process is to determine how closely we agree in our judgments. After evaluating the 25 papers, we will compare our score sheet for each student in order to determine the inter-rater reliability of the scoring system. In the cases of score-sheet items that we rated differently, we will discuss our differences and try to clarify the scoring-booklet directions (perhaps add more examples) in a manner that enables us to agree in at least 90% of our decisions about the particular technical feature. From our inspection of the 25 papers, we can also add to our classification system any kinds of errors not already identified on the score sheet. The scoring booklet and score sheet will then be revised and refined for use with the remaining 400 writing products.

Undoubtedly our inter-rater agreement will be higher for technical errors than for style deficiencies, since style depends more on personal taste than do technical aspects. Therefore, I expect to be obliged to accept a lower level of agreement in matters of style.

Third, I, myself, will score the remaining 400 papers.

Fourth, each of the 400 score sheets will not only describe the kinds of errors found on the particular paper but also the number of each kind. Therefore, the total number of each kind of error can be calculated for the entire collection of 425 papers. As a result, I can report the frequency of each type of error for all papers combined.

Reporting the error-survey results. The chapter of the dissertation in which the writing-analysis results are reported will address every technical aspect and every style characteristic in turn, describing the nature and frequency of each error or deficiency, along with illustrative examples from the students' papers.

Applying the survey results. The results will provide the basis for my constructing a six-week functional English-usage course-of-study that focuses on correcting the technical and style inadequacies found in the survey of high-school students' writings.

Juvenile Delinquents' Lifestyles

Salient Features: This dissertation writer's search for the most effective ways to reform juvenile lawbreakers involves a qualitative content analysis of court cases to identify conditions in the lives of 100 delinquents as those conditions relate to the success of treatments applied to the offenders by the justice system. The pattern of relationships among such variables is estimated both by means of the researcher's intuitive (qualitative) judgment and by quantitative computation (statistical correlation analysis).

Dissertation title. Matching Treatments to Offenders' Circumstances

Background setting. In the criminal-justice system, a question which has never been answered to everyone's satisfaction has been: "What treatment of juvenile law breakers is most effective for turning errant youths into law-abiding individuals?" Among people who write and speak about such matters, some advocate a hard-line approach, including such measures as strict jail terms for first offenders, longer jail terms for repeat offenders, and "scared straight" programs in which delinquents are required to visit prisons where hardened inmates attempt to frighten them into reforming. At the opposite extreme are people who favor soft-line methods—probation, second chance, sympathetic counseling, and eliciting from offenders sincere apologies and promises to mend their ways. Still other people suggest that the best kind of treatment for wayward youths depends on the circumstances in the particular case at hand. I find this third viewpoint—individualized treatments that depend on the circumstances—to be the most convincing. However, the question now to be asked is: "How do you recognize which circumstances warrant which kind of treatment?" In the professional literature bearing on such matters, there appears to be little agreement about what constitutes a proper answer. The purpose of the following research project is to offer a contribution toward a better answer than is now available.

The overall research plan. This project is a correlational study which attempts to determine the extent of relationship among three factors: (1) certain conditions in teenage lawbreakers' lives, (2) different ways such lawbreakers are treated in the criminal-justice system, and (3) those teenagers' subsequent habitual behavior. The study involves the analysis of case records of juveniles (ages 10-17) found guilty of crimes and sentenced to various punishments and treatments. Certain life conditions (home background, school behavior, expressed attitudes, type of crime, and more) in each case are compared (1) with the treatments applied in the cases and (2) with the subsequent behavior of the juveniles. The aim of this procedure is to identify which treatment is most successful in promoting law-abiding behavior among juveniles whose lives display a similar pattern of conditions.

The source of data. In my capacity as a probation officer for the County Correctional Department, I have access to case-records of juveniles, past and present, who have been arrested for different violations and sentenced to various kinds of treatment (probation, placement in a foster home, periodic counseling, short time in juvenile hall, long-term incarceration, and more). The records also include follow-up information about the juveniles' behavior after their official treatment period ended. I am authorized to use these cases in a research project so long as no names of individual juveniles are released. I intend to include around 100 cases in this project.

The research procedure. The process of be followed in carrying out the project is made up of five stages.

Stage 1. Pre-analysis preparation. I have already studied more than 30 books and journal articles that discuss the success of methods of treating lawbreakers, including juvenile offenders. From this study, I have collected a series of life conditions and lifestyles that have been considered by various members of the criminal-justice system to be significant guides to the suitable treatment of offenders. I intend to survey more books and articles so as to collect additional conditions that have been proposed as helpful in suggesting how offenders can best be handled.

Stage 2. Selection of conditions. From among the collection of conditions and from my own experience, I will select those life circumstances that seem potentially to have the greatest influence on the effectiveness of different treatments. I am not only interested in individual conditions (such as one-parent versus two-parent family, good versus bad record of school attendance, or type of crime), but I am also interested in different patterns or combinations of conditions.

Stage 3. Creation of a record form. I will prepare a form on which to record each juvenile's profile of (1) status on each of the conditions selected at Stage 2, (2) type of treatment administered by the justice system, and (3) behavior subsequent to treatment (particularly the extent and types of further delinquency and the youth's level of success in school).

Stage 4. Estimation of the relationship among the variables. Two methods will be used to estimate the connections among life conditions, kinds of treatment, and post-treatment behavior. The first method will be intuitive, in the sense of my inspecting the record forms in order to identify lifestyle or life-circumstance patterns that seem to relate to the success of different treatments. The second method will be statistical—the analysis of the extent of relationship between the success of a treatment and different life-condition patterns.

State 5: The interpretation of Stage 4 results. From the results of Stage 4, I will estimate how well the data enable me to answer the question: "What is the apparent relationship among (1) the type of treatment juvenile lawbreakers receive from the justice system, (2) particular patterns of conditions in juveniles' lives, and (3) juveniles' subsequent behavior in regard to the law?"

On the basis of that interpretation, I hope to be able to offer suggestions about improving the success rate of the justice system's treatment of juvenile offenders.

Controlling Academic Cheating

Salient Features: The following dissertation plan includes four data-collection activities—a search of the professional literature, a student questionnaire survey, a teacher questionnaire survey, and an experiment. Each activity involves both qualitative and quantitative methods. The search for books and articles about cheating yields types of cheating (qualitative) and the frequency of each type (quantitative). The student and teacher questionnaire surveys enable the dissertation's author to produce qualitative categories into which cheating and cheating-detection methods can be divided and to report the incidence of occurrences within each category. The experiment equips the researcher to (a) classify kinds of information (qualitative) that students plagiarize and the frequency (quantitative) of each kind and (b) estimate the reasons that students cheat or refrain from cheating (qualitative).

Three additional distinguishing features of this proposal are an abstract, a time schedule, and an outline of probable dissertation chapter titles and chapter contents.

Dissertation title. *The Incidence and Control of Academic Cheating in Schools and Colleges*

Abstract. Academic cheating consists of students attempting to acquire the symbols of academic accomplishment without acquiring the knowledge and skill that the symbols are expected to signify. This proposed study involves three surveys and an experiment. The surveys involve (1) a compilation and summarization of published accounts of cheating, (2) a questionnaire study of students' experiences with cheating, and (3) a combined questionnaire/interview study of teachers' experiences with cheating. The experiment investigates the effect of a teacher's informing students of the steps the teacher intends to use for discovering cheating.

The practical aim of this research is to identify ways that academic cheating can be effectively controlled.

Historical background. Academic cheating is nothing new. It has likely been going on since the earliest days of formal education. Apparently there have always been students who have sought unauthorized help with tests and writing assignments or have obtained falsified diplomas, grade reports, and transcripts of credits. However, in recent decades a variety of technological innovations have enhanced students' abilities to cheat, so that academic cheating has assumed new dimensions. The technological inventions have included such devices as photocopying equipment, electronic computers, the Internet and its World Wide Web, scanners with optical-character-recognition (OCR) software, digital cameras, language-translation software, cell phones, and hand-held pagers. Of particular importance are Internet websites (called *paper mills*) that will furnish students—usually for a price—completed book reports, term papers, or theses on whatever topics students choose. There are also websites (*diploma mills*) that will sell students fake—but authentic-looking—diplomas from respected universities.

Not only have advances in computer technology expanded students' ability to cheat, but innovations have also improved teachers' ability to detect and control cheating. For example, it is now possible for a teacher to enter a student's term paper or thesis into a program on the Internet and to receive in return an analysis that reveals passages that are identical to passages in previously published documents, thereby informing the teacher of the source of material that the student copied verbatim without giving credit to the original author. By such means, plagiarism can easily be detected.

The research methodology to be used in this study is presented under eight headings: (1) the literature survey, (2) the student questionnaire survey, (3) the teacher questionnaire/interview survey, (4) the experiment, (5) summarizing the results, (6) practical uses of the results, (7) the estimated time schedule, and (8) the dissertation's organization.

The literature survey. A library search of books and articles and a computer search of the World Wide Web will be conducted to locate information about academic cheating. In the dissertation, the results of the searches will be summarized in terms of (A) reasons students cheat, (B) methods of cheating, (C) the frequency of cheating at different levels of the education system, (D) methods used to detect and control cheating, and (E) trends over time in methods and incidence of cheating as well as in methods of detecting and controlling cheating.

The student questionnaire survey. A questionnaire survey is planned for two high schools and one college to learn the circumstances under which students have cheated, including (A) their motives, (B) the settings in which the cheating occurred, (C) how successful their efforts proved to be, (D) under what conditions they would not attempt to cheat, and (D) their feelings about cheating. Information will also be solicited regarding respondents' knowledge of other students' cheating. In order to encourage honesty in filling out the questionnaire items, the questionnaires will not ask for any participating student's name.

The teacher questionnaire/interview survey. In the two high schools and in the college, a sample of teachers will be asked to complete a questionnaire that focuses on (A) types of cheating that their students have attempted, (B) methods the teachers have used to detect and control cheating, and the apparent effectiveness of those methods, and (C) how technological innovations have influenced students' attempts to cheat and the teachers' own responses to those attempts. A subsample of the teachers who participate in the questionnaire survey will be asked to be interviewed by the present researcher so that more detailed anecdotal information can be obtained about interesting issues and practices that those teachers mentioned in their questionnaire answers.

The experiment. An experiment is planned for three high-school English classes and two college American history classes. (I am the teacher of the English classes, and I have a friend who is the instructor of the college classes.) The purpose of the experiment is to discover the effect that the use of a cheat-detection Internet service has on the frequency of students plagiarizing material for their written assignments.

In the high-school English classes, students will be assigned to write three book reports during the semester. The books on which students are to report are ones students select from a list the teacher provides. Each report is to be at least three double-spaced typed pages in length and submitted either as an e-mail attachment sent to the teacher's website, as a file on a diskette, or as a traditional paper version. The first report is due the fourth week of the semester, the second due the eighth week, and the third due the final week.

When the first set of reports has been collected, the teacher enters each report as a computer file on the Internet website of the plagiarism-detection service titled *Turn It In* (http://www.turnitin.com). Although the students have been cautioned ahead of time to do their own work and not to copy a book review—or portions of a review—that was written by someone else, they have not been told that their first report will be checked electronically for plagiarism. They have been shown, as well, how the original sources of copied material should be credited in their own written work. The e-mailed and diskette versions of reports will already be in the electronic form appropriate for submission to *Turn It In.* Any paper versions can be converted to a proper electronic version with a scanner and OCR software.

In preparation for the second book report, the teacher conducts a class session about how Internet cheat-checking services can be used for detecting plagiarism. During the session, she projects the image from her computer screen onto a large movie screen at the front of the classroom so that students can see how passages of a book review—copied from another author's work—have been marked and their original source identified. The book review used for this demonstration is a fictitious one created by the teacher for the purpose of the demonstration. The teacher then informs the class members that their second book report will be submitted to the *Turn It In* plagiarism-detection service. And if plagiarized portions are discovered in any report, the report will be rejected. The students who have submitted reports containing plagiarized passages will then be obligated to substitute a plagiarism-free review of another book.

When the second and third book reports are handed in, the teacher subjects them to *Turn It In* analysis.

The same procedure used with the high-school English classes will be used with the college American history classes.

By means of the foregoing procedure, I will obtain plagiarism analyses of each student's three book reports. Therefore, I can calculate the percentage of each report that has been copied from another author without the students' having placed the copied portions within quotation marks or having acknowledged the original source. From those results, I can calculate the extent to which the classroom demonstration prior to the second report reduced the amount of plagiarism from the first to the second and third reports. By inspecting the nature of the plagiarized segments, I can estimate the sorts of things students are likely to copy and can speculate about the probable reasons for their doing so.

Summarizing the results. The results of the four data-collection methods (literature search, student questionnaire survey, teacher questionnaire/interview survey, experiment) will be integrated in a summary designed to answer these questions:

- In what forms of academic cheating do students engage?
- What is the apparent frequency of different forms of cheating at different age levels?
- Under what conditions are students prone to cheat?
- How have recent technological innovations affected students' attempts to cheat and what has been the success of those attempts?
- By what methods do educational institutions (and especially teachers) seek to detect and control cheating? How successful are those methods?

Practical uses for the results. The results of this research should aid school personnel in recognizing (A) the typical rate of different forms of academic cheating and (B) conditions that encourage cheating and conditions that discourage cheating.

The time schedule. I estimate that collecting the data and writing the dissertation will take between one-and-a-half and two years. The time period during which each activity will be performed and the amount of time each will likely require are as follows:

Questionnaire preparation, tryout, and revision: Months 1–3 (June-August)
Literature survey: Months 1–11 (June-April)
Student questionnaire survey: Months 4–6 (September-November)
Teacher questionnaire/interview survey: Months 8–10 (January-March)
Experiment: Months 4–7 (September-December)
Data analysis (surveys, experiment): Months 8–16 (January-September)
Writing and revising the dissertation: Months 17–21 (October-February)

The dissertation's organization. The following is a tentative version of the dissertation chapters.

Chapter 1: Introduction
    Objectives of the Study
    A Brief Historical Sketch of Academic Cheating
    An Overview of the Study's Methodology

Chapter 2: The Research Design
Foundational Assumptions about Cheating Behavior
The Nature of the Four Data-Collection Methods
The Interlinking of the Methods
Chapter 3: The Literature Search
Purpose and Procedure
The Search Results
Strengths and Limitations
Summary
Chapter 4: The Student Questionnaire Survey
Purpose, Advantages, and Limitations
Creating and Testing the Questionnaires
The Nature of the Participants
Administering the Questionnaires
Organizing and Tabulating Questionnaire Responses
Summarizing and Interpreting the Results
Chapter 5: The Teacher Questionnaire/Interview Study
Purpose, Advantages, and Limitations
Creating and Testing the Questionnaires
The Nature of the Participants
Administering the Questionnaires
Planning and Conducting the Interviews
Organizing and Tabulating Questionnaire Responses
Quotations from Interviews in Teachers' Own Words
Summarizing and Interpreting the Results
Chapter 6: The Experiment
Purpose and Underlying Assumptions
The Experimental Design
The Nature of the Participants
The Conduct of the Experiment
Processing the Data
Summarizing and Interpreting the Results
Chapter 7: The Overall Research Results
A Way to Combine the Four Sets of Results
Types and Incidence of Cheating in Schools and Colleges
Trends in the Relationship Between Technology and Cheating
Chapter 8: Implications for the Control of Academic Cheating
Suggestions for Schools and Colleges
Chapter 9: Implications for Further Research
Questions for Which Better Answers Are Needed
A Series of Potentially Useful Future Research Projects
List of References

Assessing Classroom-Management Practices

Salient Features: In this case, the author plans to conduct a semi-structured meta-analysis of published empirical studies of classroom management in order to identify the conditions under which particular management techniques are most successful. Qualitative aspects of the research take the form of (a) important assumptions the author adopts as a foundation for the study, (b) descriptions of specific classroom management problems and solutions that the author extracts from the professional literature, and (c) the classification system the author devises for categorizing problems and solutions. Quantitative aspects of the research are in the form of (a) the frequencies of different problems and solutions as reported in individual studies and as summed across studies and (b) measures of the degree of success of attempted solutions.

This proposal also includes a section in which the author explains the meanings assigned to terms that play an important role in the project.

Thesis title. Which Classroom Management Techniques Work Best?
An Analysis of Empirical Studies from Grades K–12

The research problem and its significance. Most teachers—perhaps all of them—would probably agree that the greatest problem they face in their career is that of classroom management. It's the problem of arranging the learning situation so that all students are continually mastering the curriculum contents at the optimum level of their ability and are not engaged in conflicting or idle activities. Apparently the guidance that most teachers receive for solving this problem comes from their own experience and from advice offered in teacher-education courses, textbooks, professional journals, inservice workshops, and conversations with colleagues. That advice is often in the form of specific classroom incidents or of general maxims ("Start off very strict, then gradually relax the rules" or "Give every assignment in both written and oral form"). Although these kinds of aid can be of some value, I am convinced that most teachers—and particularly inexperienced ones—would profit from adopting a system of classroom-management analysis that is founded on more secure empirical evidence. The purpose of this thesis is to develop such a system as based on empirical studies found in the professional literature.

The thesis plan is described under six headings: (1) defining key terms, (2) clarifying underlying assumptions, (3) gathering the data, (4) organizing the data, (5) interpreting the data, and (6) preparing a classroom-management handbook.

Defining key terms. The meanings intended by five important terms used in this research are as follows:

K–12 = The classrooms studied are ones from kindergarten through the final year of high school. Thus, no management problems at the post-secondary level are included. However, studies conducted in nursery schools that are essentially like kindergartens are admissible.

Classroom = A *classroom* is a location in which pupils engage in learning activities under the guidance of adults. Therefore, management problems that occur on a playground during school hours, in a gymnasium, on a field trip, in a school's vegetable garden, and the like are considered to occur in a *classroom* and thus are pertinent to the intent of this research.

Management techniques = Both the policies or rules of classroom behavior and the methods for implementing those rules are *management techniques*. The word *discipline* is frequently used in reference to maintaining order in a classroom. However, because *discipline* often carries the connotation that the behavior being referred to is *bad behavior*, the term *management* is used throughout this study to include techniques that promote students' progress rather than only techniques that are intended to control *bad behavior*.

Professional literature = Accounts of classroom management problems and solutions in academic journals, books, magazines, newspapers, unpublished dissertations, and Internet websites qualify as items of *professional literature*.

Empirical studies = For the purpose of this research, a distinction is drawn between *empirical study* and such expressions as *theoretical proposition* and *experiential impression*. For a study to qualify as *empirical*, it must be a report of a specific incident or collection of incidents in which a classroom-management problem is described, a solution attempted, and the outcome assessed. In contrast, a *theoretical proposition* is a suggestion about how to cope successfully with a classroom management problem, with the suggestion based on a theory or set of assumptions about people's actions in social situations, particularly in school settings. An *experiential impression* is a person's belief about how to cope with classroom problems, with that belief founded on the person's direct experience or vicarious experience (reading a book, seeing a movie, listening to a friend). All data collected in the present project are to be based on empirical studies. Theoretical propositions and experiential impressions reported in the professional literature are not admissible.

Clarifying underlying assumptions. This project is founded on two major assumptions. The first concerns the patterning of causal factors that influence classroom management. The second concerns the usefulness of professional literature.

Patterns of causal factors. I am assuming that classroom events are the result of a combination of causal influences rather than the result of a single factor, such as the teacher's methods of punishment or the quality of the available learning materials. Even though all of the factors that can affect classroom events are too great in number to be identified and weighed in teachers' classroom-management decisions, I believe that four of the most powerful can be considered in practical decision-making situations. I have labeled those four (1) students' personalities, (2) teachers' management styles, (3) learning facilities, and (4) school culture. Each of these factors is composed of more specific subfactors. For example, students' personalities consist of the attitudes and abilities that students bring to the learning situation. Teachers' management styles are teacher behaviors that result from such teacher characteristics as appearance (size, gender, attire), social-relation habits (ways of interacting with others), and subject-matter expertise. Learning facilities are the available equipment and supplies. A school's culture includes both the formal regulations and the unstated expectations and ways of acting that are generally understood as being appropriate in schools.

The usefulness of professional literature. I am assuming that the professional literature bearing on classroom management can offer trustworthy empirical information about (1) types of classroom-management problems, (2) the four major factors that I accept as determinants of classroom-management events, and (3) the success of teachers' attempts to solve those types of problems.

Gathering the data. The search for empirical studies will be conducted (1) in our university library (books, academic and professional journals, conference proceedings, magazines, newspapers, unpublished documents in the *ERIC* files, theses, and dissertations) and (2) on the Internet.

The search will be guided by key words and phrases often associated with classroom management (such as *discipline, student behavior, classroom organization, classroom control, learning environment*) and by words related to the four major factors (and their subfactors) mentioned in the model of classroom management described in the above assumptions section.

Organizing the data. Information from the compiled empirical studies will initially be classified under the following categories.

1. Types of classroom-management problems
2. Influential student personality traits
3. Teacher management styles
4. Learning facilities
5. School-culture characteristics
6. Patterns of interaction among items 1 through 5 (includes specific examples from empirical studies)

I cannot expect that every empirical study will contain adequate information about item 1 in the above list, nor will every study provide sufficient information about each of the four factors (items 2 through 5) of the analytical model. Therefore, when filling in item 6 (patterns of interaction), I will give priority to studies that include the most information about items 2 through 5.

I expect that there may also be useful information from the empirical studies that cannot reasonably be located in the six categories. Therefore, the four-factor analytical structure may need to be altered to accommodate such information. In other words, my original assumption about the causes of classroom-management events may require revision.

Interpreting the data. From a careful inspection of the contents of items 1 through 6 of the study's results (or of a revised, expanded version of that classification system), I will estimate the degree of consistency of information across empirical studies. In other words, I will attempt to draw supportable generalizations about each of the items in the classification system and to estimate the degree of confidence that can be placed in each generalization. In other words, I will evaluate the validity of my original model (or revised version) and estimate how effectively generalizations drawn from the empirical studies can serve as practical guides for teachers in their classroom-management decision-making.

Preparing a classroom-management handbook. The final step in the project will be that of writing a manual that can help teachers solve classroom-management problems. On the assumption that the survey of empirical studies will yield persuasive generalizations about effective classroom-management techniques, I plan to write such a manual in an *if-then* fashion. In other words, the manual would be organized around types of classroom-management problems. For each problem, various solutions would be proposed in the following form: "*If* the type of management problem you face is (such and such), and *if* the pattern of significant factors is (such and such), *then* taking (so and so) action may solve—or at least ameliorate—your problem."

Conclusion

This chapter's six proposals have shown diverse ways that qualitative and quantitative methods can be combined in research that is intended to help people cope with problems they face in their careers. For example, qualitative procedures illustrated in the proposals have included: (a) interviews to learn respondents' opinions (science-teaching experiment), (b) researchers' subjective judgments about which kinds of items to include on a test or questionnaire (science-teaching experiment, political-ad study), (c) participants' choices among options (political-ad study), (d) typologies that researchers create for classifying data (political-ad study, language-usage project, cheating project), (e) ways of translating research results into practical applications (language-usage project, classroom-management study), (f) methods of estimating the patterning of interactions among multiple variables (delinquency study), (g) descriptions of the historical development of a phenomenon (cheating project), (h) underlying assumptions on which researchers base their projects (classroom-management study).

Quantitative methods used in the six projects included: (a) achievement-test scores (science-teaching experiment), (b) the compilation of the number of people expressing a particular preference and offering types of reasons for their decisions (political-ad study), (c) the calculation of frequencies of observed phenomena (language-usage project, cheating project, classroom-management study), (d) computations of the degree of correlation among variables (delinquency study), and (e) statistical analyses of the success or failure of attempted solutions to a problem (delinquency study, classroom-management study).

9

Establishing Foundations for Planning

Research results are frequently useful as background information on which administrators or practitioners can base their plans for the future, as illustrated in this chapter's four proposals. The first example describes a public-opinion survey of community members' attitudes regarding school-voucher programs. The second example outlines a three-century historical review of a county's educational provisions. The third is intended as a source for the content of a six-week curriculum unit focusing on the culture of the region's principal Native-American ethnic group. The fourth is designed to furnish information useful in planning a school's computer-technology facilities.

Conducting a Public-Opinion Poll

Salient features. The main quantitative aspects of this study are found in the statistical results of (a) respondents' answers to questions posed in a survey of people's attitudes regarding school vouchers and (b) a numerical summary of reports of the success of voucher programs as extracted from the professional literature. The principal qualitative aspects appear in (a) the author's historical review of voucher issues and (b) quotations of opinions of selected individuals who participate in the survey.

Thesis title. The Acceptability of School Vouchers in Oceanside City

Project summary. This research involves conducting a public-opinion survey to determine the attitudes of Oceanside City residents about the desirability of furnishing public funds to families to pay for their children's attending private schools or attending public schools outside the Oceanside City school system. As a background for the survey, the research includes a study of voucher plans in the United States and of the present status of different forms of schooling in Oceanside City and in nearby communities.

The research results are expected to help Oceanside City's Board of Education and public-school administrators estimate the outcome of a possible ballot initiative that proposes a voucher program. The thesis contents may also help them analyze the advantages and disadvantages of whatever voucher plan voters might support.

Data collection. The information required for answering the research questions will be collected by means of two surveys—a literature review and a public-opinion poll. The literature review is to serve as a foundation for (a) selecting questions to be posed in the public-opinion poll and (b) guiding the interpretation of the poll results by placing the results in a historical context.

The literature survey. The author of this thesis intends to review the professional literature to answer the following questions:

1. In the realm of schooling, what has been the history of the separation of church and state in the United States?
1. What has been the history of educational voucher plans in the United States (both privately and publicly funded plans)? How successful have voucher programs been, and what criteria have been used for judging their success?
1. What arguments have people presented in support of, and in opposition to, voucher plans?
1. In Oceanside City and nearby communities, what has been the history of—and present status of—different forms of schooling (public schools, religion-affiliated private schools, secular private schools, home schooling, distance schooling, etc.) and the history of how those forms have been financed?

The public-opinion surveys. The author intends to conduct two types of public-opinion polling. One type is a telephone survey. The other is a personal-interview survey. The purpose of the telephone survey is to gather *brief-opinion* information from a wide variety of Oceanside City residents. The purpose of the personal-interview survey is to obtain *in-depth-opinion* information from a limited number of residents.

Telephone survey. A systematic sample of 200 respondents will be selected from the Oceanside City telephone book. In a telephone interview conducted by the author, each respondent will be told briefly the purpose and form of the main voucher program that has been proposed for Oceanside City school district, and the respondent will be asked whether he or she would either favor or oppose such a program, and why. If any person who is called declines to offer an opinion, another randomly selected phone number will be substituted so that the final sample will consist of 200 brief opinions.

Personal-interview survey. A sample of 20 parents of pupils who currently attend Oceanside City public schools will be asked to participate in an in-depth interview that is intended to reveal (a) which, if any, of four potential voucher plans they would endorse and (b) the line of reasoning supporting their decisions. The parents will be ones recommended by school principals as individuals who represent various ethnic and socioeconomic backgrounds.

Data classification and analysis. The results of the telephone survey will be reported in two forms: (a) as the percentages of respondents who favored and who opposed the voucher plan and (b) as a table listing, in terms of frequency, the reasons respondents offered in support of the opinions they expressed.

The results of the 20 in-depth interviews will be reported in two forms: (a) a table showing how the parents ranked the four alternative voucher plans in terms of the plans' desirability and (b) extensive quotations from the interviews to show, in parents' own words, the diversity of parents' reasoning about vouchers.

The results of the Oceanside City surveys will then be compared with a summary of the statistical and reasoning results of the studies that were collected in the literature survey. The purpose of the comparison is to show how closely the sample of Oceanside City respondents' views match the opinions of people elsewhere.

Interpretation and application. The report of the research will conclude with a summary of (a) the recent history of voucher plans in the United States, (b) the main results of the Oceanside City surveys, and (c) advantages and disadvantages of the several options that Oceanside City citizens and school administrators face as they decide which position they will adopt in regard to the plans currently under discussion.

Because the aim of this thesis is only to clarify the considerations that deserve attention in decisions about vouchers for Oceanside City, the thesis will not include a recommendation about which of the suggested plans, if any, should be adopted.

Analyzing Historical Trends

Salient features. In this dissertation, qualitative methods appear (a) in the author's choice and description of events from the past which, in the author's judgment, demonstrate significant interactions between educational institutions and the society in which those institutions are imbedded and (b) in the author's interpretation of how the interactions operated. The project's quantitative aspects assume the form of (a) statistical information about the society and the schools and (b) comparisons of quantitative change from one historical era to another.

Dissertation title. *Patterns of Educational Development—*
A History of Schooling in Shoshone County—1700-2000

Dissertation purpose. This study is designed to answer three principal questions about Shoshone County over the years between 1700 and 2000.

1. What changes occurred in the county's broader society that most significantly affected the lives of the residents?
2. What changes occurred in the county's educational institutions?
3. What symbiotic relationship obtained between social conditions and the schools? In other words, how did societal changes affect the county's schools, and how did events in the schools influence the broader society?

Significance of the research. The dissertation is intended to make three contributions to knowledge.

- Furnish a historical record of educational trends in Shoshone County. (No single continuous record for the period 1700-2000 exists at present.)
- Clarify the interaction between societal conditions and schooling in order to illustrate the interdependence of Shoshone County's social/political setting and its educational institutions.
- Identify trends in past societal and educational developments that can help public officials, business leaders, social-welfare personnel, and educators plan for the future.

The overall research plan. By examining various kinds of published resources and by interviewing long-time residents of Shoshone County, the writer will first collect information from the period 1700-2000 regarding (a) major events and trends in the United States, (b) major events and trends in Shoshone County, and (c) the conduct of education in Shoshone County. While collecting such data, the writer will begin to identify ways that those three kinds of events appear to have influenced each other. When all of the data have been compiled, the gradually evolving picture of society/school interaction will be refined, and a line of reasoning will be developed to support the hypothesized symbiotic relationship among national societal trends, Shoshone County societal trends, and Shoshone County educational practices. Finally, predictions will be offered about what this picture of past trends suggests for the future of Shoshone County and the county's educational institutions.

The form of the information search. To reduce the task of surveying three centuries of history to a manageable size, the writer plans to (A) divide the 300 years into *nine successive periods*, with each period approximately 25 to 35 years in length, (B) gather information about *significant societal conditions* during each period, and (C) gather information about *significant educational conditions* in the nation and in Shoshone County for each period.

The sources of information for the literature review will include American history books and journal articles, Shoshone County newspaper archives, books and magazines about Shoshone County (local libraries), Shoshone County schools' records, and computer Internet websites. The people to be interviewed are long-time county residents who likely have personal information about societal or educational conditions over the past few decades.

The following societal conditions will be the focus of the literature search and the interviews about the nation and about Shoshone County. These conditions have been selected because of their assumed influence on educational provisions for the nation in general and for Shoshone County in particular. Further conditions that come to the writer's attention during the process of searching the literature and conducting interviews may be added to this list.

- Population size, geographical distribution, ethnic composition, religious affiliation
- Occupational structure—including percent of men and women in different occupations
- Social-class (socioeconomic) structure
- General economic conditions (incomes, employment rates)
- Available technology—particularly for communication and transportation
- Health and safety
- Peace and amity versus societal disorder—particularly disorder that accompanies war, civil strife, crime, and poverty

Educational conditions that will be the focus of the literature search and interviews are listed below. These conditions have been chosen as ones that are strongly influenced by societal change and, in turn, affect the general society. Other educational factors that appear during the process of searching the literature and conducting interviews may be added to this list.

- Types of educational institutions and opportunities (formal and informal, public and private)
- Enrollments in each type of institution (including the percentage of each age group, ethnic group, and gender)

- Laws regulating educational aims and practices
- Stated objectives of institutions
- Institutions' organizational structures and lines of communication
- The financing of education
- Curricula (subjects taught)
- Facilities (buildings, equipment, supplies)
- Methods of instruction
- Educational personnel (by types, duties, training, gender, remuneration compared to other occupations in the society)
- Ways of evaluating learners, educational institutions, and educational personnel

The process of analyzing interactions. The method to be used in estimating the reciprocal influence of the society and its educational provisions is based on the assumption that such influence is extremely complex and involves more conditions than a researcher could identify completely or measure precisely. Therefore, the best that can be hoped for is that a number of the most significant factors will be discovered and their interactions approximated so as to yield an informative—although still inexact—account of how a society and its educational provisions affect each other. Consequently, the process of analyzing interactions involves a substantial measure of personal judgment—a combination of intuition and logic—on the part of the researcher. Quantitative information can be of great value in this process by showing how much conditions changed over a time period, such as how the percentages of females earning high-school diplomas differed from one 25-year period to another. Then qualitative information about societal conditions prior to and during that period can suggest why the percentages changed in the observed manner. The process of explaining how societal conditions affected educational conditions can, therefore, be guided by such questions as:

- Which educational conditions (such as enrollment patterns, curricula, teaching methods) changed from one era to another?
- What societal conditions—prior to and during the educational change—were altered, why, and by what process did those alterations affect educational practices?

In like manner, the act of explaining how schooling influenced the society can be guided by the following question:

- What changes occurred in educational conditions from one era to another, and in what ways was the broader society subsequently affected by those changes?

The author's final responsibility then becomes one of constructing a persuasive line of reasoning to support the kind of causal connections the author has proposed between the society and its educational institutions.

Predicting the future. Because the main practical purpose for carrying out this historical study is to help Shoshone County educators plan for the years ahead, the dissertation will close with a section speculating about the likely future of societal conditions and about the kinds of problems and opportunities the educational community may face as a result of those conditions. The speculation will essentially consist of a projection into the future of trends from the past in societal conditions and educational practices.

Producing Curriculum Source Material

Salient features. This study of a Native-American people's culture depends predominantly on qualitative research techniques—the content analysis of book and journal materials and of interviews conducted with individuals well versed in Cherokee culture. Qualitative decisions are also required in the author's fashioning a narrative out of the information gathered from the literature search and interviews. Quantitative methods are limited to (a) the collection of census data about the population and geographical distribution of Cherokees and (b) the numbers of different sources of information the author used as the foundation for the narrative account, as reported in an appendix at the end of the dissertation.

Another distinctive feature of this proposal is the doctoral student's adapting a descriptive model from the anthropological literature to serve as the framework for the dissertation.

Dissertation Title: Furnishing Content for the Study of a Region's Native-American Culture

The Need for Research: The school in which I teach is located in a region whose substantial number of Native Americans are predominantly Cherokee. In order to acquaint all sixth-graders in our school district with the cultural history of the Cherokees, the district's curriculum-development personnel plan to create a four-week study unit focusing on life among the Cherokees, past and present. What is now needed for implementing the plan is a reliable source of content for the unit. I propose to meet that need by preparing a cultural history of the region's

Cherokees, a history that provides a general structure for the unit as well as detailed information about important aspects of Cherokee culture.

The process of carrying out this project consists of four major stages.

- Stage 1: A descriptive model is adopted for determining which kinds of information about Cherokee culture should be collected.
- Stage 2: Sources of information about Cherokee culture, past and present, are identified. Those sources include published books and articles and people who are intimately acquainted with Cherokee life.
- Stage 3: The desired information is collected from the sources by means of a literature search and interviews.
- Stage 4: The information is presented as a series of narratives that are organized according to the descriptive model.

The descriptive model. The term *descriptive model*, as intended here, means a pattern or template that dictates the form in which a phenomenon will be portrayed. Rather than attempting to create a model by myself, I hunted through anthropological, sociological, and educational books and journals for models or frameworks that had already been successfully used for depicting important aspects of culture. The model that I adopted was one that had been used in the South Pacific's Samoan Islands as the guide to teaching Samoan culture in the islands' schools. Although the journal article in which the Samoan study was described used Samoan-culture examples to illustrate the application of the scheme, the model itself was a general or generic one that could be used to depict any culture, including that of the Cherokees.

The definition of *culture* underlying the structure of the model is one offered by Hofstede (1980, p. 25):

> Culture can be seen as behavior unique to human groups, including material objects involved in such behavior, as well as language, ideas, beliefs, customs, strategies, codes, institutions, tools, techniques, works of art, rituals, ceremonies, pastimes, and the like. Culture reflects "the collective programming of the mind which distinguishes the members of one human group from another."

The following model is an revised version of the framework that was published in an article entitled "A Pattern for Teaching Indigenous Culture" in the journal *Comparative Education*, Volume 10, No. 1, 1974.

The framework is divided into seven sections that reflect viewpoints toward culture as expressed by anthropologists, biologists, political scientists, sociologists, social-psychologists, and historians. The sections treat matters of:

1. People's roles or positions in Cherokee society, including occupations and positions in the system of governance
2. Material culture—objects employed in a Cherokee lifestyle
3. Graphic arts, music, and dance
4. Ceremonies, religious beliefs, and practices
5. Games, sports, recreation, and entertainment
6. Plant life and animal life
7. Significant non-living elements of the environment

The contents of each section assume a three-dimensional form. The first dimension, labeled *types of items*, consists of descriptions of important kinds of items belonging in the particular section. For example, Section 7 lists such important nonliving elements in Cherokee culture as land formations, rivers and seas, sun and moon, rain and drought, changes of seasons, minerals and stones, and more. Section 5 lists all Cherokee forms of recreation and entertainment.

The second dimension, called *item characteristics*, focuses on important kinds of information about each of a section's item types. Thus, under Section 1, the following sorts of information are described for each role or position in Cherokee society:

(a) The role's name
(b) The responsibilities assigned to the role
(c) Privileges and rewards associated with the role
(d) Functions of the role in the society (what service the role performs for the society or for particular members of the society)
(e) By what means a person achieves and retains the role
(f) The traits or skills needed for performing the role
(g) The behavior considered proper and improper for people in that role
(h) Ways a person can lose the position or be removed from it

As another example, consider the kinds of information to be obtained about the items in Section 2: Material Culture (tools, weapons, buildings, home furnishings, foods, food-preparation equipment, clothing, items of personal adornment, handicrafts, and more).

(a) A description of the item and its estimated origin
(b) The purpose or function of the item in Cherokee society
(c) The materials from which the item was made, including advantages and disadvantages of those materials
(d) Who prepared the item, including what skills were needed and how those skills were acquired
(e) Who used the item and under what circumstances
(f) The kinds of standards applied in judging the quality of the item

The third dimension in the description of Cherokee culture is labeled *historical time*. It involves answering the two-part question: How did each cultural element change over the decades, and what were the apparent forces that caused such change?

The way a section's three dimensions fit together is illustrated on the following page for the contents of Section 3: Graphic Arts, Music, and Dance (see Figure 1). As the diagram shows, each cell in the model represents a set of artistic components of the culture. The types of components are listed across the top, the characteristics of components that need to be described are listed along the left side, and the historical development of each type is represented along the vertical axis. Therefore, my task, as defined by the model, is to search for the information that describes the characteristics of each kind of artistic endeavor found under each of the types listed across the top of the cube. Similar cubes can be constructed to represent the three-dimensional character of all of the other sections of the model.

As explained earlier, the data needed to fillout the descriptive model will be sought by hunting through published materials about life among the Cherokees, past and present, and by interviewing people who are well versed in the nature of Cherokee life.

The literature search. The three main sources of information will be university and public libraries, the Internet's World Wide Web, and archives maintained by each of the region's newspaper publishers.

The literature review will be guided by the questions implied in the descriptive model. For example, information will be sought to answer such questions as the following about Section 1: People's Roles in Cherokee Society.

- What were the names or titles of different roles or positions in the society? How and why did names or titles change over time?
- What were the duties or activities that each role involved? How and why did the activities change with the passing of time?
- What were the privileges and rewards that each role entailed? How and why did those privileges and rewards change over time?
- etc.

The information from the search will be recorded in several ways. My handwritten notes taken in a library or archive from books and periodicals will later be typed into a computer file. Whenever possible, I will take my laptop computer to libraries so my notes can be entered immediately into the computer rather than first being written by hand. Photocopies of articles or book chapters will be entered into the computer with the use of a scanner and optical-character-recognition software. A separate computer file will be established for each section of the descriptive model, with the file divided into subsections defined by the model's components. For example, the file on Section 3 will be divided into types of artistic activities, characteristics of each type, and historical changes in each type. Consequently, when I set out to write the dissertation, all of the information I need about a particular topic will be in the same file.

Figure 1

A Model of Artistic Aspects of Cherokee Culture

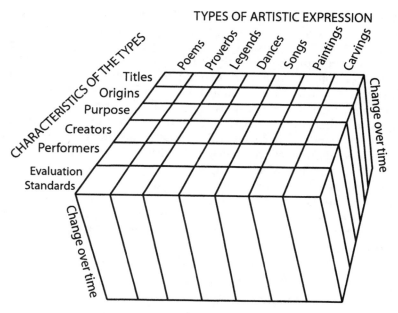

Adapted from: R. M. Thomas. (1974). "A Pattern of Teaching Indigenous Culture," *Comparative Education*, Vol. 10.

The interviews. The interview phase of data collection will involve four steps: (a) preparing an interview procedure, (b) identifying and gaining the cooperation of suitable interviewees, (c) conducting the interviews, and (d) recording the results.

(a) The conversations with informants will be *guided interviews* rather than *casual, undirected interviews.* In other words, I will ask the participants specific questions that derive from the descriptive model rather than simply asking them to "Tell me what Cherokee life used to be like and what it's like today." Therefore, my pattern of questioning will be directed by a printed set of questions that I take with me to the sessions.

(b) I plan to use three methods for locating knowledgeable interviewees—ask Cherokees with whom I am already acquainted, contact Cherokee leaders in our region who can suggest appropriate informants, and search the Internet's World Wide Web (which contains nearly 13,000 web sites that furnish Cherokee information, including genealogies and the names of Cherokees in our region).

(c) I intend to carry out both face-to-face interviews and telephone interviews.

When conducting an interview, I will first explain the purpose of my dissertation research by asking for the respondent's help in this venture. Then I'll ask if the informant minds my tape-recording our conversation so that I won't forget any of the information he or she gives me. If the individual objects, then I won't tape record the session but will take handwritten notes. I expect that during the interviews some informants will not stick strictly to the questions I ask but, instead, will occasionally digress to other topics. Because those digressions may contain valuable information about Cherokee culture that I had not envisioned, I won't try to direct them back to the original question but will record what they have to offer. Only when a digression is clearly irrelevant will I try to steer the conversation back to my list of questions.

(d) Because the job of typing into a computer the entire verbatim conversation from a tape recording would be unduly burdensome, I intend to listen to each tape and then type (1) a summary of the answer to each interview question and (2) any exact quotations that are of particular interest—ones that deserve to be stated in the informant's own words.

Presenting the cultural history. The final stage of this project consists of my writing a narrative that is interesting and accurate (worth reading its own right) and that can serve as the source material for an instructional unit on Cherokee culture for our region's sixth-grade pupils.

Here is a tentative set of chapters for the dissertation.

Part I: Backgrounds of the Study
Chapter 1: The Need for a History of Cherokee Culture
Chapter 2: The Research Methodology
Part II: Cherokee Culture, Past and Present
Chapter 3: A Brief History of the Cherokees
Chapter 4: How the Cherokees Have Governed Themselves
Chapter 5: People's Roles in Cherokee Society
Chapter 6: Cherokee Material Culture
Chapter 7: Forms of Art in Cherokee Culture
Chapter 8: Cherokee Ceremonies and Religious Practices
Chapter 9: Cherokee Recreation and Entertainment

The above proposed structure is properly viewed as "tentative" because, during the process of collecting data and organizing it, I may discover that the original descriptive model needs revision. Consequently, the pattern of chapters in the final version of the dissertation may also need to be changed.

When writing chapters 3 through 10, I need to identify for readers the sources of my data about each portion of each chapter. That is necessary because readers have a right to know (a) where the data came from and (b) on how many sources the content of a given section has been based. In order to furnish that information without continually interrupting the flow of the narrative, I plan to place superscript numbers at appropriate places in each chapter (such numbers as [14] or [27]). Those numbers relate to *endnotes* in Appendix A at the end of the dissertation. The endnotes identify both (a) the types of sources of the data adjacent to the superscript numbers in the text and (b) the number of sources (books, articles, interviews) on which those data were based.

Identifying Computer-Technology Needs

Salient features. Qualitative aspects of this project include descriptions of computer-technology equipment and services gathered from a search of the professional literature, a questionnaire survey, interviews, and visits to schools. The quantitative component of the project is found in a series of tables showing the frequency of different answers that the data collection provided for seven questions that guided the research.

An additional noteworthy characteristic of this proposal is the author's including specific examples of the literature sources to be consulted and telling where the names of suitable questionnaire recipients will be found. Such specificity is intended to help convince the author's dissertation supervisors that the author has, indeed, "done his homework" and is well prepared to carry out the study.

Dissertation title.   *Hardware and Software Considerations in Planning a School's Computer-Technology Facility*

The dissertation's purpose. As the Central City Unified School Districts moves into the computer era, administrators need to learn what kinds of computer-related hardware, software, and services schools should offer in order to be up-to-date. To meet this need in a systematic manner, I plan to carry out a study that helps school personnel make decisions about computers, peripheral equipment, and computer-associated services in school settings.

Overview of the research plan. The study is designed to answer seven principal questions.

1. What services can computers and computer-related equipment provide in a school?
2. What kinds of hardware (machines, equipment) and software (programs that instruct machines in how to carry out functions) can provide the services identified under question 1?
3. What are the best sources of information for answering question 2, and how does one find those sources?
4. What factors should be considered in arriving at a decision about whether a particular item of hardware or software should be acquired?
5. Once an item of hardware or software has been obtained, how can the effectiveness and efficiency of that item-in-use best be evaluated?
6. What are examples of wise decisions made in the acquisition and use of hardware and software?
7. What are examples of unwise decisions made in the acquisition and use of hardware and software? How might those unwise decisions have been avoided?

Answers for the seven questions will be sought by means of four information-gathering methods—(1) a search of the professional literature, (2) an e-mail questionnaire survey sent to school systems, (3) telephone follow-up interviews with a selected set of the school systems that responded to the e-mail survey, and (4) observations and interviews that I carry out during visits to schools and to school-districts' central technology-services sites.

Finally, the information collected by the above four methods will be synthesized into a report that provides detailed answers to the seven research questions. It is conceivable that during the information-gathering process, additional important guide questions will emerge. Those questions will also be answered in the final report.

The professional-literature search. The literature useful for the purposes of this study will be found mainly in libraries and on the Internet. In addition, I will collect catalogues issued by companies that sell computers, peripheral equipment (scanners, digital cameras, photocopy machines, and others), and software in order to compare types of items and their costs. Examples of sources that will be of particular interest are the National Educational Technology Standards (cnets.iste.org) and such periodicals as *Educational Technology & Society* (ifets.ieee.org/periodical), *Education Week, The Chronicle of Higher Education,* and the online journal *Educational Technology Review* (aace.org/pubs/etr).

The main search engines to be used in surveying the World Wide Web are Google, Teoma, and Altavista. Typical key words and phrases to guide the survey are *educational technology, computers in education, computer assisted instruction, digital photography,* and *educational communications.*

The e-mail survey. The names of appropriate people to participate in the e-mail survey will be found in two ways. First, the literature search can provide the names of authors who have written informative articles and books on the topic of this dissertation. I will try to locate the authors' addresses (postal and/or e-mail) and ask the authors to participate in my questionnaire study. I will also ask authors to suggest the names of other potential informants. Second, I will contact officials in organizations that specialize in the kinds of information that I need and will ask for the names and addresses of suitable participants for the survey. Two such organizations are the International Society for Technology in Education (www.iste.org) and Association for Educational Communications and Technology (www.aect.org). A further source is the Office of Educational Technology (www.ed.gov/Technology) at the U.S. Department of Education.

The questionnaire, designed to answer the seven research questions, will contain both multiple-choice items and open-ended questions. A copy of a temporary version of the questionnaire accompanies this proposal as Attachment A. This version is based on the results of an initial search of the literature and my interview with the director of technology services for the Central City School District. I plan to do a tryout study of the questionnaire by sending it to 10 teachers, six school principals, and three heads of technology-services departments in nearby counties. On the basis of their suggestions about the content and form of the questionnaire, I will revise the questionnaire, putting it in the form that will be sent to the final participants whom I select by the method described in the above paragraph.

Because the Central City school system includes students from kindergarten through the two-year community college, the participants in the survey need to include individuals who are well acquainted with the kinds of computer-technology equipment and services useful at the different steps of the schooling ladder.

The telephone-interviews. Participants' responses to the e-mail survey can alert me to school systems that appear to warrant my talking directly to certain of the participants to learn in greater detail about their situations. Therefore, in the respondent-identification portion of the e-mail questionnaire, I will include a space for the participant's phone number. When I phone a respondent, I will explain the purpose of my call (my interest in their technology program) and ask if we might discuss points of interest, either now or at a later, more convenient time. I will also ask if it is all right for me to tape record our conversation so that I will be able to recall the information accurately.

Therefore, by means of telephone interviews, I hope to gain a more detailed understanding of the matters treated in the e-mail survey.

The site visits. Information about some aspects of a school's educational-technology services can best be obtained by direct observation and face-to-face discussions with teachers, administrators, and computer-technology personnel. Consequently, from my literature survey, e-mail questionnaire results, and telephone conversations, I will select several school districts to visit personally. I plan to take a camera with me on those visits in order to photograph equipment and facilities of particular interest. The most informative of those photographs can be included in the dissertation.

The final report. According to my tentative plan, the final version of the dissertation will contain three sections.

The first section will describe the need for the study, the data-collection process, and how the final report was prepared.

The second section—and by far the longest of the three—will answer each of the seven research questions in turn. The section's contents will be a combination of qualitative and quantitative information. The qualitative portion will consist of descriptions of different ways the research question has been answered (various options) in different school systems. The quantitative portion will consist of the frequency with which each option has appeared in the data derived during literature search, questionnaire survey, interviews, and site visits.

By way of illustration, consider the first research question: "What services can computers and computer-related equipment provide in a school?" The types of services will be listed according to the frequency with which they were reported in the collected data—with the most frequent service placed first and the least frequent last. For each question, two kinds of tables will be prepared. The first kind will show the *overall* frequency for all levels of the schooling ladder. The second type will show the frequency of services in terms of five grade-level groups: (1) kindergarten through grade 2, (2) grades 3–6, (3) grades 7–9, (4) grades

10–12, and (5) grades 13–14 (two-year community college). The intention of the five-level tables is to indicate differences in services for different levels of the schooling hierarchy. Similar tabular information will be presented in the reports about the remaining six research questions.

The third section of the dissertation will suggest (1) how the information in the second section can be used by the people who plan and use computer-technology services in the schools, (2) cautions to be observed in incorporating computer-technology in educational institutions, and (3) kinds of additional research needed about the topic of the dissertation.

Conclusion

The purpose of this chapter has been to demonstrate four types of research that furnish background information useful in preparing plans of action.

Qualitative aspects of the illustrative cases have included: (a) surveys of the literature to trace a topic's historical background (school vouchers, schooling in Shoshone County, Cherokee culture), (b) quotations of people's opinions about controversial issues (school vouchers), (c) individuals' descriptions of their experiences (Cherokee culture, computer technology), and (d) the manner in which researchers report their findings (all four studies).

Quantitative aspects have consisted of: (a) reported frequencies of people's expressed opinions (school vouchers), (b) frequencies of practices (school vouchers, Cherokee culture, computer technology), (b) quantitative changes in social conditions over time (vouchers, Shoshone County schooling, Cherokee culture), (c) comparative costs (vouchers, computer technology), and (d) totals of the sources of information about the research topic (Cherokee culture, computer technology).

10

Applying, Testing, and Generating Theories

A key purpose of some research projects is to demonstrate the real-life application of a theory, to test how adequately a theory explains some aspect of life, or to create a theory out of the research data. The four proposals in this chapter illustrate different ways that qualitative and quantitative methods can be combined in applying, testing, or generating theories.

At the outset, it is important to recognize how the word *theory* is used throughout the chapter. A theory is an estimate of (a) which components of an event are involved in the event and (b) how those components relate to each other. Two sorts of theories illustrated in this chapter are the *explanatory* and the *classificatory.*

The purpose of explanatory theories is to identify the causes of events and to describe how the causes operate. The key components of explanatory theories are the factors that interact to produce an event (the causes) and the outcomes of those interactions (the effects). For example, in the field of psychology, the major causal components in B. F. Skinner's (1974) theory of learning are (1) the learner's needs or drives that determine what the learner seeks in the environment and (2) the environmental consequences that follow the particular behavior that the person displays in a learning situation. As for the *interaction* between the person and consequences, if the person finds the consequences of a behavior rewarding (*reinforcing*), the person will tend to display that same behavior in similar future situations. But if the person finds the consequences unrewarding (either *punishing* or simply *nonreinforcing*), he or she will tend to avoid exhibiting that behavior in the future. Hence, in Skinner's theory, the effects are the behaviors the person has learned to habitually display as a result of the consequences experienced in the past. Thus, in such a manner, researchers use explanatory theories to account for why events happen as they do.

Classificatory theories are proposals about useful ways to categorize components of events. Such proposals are usually referred to as *typologies, taxonomies,* or *classification systems.* In such systems, the components of events are organized into groups, with each group defined in terms of selected ways that the members of the group are alike. An example of such a taxonomy is found in the *Diagnostic and Statistical Manual of Mental Disorders—IV* (American Psychiatric Association, 2000). The manual was created to guide psychotherapists' decisions about how to treat people who suffer behavioral disorders. A key assumption behind the DSM classification scheme is that patients whose observable symptoms and life conditions are much alike are people who share the same underlying illness, so that the same kind of therapy should be suitable for all patients within their assigned category. Thus, the events that are classified by means of the DSM are people's typical ways of acting in various situations. Researchers use classificatory theories for assigning aspects of events to categories that render the components readily compared.

In the following pages, the first of the research plans demonstrates the application of two theories for explaining an assumed causal relationship between a society and its educational institutions. The second plan illustrates a research project designed to test the validity of a theory. The third describes a method of generating a theory (a *grounded* theory) from information the researcher has compiled. The fourth demonstrates a way the author intends to derive a classification system from data collected in the author's envisioned project.

Social Environments and Human Development

Salient features. The author of this proposal combines two theories of human development as a foundation for a study of how selected conditions of a society can affect people's beliefs and actions at different stages of their lifespan. The quantitative aspects of the project are in (a) the scores derived from an attitude questionnaire that participants complete, (b) the amount of discrepancy between participants' scores, and (c) statistics from published surveys of people's opinions about four controversial issues—sexual behavior, the use of marijuana and of alcohol, and warfare. The qualitative aspects include (a) participants' opinions expressed during interviews about how they developed their attitudes toward the controversial issues and (b) the researcher's interpretation of the questionnaires and interviews in relation to the pair of theories on which the study is founded. This proposal is an example of a dissertation plan in considerably more detail than the others in the chapter.

Proposed Dissertation Title:
The Influence of Societal Conditions on Individuals' Attitude Development

Synopsis

There appears to be widespread agreement among social scientists that general conditions in a society at any given time strongly influence the beliefs and behavior of individual members of the society. However, the process by which that influence is exerted has not been adequately explained. The purpose of this research project is to contribute to the explanation of that process by studying the expressed attitudes and beliefs of eight youths, their parents, and their grandparents regarding four public issues—sexual behavior, smoking marijuana, drinking alcohol, and warfare.

The Aim of the Study

The two-fold aim of the project is to

- Empirically demonstrate one way that theories can be combined to explain how societal events affect individuals' attitudes at different times in those individuals' life spans.
- Assess how effectively the present author's questionnaire/interview data-collection method provides the information needed for interpreting people's attitude development from the perspective of the two theories.

Theoretical Foundation

The approach adopted in this study is based on an integration of two models that are intended to explain how societal conditions affect people's beliefs and behavior.

Bioecological theory. The first theory is Bronfenbrenner's (1979, 1993, 1995) bioecological model that focuses on environments (called *behavior systems*) with which a person interacts. Bronfenbrenner identified four levels of such systems, each defined in terms of how directly the level impinges on the developing person. The settings that affect the individual most intimately are called *microsystems.*

> A microsystem is a pattern of activities, roles, and interpersonal relations experienced by the developing person in a given face-to-face setting with particular physical, social, and symbolic features that invite, permit, or inhibit engagement in sustained, progressively more complex interaction with, and activity in, the immediate environment. (Bronfenbrenner, 1993, p. 15)

Figure I charts four microsystems in the life of a hypothetical 17-year-old—her family, her high school, the agemates with whom she spends time, and the Internet which she accesses by means of the personal computer in her bedroom.

At the next environmental level, the four microsystems are encompassed by a *mesosystem* which constitutes the "linkages and processes" that operate between two or more of the developing person's behavior settings. In our example, the 17-year-old's actions in the classroom and on the street any given day are influenced by her impression of how her parents and peers would regard those actions.

The environmental unit beyond the *mesosystem* is the *exosystem*, consisting of the processes operating between two or more environmental settings, "in which events occur that indirectly influence the processes within the immediate setting in which the developing person lives" (Bronfenbrenner, 1993, p. 22). Four illustrative exosystems in Figure I are the workplaces of the 17-year-old's parents, the neighborhood in which the family's home is located, the school's governing board that passes regulations affecting the students, and the kind of browser in the girl's computer that constrains the sites she can visit on the World Wide Web.

Finally, the source of influence most remote from the 17-year-old's immediate experiences is the array of physical conditions, attitudes, practices, and convictions shared throughout the society. The macrosystem is the cultural milieu, represented in Figure I as the large box encompassing the microsystems and mesosystems. Bronfenbrenner's microsystems serve as the immediate transmitters of culture to the growing 17-year-old. In other words, the family, school, and companions—along with such mass communication media as books, television, and the Internet—are the functionaries that carry society's messages directly to the individual.

Sociohistorical life-course theory. The second theory used in this research is Elder's (1996; Elder, Modell, & Parke, 1993) model which explains an individual's development in terms of (a) the history and present conditions of the society, (b) the history of the individual's own development, and (c) ways that these two histories interact to determine the person's present and future beliefs, attitudes, and behavior.

Central to Elder's theory are four propositions which identify theory components and their interaction.

- *Social stability and social change.* Each person is raised in a society that moves through phases of stability and change that can significantly affect that person's development. Those phases include changes in such things as (a) public order and safety (peace/war, strikes, crime), (b) sexual-relationship patterns (marriage/cohabitation, heterosexuality/homosexuality) (c) economics (prosperity/de-

Figure I

Bronfenbrenner's Bioecological Model

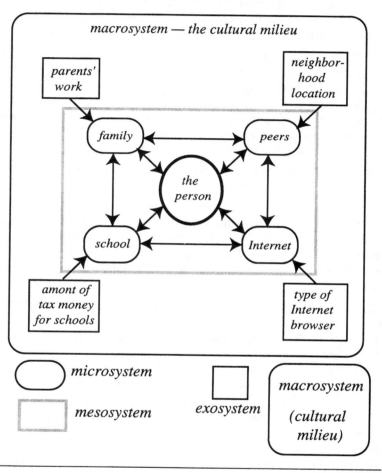

pression), (d) the society's ethnic patterns, (e) health conditions and medical practices, (f) religious affiliations, and more.

- *Time and place.* Each person is at a particular time and place in relation to society's phases. This linking of time and place produces a life-stage principle which states that "the influence of a historical event on the life course depends on the stage [of life and place] at which the individual experiences the event" (Elder, 1996, p. 52).

- *Mediators.* The impact of societal characteristics on development is transmitted to the person by mediators or agents with whom that individual directly interacts. Typical mediators are parents, other family members, neighbors, companions, teachers, and mass-communication media (books, television programs, videos, computer networks) that convey to, and interpret for, the developing person the significance of events in the broader society.

- *The individual's developmental history.* Within each person's life course, time operates in a cumulative fashion. The passing years furnish a continuing stream of new experiences from which the individual extracts knowledge, attitudes, and skills that are integrated into the ones that have accrued over past years. Consequently, the description of an individual's life course is a historical account of this cumulative process.

Adapting the theories. How the Bronfenbrenner and Elder models are combined in this dissertation is reflected in the project's methodology.

The Research Methodology

In the following section, the methods for carrying out the research are described under six headings: (a) general research design, (b) essential assumptions, (c) the selection of participants, (d) instrumentation, (e) interviews, (f) literature search, (g) data processing, and (h) interpretation of the results.

General research design. The participants in the study will consist of eight youths (ages 18-20), their parents, and one or two of each youth's grandparents. Thus, eight three-generation *family clusters* will form the objects of study.

All of the participants will complete a 20-item attitude questionnaire reflecting their present opinions about the study's four controversial issues—sexual behavior, smoking marijuana, drinking alcohol, and warfare (five items per issue). In addition, the parents and grandparents will fill out the same questionnaire in the way they think they would have responded when they themselves were around age 18 to 20.

The completed questionnaires will be compared to determine the extent of attitude agreement between (a) the youth and each parent (present time), (b) the youth and each grandparent (present time), (c) each parent (present time) and spouse (present time), (d) parent (present time) and grandparent (present time), (e) the youth and each parent (past time), (f) the youth and each grandparent (past time), (g) each parent (present) and herself or himself (past), (h) grandparent (present) and herself or himself (past), and (i) parent (past) and grandparent (past).

Calculating the extent of agreement for each of the foregoing combinations of respondents is the initial step toward estimating how societal conditions may influence an individual's attitudes at different junctures in the lifespan.

As a second step, the questionnaire results will be used as the focus of discussion in a subsequent interview with each participant. During the interview, the researcher will use each interviewee's questionnaire answers as a guide to seeking information about why the interviewee believes he or she currently subscribes to the attitude reflected in his or her answer to particular items on the questionnaire. Information will also be sought from parents and grandparents about what influences in their lives apparently account for whatever change (or lack of change) occurred between their present-day attitudes and their recalled attitudes from the time of their youth.

In addition, a search will be conducted for published broad-scale public-opinion surveys that focused on the present project's four controversial issues. The purpose of the search is to determine how the attitudes of the participants in the present project compare with the attitudes of larger numbers of Americans.

The results of the information gathered by the above methods will then be interpreted in terms of the Bronfenbrenner and Elder theories.

Essential assumptions. Two beliefs on which this study is based are that

- Participants will usually answer the questionnaire items and the interview questions as honestly as they can.
- People's recall of the attitudes they held two or more decades in the past will not be precise, yet will still tend to reflect the general nature of their beliefs at that time.

The selection of participants. Obviously, this project's research design places rather strict requirements on the types of subjects who can take part in the study. Each of the eight youths who serve as the central focus of the investigation must have two parents by whom the youth was raised and at least one grandparent with whom the youth spent considerable time during childhood and adolescence. Furthermore, the youth, the parents, and the grandparents must be willing to complete the attitude questionnaire and to be interviewed about the issues treated on the questionnaire. I intend to recruit eight university students with the help of professors who teach undergraduate university classes and perhaps with the help of fraternities and sororities. Potential candidates —youths (ages 18 to 20), their parents, and their grandparents—will be given a detailed written and oral description of the purpose of the study, the questionnaire, and the nature of the interview so that they will clearly understand the intent of the study and the responsibilities they assume by agreeing to take part. They will be assured that fictitious names will be substituted for their own names during the recording of information and in the writing of the final report so that their identities can be kept secret. If they do not wish to have their identities kept secret, then their names will be gratefully recognized on the acknowledgment page at the beginning of the dissertation. Each participant will be furnished a copy of the dissertation in its final form.

Instrumentation. The questionnaire will consist of 20 items, with five items for each of the controversial issues—sexual behavior, smoking marijuana, drinking alcohol, and warfare. Those issues were selected for the following reasons.

(1) News reported in the public press often relates to those issues.
(2) There is marked disagreement within American society about the proper attitudes to adopt toward the issues.
(3) People's welfare can be strongly affected by their own attitudes and by others' attitudes regarding the issues.
(4) Public-opinion polls conducted over the past 60 years reveal significant changes in attitudes toward the four issues from one period of time to another.

The questionnaire consists of 20 statements to which participants are to respond by indicating how strongly they agree or disagree with each statement. Their response is in the form of circling one of five code-letter choices that represent different levels of agreement. The five code letters are defined as follows:

AA = Absolutely <u>agree</u>, with no exceptions.
 A = <u>Mainly agree</u>, but with some exceptions.
A/D = <u>Half</u> agree and half disagree. Or undecided.
 D = <u>Mainly disagree</u>, but with some exceptions.
DD = Absolutely <u>disagree</u>, with no exceptions.

The code system will be explained, along with an illustrative example, at the beginning of the questionnaire. The way items will appear on the questionnaire is shown by the following three examples.

AA A A/D D DD Our nation should wage war against another nation only if our country is directly attacked.

AA A A/D D DD Growing marijuana and smoking it should be made legal, just as smoking tobacco is legal.

AA A A/D D DD   When, how, and with whom people have sexual intercourse is their own business. It's not a matter that should concern the government or general public.

Interviews: The eight youths, their parents, and their grandparents will be interviewed after their questionnaire results have been tabulated. The interviews will consist of the researcher using a participant's questionnaire answers as a guide to which questionnaire items will be discussed. To prevent an interview from using an inordinate amount of the participant's time, the discussion will focus on only a limited number of questionnaire items. The selected items will include (a) at least one focusing on each of the four controversial issues, (b) ones in which the interviewee's attitude was markedly different from the attitudes of other family members (a difference between the youth, parents, grandparents), and (c) ones in which the interviewee agreed closely with one or more of his or her other family members. The discussions will center on questions about (a) what people or media (school, church, books, movies, television, etc.) seemed to exert significant influence on the participant's expressed attitude and (b) how and why that attitude may have changed with the passing of time.

Literature search. In a study of the relationship between the broader society and individuals' attitudes, it is useful to understand the extent to which a particular person's attitudes are typical of those held in the general population. Therefore, this project includes a search for published public-opinion surveys that have treated the same topics as those in the present study. The search will employ library sources and the World Wide Web. An effort will be made to find polls conducted around the present time as well as ones conducted around 20 years ago and 40 years ago when the parents and grandparents in the present study were around ages 18-20.

Data processing. The information collected by means of the questionnaires, interviews, and literature search will be organized and summarized in the following manner.

Questionnaire analysis. The letter-codes that participants used to express their agreement/disagreement with questionnaire statements will be converted to numbers that form a five-step scale (AA=1, A=2, AD=3, D=4, DD=5). Thus, the extent to which a youth and parent agreed with each other on a particular item can be expressed as a *discrepancy score* (the difference between the youth's and parent's opinion). A discrepancy score of 0 means the youth and parent held the same attitude. A score of 4 means the youth and parent held radically different opinions about the statement. Summing the discrepancy scores for all 20 questionnaire items produces an overall numerical picture of the extent of youth/parent attitude agreement about the issues treated on the questionnaire.

In like manner, discrepancy scores can be calculated for all nine of the family-cluster pairings identified above in the description of the overall research design.

Interview analysis. The results of the tape-recorded interviews will be summarized in two forms—as frequencies and as illustrative quotations.

First, I will listen to each interview in order to identify (a) *mediators* (people, institutions, mass-communication media) that the participant cited as influencing her or his attitude toward a particular issue and (b) when and where that influence was exerted. From the interviews, I will create categories in which to classify the mediators, times, and places. Then tally marks will be used to identify—for all interviews combined—the frequencies of mediators, times, and places.

Because numerical summaries fail to reveal how the development of attitudes assumes different patterns in different individuals' lives, selected segments of interviews will be extracted to demonstrate the diversity of such patterns.

Literature search. Statistics from public-opinion polls bearing on this study's controversial issues will enable the researcher to estimate how comparable the attitudes of individuals in the present study are to the attitudes of the people who took part in present-day published polls and in surveys 20 and 40 years ago.

Interpretation. The final two steps in the project consist of my summarizing the results of the data processing and proposing what those results appear to mean in terms of the Bronfenbrenner and Elder theories. This process of assigning meaning to the data will involve a large measure of qualitative judgment and hermeneutic skill.

References

The following are the literature sources cited in this proposal:

Bronfenbrenner, U. (1979). *The ecology of human development.* Cambridge, MA: Harvard University Press.

Bronfenbrenner, U. (1993). The ecology of cognitive development: Research models and fugitive findings. In R. H. Wozniak & K W. Fischer (Eds.), *Development in context. Acting and thinking in specific environments.* Hillsdale, NJ: Erlbaum.

Bronfenbrenner, U. (1995). Developmental ecology: A future perspective. In P. Moen, G. H. Elder, Jr., & K. Luscher (Eds.). *Examining lives in context.* Washington, DC: American Psychological Association.

Elder, G. H., Jr., (1996). Human lives in changing societies: Life course and developmental insights. In R. B. Cairns, G. H. Elder, Jr., & E. J. Costello, *Developmental science.* Cambridge, England: Cambridge University Press.

Elder, G. H., Jr., Modell, J., & Parke, R. D. (1993). Studying children in a changing world. In Elder, G. H., Jr., Modell, J., & Parke, R. D. (Eds.), *Children in time and place.* Cambridge, England: Cambridge University Press.

Testing a Moral-Development Theory

Salient features. The author's purpose in conducting this study is to discover how adequately a theory espoused by Harvard Professor Carol Gilligan predicts the moral judgments of two categories of people (suburban and inner-city high school students) whose beliefs have not been studied before.

Examples of qualitative methodology in the project are (a) the author's choice of moral dilemmas that the study's participants are to judge, (b) the definition of *social class* used for selecting the two high schools from which participants will be drawn, (c) the two schemes that the author devises for classifying students' questionnaire responses, (d) reasons the author proposes for the pattern of answers found in students' judgments of eight cases of wrongdoing, and (e) the author's interpretation of what implications the study's results hold for the validity of Gilligan's theory of moral development.

The chief quantitative components of the plan are (a) the frequencies of high-school students' different preferences for consequences to be faced by wrongdoers, (b) the frequencies of different reasons students propose in support of their preferences, and (c) statistical comparisons between genders and social-class levels in terms of variables (a) and (b).

Dissertation title. Females' and Males' Moral Judgments: An Assessment of Gilligan's Model

Introduction. Over the past two decades, controversy has continued about the question of whether females and males base their judgments of moral events on the same values. The most frequent focus of the controversy has been on the difference between the theory of moral development advanced by Lawrence Kohlberg (1984) and one proposed by Carol

Gilligan (1982). Kohlberg contended that mature moral judgments are founded on (a) people reaching an agreement about rules of justice and (b) the even-handed application of those rules to all members of society. Kohlberg's theory was originally constructed out of the responses that a sample of adolescent boys gave to nine moral dilemmas—brief stories about people in moral-decision situations. Subsequently the theory was used for interpreting the answers offered for the nine dilemmas by people in a variety of cultures.

However, Gilligan contested the universality of Kohlberg's position and proposed, instead, that males and females tend to found their moral decisions on different philosophical values. On the basis of her interviews with expectant mothers, Gilligan concluded that while males' judgments are based on a concept of even-handed justice, females' decisions place more emphasis on compassionate caring. Gilligan asserted that as boys grow up, they become increasingly concerned about rules and about how to apply rules fairly to solve conflicts. In contrast, girls are more tolerant of altering rules and making exceptions in order to accommodate people's feelings and interests. Although Gilligan did not consider it inevitable that females assume a caring orientation and males assume a justice position, she suggested that such is usually the case (Gilligan & Wiggins, 1988).

In both the academic literature and the popular press, Gilligan's theory has met with mixed reviews. She has been praised for drawing attention to the importance of compassion as a significant moral virtue that had been neglected by writers who defined morality exclusively in terms of justice and equal rights (Haste & Baddeley, 1991). On the other hand, critics have charged that moral development depends on far more variables than sex differences, so that Gilligan unduly emphasized gender and thereby offered a simplistic and misleading interpretation of moral matters (Diver-Stamnes & Thomas, 1995).

My purpose in this research project is to add to the existing knowledge about moral development by testing Gilligan's theory with (1) a different sample of participants than those used in past studies and (2) a different method of investigation than the approach used by Gilligan and her colleagues in studying such matters (Gilligan, Ward, & Taylor, 1988).

The participants. An aspect of moral decision-making that apparently has not been investigated sufficiently in the past is reflected in two questions:

- Do youths from different social-class backgrounds base their judgments of moral situations on the same moral principles?
- Do adolescent girls more often base their moral judgments on the principle of compassion than do adolescent boys?

The participants in the study will be around 100 students (50 girls, 50 boys) who attend an upper-middle-class, suburban high school and around 100 (50 girls, 50 boys) who attend a high school located in a high-crime-rate, poverty-ridden district of a large city.

The project's focus. The main questions to be answered in this study include:

(1) Do adolescent girls more often base their moral decisions on principles of compassionate caring than do adolescent boys?

(2) Do adolescent boys more often base their moral decisions on principles of even-handed justice than do adolescent girls?

(3) Are there significant differences between students in a suburban high school and an inner-city high school in their opinions about the way that the people in eight cases of wrongdoing should be treated?

(4) Are there significant differences between students in a suburban high school and an inner-city high school in the reasons they propose to support their opinions about the way the people in eight cases of wrongdoing should be treated?

(5) What are likely reasons for the pattern of answers found for questions 1 through 4?

The data-gathering method. Students' judgments of moral situations will be collected by means of questionnaires that are completed during a single class session in the high school they attend. The teacher of the class and I will administer the questionnaires together.

Each student will be asked to complete a printed questionnaire (opinionnaire) that contains the descriptions of eight cases involving moral decisions. Each case describes a moral dilemma in which the student is to choose between two solutions (or to add a third solution) and to tell why the chosen option is better than the rejected one.

This method of collecting information differs from the methods used by Kohlberg and Gilligan in their original studies. Whereas Kohlberg did pose moral dilemmas for interviewees to judge, the dilemmas were different in nature from the ones I intend to use. Gilligan's data were gathered by means of interviews and did not pose the sorts of dilemmas used in either Kohlberg's study or in the one that I propose to carry out.

The nature of the dilemmas planned for the present project is illustrated with the following example.

Sample moral-dilemma. The instructions for completing the questionnaire will be as follows:

Directions: For each incident below, first read the incident. Second, mark an X on the line in front of the action that you think is better for that case. Third, write why you think the action you chose is better than the other suggested action.

Incident 1: "A 13-year-old boy was caught one night by police officers as he stole an auto radio from a car in a parking lot. When the officers began questioning him, the boy hit one officer across the face with the iron pipe he had used to break open the car window, and the blow broke the officer's nose and jaw. After the boy was taken to the detention hall for juveniles, a social worker reported that the boy did not live at home but, instead, had left home and now lived on the streets. When the social worker spoke with the boy's parents, they said they had put their son out of the house because they could not control him."

Your task is to choose from the following two actions the one you believe is the better one. Then you are to explain why you think it is better than the other action. Or you can suggest a third kind of action that you believe is better than either 1 or 2.

_____1. The boy should be kept for at least a year in a juvenile detention facility, as provided by law.

_____2. The boy should be put in a foster home, be enrolled in school, and helped by a friendly counselor.

_____3. Other (Suggest another kind of action that you like better than 1 and 2.)

Finally, tell why you think your choice is a good one:

The data-analysis plan. When the completed questionnaires have all been collected, I will divide students' answers into two main categories. One category will contain the various solutions suggested for each of the eight moral-dilemma cases. The other category will contain the kinds of reasoning—including the moral principles—that students offer in support of their solutions. Under each category, there will be different types of student answers.

Therefore, in order to classify students' responses into different types, I will need two classification systems. I haven't yet decided on the subtypes (subcategories) that each system will contain, because I do not know yet the diverse answers students will give. In searching the moral-development literature I found several typologies used by other researchers. However, I am not convinced that their schemes will fit my needs. Therefore, I have collected some ideas from the literature, but I will have to wait until the completed questionnaires are analyzed before I can settle on my final way of categorizing students' responses.

In classifying the students' reasons for their preferences, I will need to differentiate among (a) reasons representing an even-handed-justice principle, (b) reasons representing a compassionate-care principle, and (c) reasons representing other principles. In order to make these distinctions, I need to be guided by criteria in the form of *indicators* of moral-judgment principles. Here are examples of such indicators as reflected in respondents' reasons for their opinions in the eight cases.

Compassionate-Care Emphasis. (1) The usual punitive consequences assigned for the sort of misconduct found in this case should be reduced or eliminated if the wrongdoer suffers a particularly difficult social or personal plight.

(2) Sympathy should be a strong component of any decision about how best to handle cases of wrongdoing.

Even-Handed-Justice Emphasis. (1) People who knowingly disobey rules and laws should all be subject to the sanctions that society has established for such wrongdoing. Individuals should not be excused from punitive consequences of their actions on the basis of their social-class status, income, friendship with authorities, ethnic status, gender, or expressions of remorse.

(2) A society operates best and is fairest whenever people receive equal opportunities and equal treatment based on the nature of their actions. In short, people deserve to be treated alike.

The data interpretation. The results will be interpreted from the viewpoint of Gilligan's theory by comparing

- the solutions to the moral dilemmas suggested by girls with the solutions suggested by boys (each school separately and both schools combined),
- the reasoning offered by girls in support of their decisions with the reasoning offered by boys (each school separately and both schools combined),
- the solutions suggested by students in the suburban school with those of students in the inner-city school (girls and boys separately and both genders combined), and
- the reasoning to support their decisions offered by students in the suburban school with the reasoning offered by students in the inner-city school (girls and boys separately and both genders combined).

Those four sets of comparisons will enable me to answer the project's five guide questions and to propose what implications the results suggest for the validity of Gilligan's theory.

(1) Do adolescent girls more often base their moral decisions on principles of compassionate caring than do adolescent boys?

(2) Do adolescent boys more often base their moral decisions on principles of even-handed justice than do adolescent girls?

(3) Are there significant differences between students in a suburban high school and an inner-city high school in their opinions about the way that the people in eight cases of wrongdoing should be treated?

(4) Are there significant differences between students in a suburban high school and an inner-city high school in the reasons they propose to support their opinions about the way the people in eight cases of wrongdoing should be treated?

(5) What are likely reasons for the pattern of answers found for questions (1) through (4)?

Bibliography: The sources referred to in this proposal are:

Diver-Stannes, A. C., & Thomas, R. M. (1995). *Prevent, repent, reform, revenge: A study in adolescent moral development.* Westport, CT: Greenwood.

Gilligan, C. (1982). *In a different voice.* Cambridge, MA: Harvard University Press.

Gilligan, C., & Wiggins, G. (1988). The origins of morality in early childhood relationships. In C. Gilligan, J. V. Ward, & J. M. Taylor, (Eds.). (1988). *Mapping the moral domain.* Cambridge, MA: Harvard University Press.

Gilligan, C., Ward, J. V., & Taylor, J. M. (Eds.). (1988). *Mapping the moral domain.* Cambridge, MA: Harvard University Press.

Haste, H., & Baddeley, J. (1991). Moral theory and culture: The case of gender. In W. M. Kurtines & J. L. Gewirtz (Eds.), *Handbook of moral behavior and development: Vol. 1. Theory* (pp. 223-249). Hillsdale, NJ: Erlbaum.

Kohlberg, L. (1984). *The psychology of moral development.* San Francisco: Harper & Row.

Theorizing About a Pair of Twins

Salient features. The author of the following proposal intends to study the lives of Glenis and Mavis Miller, twin sisters who gained distinction for their talents but whose lives moved in very different directions. The author's purpose is not only to trace the course of those lives, but also to devise a theory that explains why the two lives took the particular turns they did. The proposal draws chiefly on qualitative research methods, with only modest input from quantitative techniques. The qualitative methods consist of the content analysis of publications and interviews, the estimation of factors that influenced the lives of the twins, and the formulation of a theory that patterns those factors. The quantitative aspects of the study include records of the twins' grades in school and college, of the numbers of their publications, of the comparative popularity of those publications, of the twins' socioeconomic status, and of how high each twin ranked in her profession.

Dissertation title. *Explaining Linked Lives: Likenesses and Differences Between Remarkable Twins*

Background of the study. Three years ago a woman named Mavis Miller died at age 73. Her twin sister, Glenis, had died two years earlier at age 71. I find these two women interesting, because both became very prominent, yet their lives advanced down very different paths. By their appearance, they must have been identical twins, sharing the same genetic inheritance from their parents. However, they grew up to be distinctly different from each other in both their vocational careers and personal lives.

Mavis Miller became a highly respected novelist and poet. In contrast, Glenis Miller became a university professor, a noted research entomologist specializing in the study of mosquitoes. Mavis was twice married and had four children, two with her first husband—a struggling writer whom she divorced—and two with her second husband, a business executive with whom she lived the rest of her life. Glenis never married, but from her early forties until her death she shared her home with a woman companion, 16 years younger, who had been one of her students at the university. Mavis had dropped out of college after her junior year to marry the fellow student who would become her first husband. Glenis not only earned bachelor and master degrees with top honors, but also a PhD in biology that won her a faculty appointment at that same university from which she had graduated. She remained a member of the faculty until retirement. Throughout their lives, Mavis and Glenis maintained a desultory personal relationship with each other, sometimes very intimate and loving, other times distant and antagonistic.

Because the Miller twins spent most of their lives in or near the city in which I grew up (and where my parents still live), I have access to sources of information about the Millers that enable me to study the development of their lives. Mavis's first and second husbands still live in the area, and Glenis's life companion is in the region as well. Furthermore, many of the people who knew the pair are still around, and the archives of the city's two newspapers contain articles about the two sisters' accomplishments. Therefore, doing a dissertation that focuses on the Miller twins' development seems feasible.

The aim of the research. This study has two main purposes:

- To chronicle significant events in the lives of a pair of remarkable twins in a manner that identifies likenesses and differences between them in their development from early childhood until their death.

- To generate a theory that explains in a convincing way why those two individuals developed the way they did.

Consequently, the dissertation is intended to make a twofold contribution: (A) provide a record of the two women's lives and (B) offer a theory that identifies the patterning of causal factors that account for the way those two linked lives evolved. I would hope that the theory which results from this study might be useful to other researchers who are also interested in the methodology of comparative biography.

Information-collection sources. Information about the biographees will be gathered from seven main sources:

1. *Libraries.* Books and articles (journals, magazines, conference proceedings) written by the Millers or written about them and their works.

2. *School records.* Grades and honors the Millers earned in schools and higher-education institutions, types of classes in which they enrolled, and yearbook and school-newspaper pictures and comments.

3. *Newspaper archives.* Articles about and by the Millers, as found in the archives of the city's two daily newspapers.

4. *Letters and memorabilia.* Letters to or from the Millers held by friends and relatives; other objects of interest that are connected with the Miller twins.

5. *The Internet.* Websites that include Glenis's and Mavis's names and references to their works.

6. *Interviews.* Face-to-face and telephone conversations with friends, relatives, colleagues, and knowledgeable people in the fields to which the Miller's contributed.

7. *Written correspondence.* Inquiries that I send to knowledgeable people by means of regular mail or e-mail.

Information-collection guide questions. The process of searching the sources for information will be guided by a series of questions. The following list illustrates the kinds of questions that will be posed. The numbers in brackets following each question identify the sources in the above list that probably can furnish answers to the question. The *what* kinds of questions are designed to elicit information about events that will be used in writing the chronicle of their lives. The *why* kinds of questions are intended to reveal potential causal factors that may be helpful in devising the theory that I hope to produce.

Under what circumstances did you know (Glenis Miller, Mavis Miller)? [6, 7]
What do you remember most about (Glenis Miller, Mavis Miller)? [6, 7]
Can you think of any specific incidents that helped you understand what (Glenis Miller, Mavis Miller) was like? [6]
In the incident that you just now described, why do you think (Glenis, Mavis) acted as she did? [6]

Please look at this list of words and check ones that you think fit (Glenis's, Mavis's) personality? (The list of adjectives includes such terms as *friendly, hard-working, quick-thinking, quiet, talkative, humorous, short-tempered, competitive,* and more.) [6, 7]

What were (Glenis's, Mavis's) hobbies and interests? What did she do for entertainment at different times in her life? Why did she choose such activities? [1 through 7]

How well did (Glenis, Mavis) perform academically in different subject-matter fields? [2]

In what extracurricular activities did (Glenis, Mavis) engage in school and college? How did those activities seem to influence her later life? [1,2, 4, 6, 7]

How many friends did (Glenis, Mavis) have in school and in adult life? What kinds of people were those friends? What do you believe was the basis for the bond between (Glenis, Mavis) and those friends? In other words, why did they become friends? How long and why did the friendships last? [1, 2, 4, 6, 7]

What was (Glenis's, Mavis's) relationship with her parents? [1, 4, 6, 7]

What was the nature of the twins' relationship with each other? [1, 4, 6, 7]

What did (Glenis, Mavis) publish? What quantity of published works did (Glenis, Mavis) produce? What was the quality of those works? [1, 3, 5]

What honors, awards, or other of types of public recognition were given to (Glenis, Mavis)? [1 through 7]

What were the most important influences in determining the course of (Glinis's, Mavis's) life at different points in her lifespan? [1 through 7]

What was (Glenis's, Mavis's) socioeconomic status at different times in her life? [3, 4, 5, 6, 7]

During the process of my gathering information, additional relevant questions will undoubtedly arise and then be added to the list.

Organizing the information. As I collect data, I intend to organize it in the following way.

A computer file will be set up for each of the twins. The file will be divided into eight chronological segments, with each segment representing a decade in the life of the particular twin. As I collect information, I intend to enter it into the appropriate decade. I also plan to add a *miscellaneous* segment in each file, thereby providing a place to store information that is not associated with a particular period of the person's life. Within every decade—as far as is feasible—I intend to organize the information in terms of the question (or questions) that the information answers, thereby putting together in one place the information about each topic that has been the focus of a guide question, such as the topic of school success, of the relationship of the Miller parents with their daughters, and of the twin's publications.

The process of generating the theory. After I have compiled all of the data in the above manner, I will compare the information, decade by decade, to identify likenesses and differences between the twins. During this procedure, I will estimate what influences have caused such likenesses and differences. That is, I will try to identify what factors in the twins' lives (people, incidents, experiences, choices among options, personality traits, interests, and such) and what interactions among those factors determined (at least partially) the direction that the sisters' lives followed. From this process, I hope to discover themes and patterns of influence that explain why Glenis and Mavis Miller grew up to be in some ways alike and in other ways different. Those themes and patterns will be my theory.

I assume that arriving at such a theory will require both logic and intuition. The test of whether the theory is sound will be how reasonable and convincing my explanation appears to readers of the dissertation.

The writing process. Because it will be impractical to include in the dissertation all of the information that I collect about the twins, I will need to choose carefully what I use in the final narrative. I intend to organize that narrative around my theory. That is, within each portion of the narrative, I plan to describe an influential factor or a theme from the theory, then liberally illustrate that factor with specific information from my collected data—information which supports that particular portion of the theory. As I see it, the trick will be to write the narrative in a way that supports the elements of the theory and, at the same time, traces the chronological development of the two women's lives. I will have to wait until I have collected and organized all of the data before I decide exactly how I can accomplish both of those purposes.

A Typology of Help-Seeking Behavior

Salient Features: A key outcome of this research project is to be a three-part scheme for classifying (a) types of social services, (b) the life conditions of needy persons, and (c) individuals' reasons for either obtaining or not obtaining social services. The principal qualitative aspects of the project are found in the author's interview methods and in the author's extracting from interview records the categories that will make up the classification scheme. The quantitative portion of the study is found in the frequency with which each type of social service, life condition, and reason appears in the 80 interviewees' responses.

Thesis title. Who Uses Social Services and Why?

The nature of the problem.   Those of us who are social-case workers in the city's Department of Social Services have a general and rather spotty impression of why some people who need our services and who qualify for those services are not getting them. However, we really do not have a clear, well-organized understanding of all the reasons for this state of affairs or of the frequency of different reasons.

The dual purpose of the study.   The two goals of this research are to:

- Collect information from qualified individuals about why they do or do not avail themselves of the assistance offered by the Department of Social Services. This information should help Department personnel determine how to carry out their mission more satisfactorily.
- From the information provided by informants, create a system for classifying individual's reasons for either obtaining or not obtaining the Department's services. At present, there appears to be no suitable system for categorizing people's reasons. Having such a system available should equip the Department to conduct its business more efficiently.

The methodology.   I plan to interview around 80 individuals whose life conditions suggest that they might need the kinds of help that social-service agencies offer. Around half of the interviewees will be ones who currently are availing themselves of an agency's assistance. The other half are ones who are not taking advantage of such aid.

After the interview results have been collected, I will organize the respondents' answers under three categories that represent the kinds of information that the Department can profitably use: (a) types of social services that would be suitable for needy persons, (b) life conditions that would appear to warrant people's seeking social services, and (c) types of reasons that people either do or do not use such services. Then, under each category I will create a list of types of responses (or *taxa*, as they are referred to in taxonomies) that will accommodate all of the information furnished by the interviewees.

The people to interview.   The individuals who are already receiving social services will be selected randomly from the files of the Department and of private church-related and philanthropic agencies. Each of the selected persons will be contacted, told the nature of the research, and asked if he or she is willing to be interviewed. To replace those who are unwilling to participate, others selected at random from the files will be substituted.

Three methods will be used to locate individuals who are not receiving social services but would appear to need and deserve them. First, persons who have been on social-service-agencies' rolls in the past but now are no longer involved will be asked to participate in the study. Second, current social-service recipients will be asked for the names of acquaintances who could profit from agencies' services but are not getting those services. The identified individuals will be asked to be interviewed. Third, hospital emergency-room personnel and the police will be asked if they know of individuals who need social-service help but are not getting it. Such individuals will be invited to participate in the project.

The interview process. According to my tentative plan, the interviews will involve three steps. (1) With a list of Department services in hand, I will describe each type of service and ask whether the interviewee would find that service useful. (2) If the person says a service would be useful, but the person is not currently receiving that service, I will ask why? (3) If the person says the service would not be useful or else not feasible, I will ask why?

The interviews will take place at whatever locations the participants prefer. I plan to tape-record each interview so as to have an accurate record of participants' responses. If an individual does not want the interview to be taped, I will take handwritten notes instead.

The pilot study. Before I conduct the interviews with the 80 participants, I plan to carry out a pilot study with 12 people in order to determine how well my interview approach produces the kinds of answers I need for developing the social-services typology. For the pilot tryout, I will interview eight people who are now getting services but who will not be part of the final 80 interviewees. The other four tryout interviewees will be ones suggested by any of the first eight who are willing to identify acquaintances who might qualify for Department assistance but who are not receiving services.

On the basis of the pilot study, I will make any necessary adjustments in the interview process and will use the responses from the tryout to begin developing the three-part classification system.

The official data-gathering phase. Upon completing the pilot study, I will conduct interviews with the 80 individuals whose responses will be used as the basis for the classification schemes and for the report of the frequency of (a) the use of different services, (b) life conditions that warrant services, and (3) reasons that potential service-recipients have not taken advantage of the Department's programs.

The analysis of the results. The interview responses will be analyzed by means of a two-stage procedure.

Stage 1. The first stage consists of my reading all interview records in order to devise the three classification schemes. As I read a response, I will first decide what type of social service the response reflects. Frequently, those types will already be among the ones on the list I use for conducting the interviews. However, it is likely that the respondents' expressed needs will reflect other sorts of service beyond those on my list. Those extra types will be added to the list. From the study of all 80 interview reports, I will thus derive the items for the first of the three typologies—kinds of social services suitable for needy persons

Second, from the interview reports, I will infer the conditions of people's lives that could warrant their needing the kinds of services identified in the first typology. Such conditions will include poverty, conflict among family members, unwanted pregnancy, drug abuse, divorce, and more. The conditions will be organized as a list of types that compose the second of the typologies.

Finally, in answer to my questions about why interviewees do or do not avail themselves of social services, I will extract the types of reasons that will become the items in the third typology.

As guidance for people who later may wish to use the typology in their own research, under each subcategory of the typology I will include three or four phrases taken from interviews to illustrate the sorts of comments that belong in that subcategory. For example, in the system for classifying people's reasons for using social services, one subcategory might be *Lack of Knowledge.* That item in the typology might be defined as follows and then clarified with three quotations from interviews.

> *Lack of Knowledge:* People seek social services because they lack the kind of information they need to accomplish some goal.
>   Examples: "I didn't know the right way to fill out the job-application form."
>   "My ex-husband was trying to get the kids away from me, and I didn't know if the law would let him do such a thing."
>   "I didn't understand exactly the ways people could get HIV and AIDS or how to treat HIV if you did get it."

Stage 2. The second stage consists of my reading all 80 interview reports again in order to tabulate the number of cases in which each type of item on the three classification lists appeared. Therefore, I will end up with three numerical tables—one showing the frequency of different types of services, another showing the frequency of relevant life conditions, and a third showing the frequency of different reasons that services have been used, or have not been used, by the interviewees.

The Presentation of the Results: The final written version of the thesis will consist of four parts: (1) an explanation of the purpose of the research and of the methodology, (2) a description of the three typologies, (3) three tables showing how often the different items on each typology appeared in the 80 interviews, and (4) suggestions about how the research results might be used to improve the effectiveness of the Department of Social Services.

Conclusion

The examples in this chapter have focused on four ways theories can be involved in thesis and dissertation research. That is, a researcher can

- combine two or more theories to provide a perspective from which to collect and analyze evidence,
- test the validity of a theory under new conditions,
- generate—from information that is collected—an explanation of the causes that account for the nature of that information, or
- generate—from information that is collected—a system for classifying the kinds of information embedded in those data.

Qualitative characteristics of this chapter's proposals include (a) people's opinions as expressed in interviews (social environments, moral development, twins, social services), (b) researchers' interpretations of what collected information means in relation to existing theories (social environments, moral development), (c) researchers' content analyses of publications and interviews (social environments, moral development, twins, social services), (d) researchers creating new explanations for why events occur as they do (social environments, moral development, twins), and (e) researchers devising new schemes for classifying information (social services).

Quantitative features of the chapter's four cases have included (a) scores derived from questionnaires (social environments, moral development), (b) the frequency of subcategories of phenomena that have been studied (social environments, moral development, twins, social services), (c) quantitative comparisons between groups of questionnaire and interview respondents (social environments, moral development, social services), (d) published statistics from earlier research (social environments, moral development), and (e) numerical information about individuals' lives (twins).

11

Contributing to Research Methodology

Sometimes the most important contribution made by a thesis or dissertation is a methodological innovation that the author introduces. Such innovations can be of various kinds—a data-gathering process, an instrument for collecting information (test, questionnaire, interview plan), a statistical treatment, a computer program, and more. The author's novel method is often considered more significant than the actual data he or she collects, because the method can be adopted by other researchers who will then add further information to the world's storehouse of knowledge.

This chapter's proposals illustrate three kinds of methodological contributions—a data-collection instrument (graphic-arts preference inventory), a way of comparing alternative methods of taking research notes, and a comparison of three ways to improve the rate at which participants in questionnaire surveys return completed questionnaires.

A Graphic-Arts-Preference Inventory

Salient features. The author of this proposal in the field of art education intends to develop a new procedure for assessing people's likes and dislikes in such graphic arts as drawing, painting, and photography. The author has been required to make qualitative decisions about (a) which characteristics of art products will be appraised by means of the author's preference inventory, (b) which pictures will be used for investigating people's preferences, and (c) which artists' styles will be featured in the inventory. Qualitative judgments are also required of people who take the inventory and of analysts who interpret people's choices. The quantitative aspects of the project are found in the statistics used for (a) plotting the preference patterns of individuals and groups and (b) describing the extent to which individuals and groups agree with each other in their preferences.

A further noteworthy feature of this proposal is the detail in which the author describes the project. Some thesis and dissertation advisers require that students plan in great detail so as to ensure that the student has clearly thought through the specifics of the project ahead of time and thus knows at the outset precisely how data are to be gathered and interpreted.

Dissertation title. A Method of Appraising People's Graphic-Arts Tastes

The need for a new approach. For at least eight decades, art educators and psychologists have been attempting to create satisfactory ways to appraise people's artistic abilities. Included among these attempts have been tests intended to measure individuals' skills and knowledge in the field of two-dimensional graphic arts, particularly drawing and painting (Graves, 1948; Horn, 1953; Knauber, 1935; Lewerenz, 1927; Lowenfeld, 1957; McAdory, 1929; Meier, 1942; Varnum, 1946; Welsh, 1949). The principal aim of such instruments has been to determine people's aesthetic sensitivity or "good taste" and to predict students' success in art courses. However, currently existing tests display a variety of shortcomings. They measure too few of the factors that apparently affect people's art preferences. Too many of the tests assume that there is a single standard of "good art." Too many fail to distinguish among abilities to appreciate, to judge, and to produce art. And none appears to provide for discovering people's reasons for preferring one art product over another. A key aim of this dissertation is to develop a graphic-arts-preference inventory that copes more adequately with such shortcomings than do the presently available art-judgment measures.

The sections of the following proposal are presented in this sequence: (A) specific objectives, (B) adopted assumptions, (C) the construction of the inventory, (D) the answer booklet, (E) the guidebook for administering the inventory and interpreting the results, (F) the inventory tryout, (G) the final data collection, (H) data-compilation methods, (I) data-interpretation methods, and (J) practical applications of the inventory.

The study's specific objectives. The aims of this research are to:

- Create an inventory useful for revealing (A) the patterning of individuals' preferences in graphic arts (drawing, painting, photography) and (B) individuals' expressed reasons for preferring certain items of art over other items.

- Furnish standards of preference held by a selection of artists and art educators—standards that can be used for comparing individuals' preferences with those of artists and art educators.
- Provide a statistical method of comparing individuals with each other, with artists, and with art educators in terms of art preferences.

Adopted assumptions. The study is founded on the following three beliefs:

- There is no single standard of what constitutes "good art." Although people posing as "authorities" often set standards, a review of the history of art over the centuries and an inspection of the expressed judgments of present-day artists and art critics demonstrates that there is no consensus about such matters. The truth of the matter appears to be that different individuals and groups hold different criteria for determining how to distinguish "good art" from "bad art" and how to separate "pleasing art" from "unattractive art."
- Frequently—perhaps always—people's likes and dislikes in art include a large measure of emotional response that cannot adequately be expressed in words. In effect, the basis for expressed preferences can be either subconscious emotion or else a combination of subconscious emotion and conscious reasons. Therefore, some people will be able to explain the basis of their preferences, whereas others will not. As a result, we cannot expect all individuals to be able to tell why they like one art product more than another. But for the purpose of understanding at least part of the basis for people's judgments, it is still useful to learn the rationales offered by those who are able and willing explain their reasons.
- Sometimes people who are confronted with a choice between two art objects will not favor one over the other. They consider both objects either equally acceptable or equally unacceptable. (Most, if not all, existing art tests fail to accommodate for such a possibility.)

The construction of the inventory. The materials needed for the application of the inventory consist of three booklets: (A) a 50-page picture booklet, (B) a four-page answer booklet, and (C) a guide to the administration of the inventory and to the interpretation of its results.

The picture booklet. Each of the 50 pages of the picture booklet will display a pair of pictures, side by side. In each pair, the picture on the left differs in some way from the picture on the right. (See Figures 1-4.) Persons whose art preferences are being inventoried are asked to choose which of the two pictures they like better and to mark that choice on the

Figure 1
Subject-matter: Portraiture versus Architecture

A

B

Figure 2

Media: Oil versus Rough Pastel

A

B

Figure 3

Style: Photographic Realism verus Stylized Realism

A

B

Figure 4

Composition: Symmetry versus Asymmetry

A

B

proper line of the answer booklet. Or, if they find the two pictures equally acceptable or equally unacceptable, they can record that decision on the answer sheet.

The 50 pairs of pictures in the booklet are designed to reveal different features of graphic-art products that can influence people's preferences. Those features are shown in Table A, which identifies the characteristics that distinguish one member of a pair from the other member.

For example, the distinction between the pair in Figure 1 is in the *subject-matter* depicted—portraiture versus architecture. Thus, the art medium (black-and-white, pen-and-ink) and the composition (one figure dominating the scene) are identical in the pair so as to elicit only viewers' preferences for subject-matter—not for media or composition. In contrast, the difference between the pair in Figure 2 is the *art medium* (oil paint versus rough pastel), with the subject-matter, composition, and colors identical in both members of the pair.

(Note: In the booklet, the pictures will be more than twice the size they are in this proposal. Furthermore, all pictures—other than the pen-and-ink, charcoal, and Conté-crayon drawings—will be in full color, thereby making the task of seeing the difference in the pair far easier than it is in this proposal. Thus, figures 2, 3, and 4 will be larger and in color. In addition, the label identifying the kind of difference in each of the following figures does not appear in the booklet version of the 50 pairs. Hence, viewers must figure out for themselves the characteristic that differentiates one member of the pair from the other member.)

The distinguishing characteristic in Figure 3 is an aspect of *artistic style*, that is, a contrast between photographic realism and stylization (the simplification or elimination of fine details). The subject-matter, composition, and color in the pair are kept identical. The distinction in Figure 4 is in the *composition* of the two scenes, with a symmetrical arrangement of objects in picture A versus an asymmetrical arrangement in picture B.

In a similar fashion, each of the remaining 46 pairs of scenes in the booklet focuses on one of the contrasting variables identified in Table 1.

So far I have prepared only four additional pages beyond the four illustrated in Figures 1 through 4. Therefore, the task I now face is that of creating 42 more pairs of pictures. I have had extensive experience in drawing, painting, and digital photography, so I am able to produce most of the pairs myself. I have artist friends who are willing to do the remaining ones. They view the opportunity as an interesting challenge. The burden of developing the pairs is made considerably easier by the computer program called Photoshop, which equips me to alter paintings and photographs in ways that simulate different art styles.

In addition to preparing the picture book, I intend to offer the 50 pairs in the form of a photographic-slide presentation by employing the Power

Point computer program which enables one to project each page in sequence onto a large screen in the front of a classroom. Consequently, an entire class of students can simultaneously complete the answer booklet without the need for individual picture booklets. Thus, there will be two options for administering the inventory—the individual picture-booklet option and the group projected-images option.

Table A

Guide to the Distinctions Between Pairs of Scenes in the Inventory Booklet

Note: The number following each item indicates the number of pages (pairs) in the booklet that exhibit the identified difference between the members of a pair.

Subject-matter
—Portraiture vs. architecture (2)
—Still life vs. landscape (2)
—Landscape vs. abstract pattern (2)
—Action group vs. posed group (2)

—Landscape vs. seascape (1)
—Human figure vs. abstract (2)
—Animals vs. humans (1)

Composition
—Dominance vs. diffusion (3)
—Tight vs. loose (3)

—Simple vs. complex (3)
—Symmetry vs. asymmetry (3)

Media
—Oil vs. pastel (2)
—Oil vs. transparent watercolor (2)
—Photograph vs. etching (1)

—Pen-and-ink vs. charcoal (1)
—Line-and-wash vs. acrylic (1)
—Pencil vs. poster paint (1)

Style
—Photographic vs. stylized (2)
—Manet style vs. classical realism (1)
—van Gogh style vs. Homer style (1)
—El Greco style vs. Rivera style (1)
—Warhol style vs. Dali style (1)

—Cubism vs. visual realism (1)
—Cézanne style vs. Picasso (1)
—Pollack style vs. Rockwell (1)
—Moses style vs. Wyeth (1)

Color
—One value level vs. another (2)
—One hue combination vs. another combination (4)

—One intensity vs. another (2)

Although the job of publishing multiple copies of a picture booklet in full color was a very expensive undertaking in the past, it is relatively inexpensive today. I can do all of the work at home with my computer, scanner, and color printer. The only recurrent costs will be for paper and ink.

The answer booklet. The subjects who take the inventory will not write their choices on the picture booklet but, rather, will record their choices in a four-page answer booklet. Providing answer booklets is more cost-effective than having subjects mark a picture booklet and thereby eliminating the possibility of using a booklet more than once. Furthermore, subjects' responses on a four-page answer booklet are more readily inspected and compiled than if the responses were marked on a 50-page picture booklet.

The directions for using the answer booklet and the format in which choices are to be reported are illustrated in Figure 5. The pairs of pictures in Figures 1 through 4 serve as the examples of items. If the inventory is being administered to several people at once—such as to a classroom of students—the person in charge of the group can read the directions aloud while group members follow the printed directions in their answer booklets. This procedure helps ensure that the subjects understand how to report their choices. It also enables subjects to ask questions about any matters they fail to understand completely.

The guidebook. A guidebook will be supplied for people who administer the inventory and who interpret the patterns of choices found in subjects' answer booklets. The guidebook's contents will include:

- The purpose and uses of the inventory
- Ways that the inventory is similar to and different from other available methods of appraising people's graphic-arts preferences
- How to administer both the picture-booklet form of the inventory and the projected-images form
- Ways of interpreting and reporting the results of subjects' answers

The inventory tryout. As soon as initial versions of the picture booklet, answer booklet, and guidebook are available, these materials will be tested out with three groups of subjects, each group consisting of 10 or 12 persons. Group 1 will be composed of fourth-grade pupils, Group 2 of tenth-grade students, and Group 3 of adults in their twenties. The two aims of the tryout are (A) to discover how well subjects at different age levels understand how to perform the tasks required by the inventory and (B) to guide my developing a method for compiling, analyzing, and interpreting subjects' responses. Not only will the tryout subjects be asked to complete the inventory, but they also will be asked to tell what problems they encountered in doing the task. Information about the subjects' problems can aid me in revising the picture booklet, the answer booklet, guidebook, and the administration procedures so as to make the

Figure 5

The Form of the Answer Booklet

Directions: Each of the numbered items below refers to a pair of pictures in the booklet you have been given. As you look at a pair of pictures, you are to decide which of the two pictures you like better—**A** or **B**. Then, in this answer booklet, find the item that refers to the two pictures you are viewing, and draw a circle around the letter that is the same as the letter under the picture you prefer—**A** or **B**. However, if you do not like one of the pictures more than the other, then draw a circle around the word "**Neither.**"

Sometimes people can give reasons for liking one picture more than another. Other times they cannot give reasons, but they simply like one better than the other. So, if you can give reasons, write those reasons on the space following the word "Reasons." But if you cannot think of reasons, it's quite all right. Just leave the space blank.

Item 1: Man and building.

I prefer: **A** **B** **Neither**
Reasons:

Item 2: White water bird

I prefer: **A** **B** **Neither**
Reasons:

Item 3: Horse and rider

I prefer: **A** **B** **Neither**
Reasons:

Item 4: Teapot and cups

I prefer: **A** **B** **Neither**
Reasons:

final version of the system more effective. The results of the tryout will also enable me, on the basis of empirical evidence, to refine my methods for analyzing and interpreting the subjects' choices.

The final data collection. The five reasons for collecting data by use of the revised versions of the inventory materials will be to:

- Reveal individuals' patterns of graphic-arts preferences
- Show likenesses and differences among three age groups in their graphic-arts preferences
- Show likenesses and differences between females and males in their graphic-arts preferences
- Compare students' graphic-arts preferences with those of art teachers and of several established artists whose works display distinctive styles and subject-matter
- Provide an initial cluster of standards against which the choices of people who complete the inventory in the future can be compared

I hope to have the final version of the inventory completed by five sorts of people: (A) around 200 fifth graders, (B) around 200 tenth graders, (C) around 200 college students (sophomores, juniors, or seniors), (D) 10 art teachers, and (E) six established artists who differ from each other in style, subject-matter, and/or media.

I plan to arrange for administering the inventory to students by appealing to art teachers in one or more elementary-school districts, high-school districts, and colleges. I will also ask those teachers to complete the inventory themselves. I have already identified six well-know artists who are willing to participate in this project.

Data-compilation methods. Participants' choices between the pair on each page and the reasons they offer for their choices will be compiled in two ways.

Numerical analysis. First, in order to record the ways students marked the *A, B,* and *Neither* options, I intend to use the *DataDesk* statistical-analysis computer program to set up five computer files labeled *Grade 5. Grade 10, College, Teachers,* and *Artists.* The way each participant marked the answer booklet will be keyed into the appropriate file. For each participant, there will be one variable containing 50 items. The three options on the answer sheet will be assigned these numbers: Neither=0, A=1, B=2. Thus, a participant's answer for a given item will be recorded as number 0, 1, or 2. As a result, the pattern of participants' answers can conveniently be manipulated statistically to yield percentages and correlations, thereby permitting comparisons across groups as well as between individuals within a group.

Participants' reasons. A separate set of five files will be set up for listing the reasons participants offered in support of their picture choices. Each file will be divided into six sections titled *Subject-matter, Composition, Media, Style, Color,* and *Miscellaneous.* Reasons that participants offered for their choice between the paired pictures will be placed under the appropriate section—*Subject-matter, Composition, Media, Style,* and *Color.* Or, if the reason fits none of those sections, it will be listed under *Miscellaneous.* As these six lists accumulate, it will become apparent that certain reasons have been cited by several participants. In such cases, that reason will not be written again, but a tally mark will be placed following the reason for each additional instance in which that reason is cited. This procedure not only saves writing time for the person who is recording the reasons, but it produces a growing count of the frequency of different reasons.

Data-interpretation methods. The data analysis will focus on answering a series of questions that derive from the research objectives. The interpretation process is a combination of quantitative and qualitative approaches. The question, as well as the types of information and judgments employed in answer them, are described in the following paragraphs. In the questions, the term *groups* refers to the five categories of participants—fifth graders, tenth graders, college students, teachers, and artists.

Part I: Quantitative Interpretations

Question 1: How much are the participants within each group similar to each other in their art preferences—both their preference within each pair of pictures as well as their general preference across the 50 pairs combined?

The percentage of individuals within a group who chose *A, B,* and *Neither* for a given picture-pair reflects the extent of agreement among the group members regarding that pair. For example, if 80% or more choose either picture *A* or picture *B,* then we conclude that there is a high level of agreement within the group. The closer the figure is to 50%, the less the within-group agreement.

Next, computing the average of those 50 percentages produces a number representing the extent of general art-preference agreement for the group.

Question 2: How much agreement is there between groups—both in their preference for individual pairs of pictures and in their general preference for all 50 pairs combined?

The percentages computed to answer Question 1 within a group can be used to reflect the agreement between groups. Imagine that, in judging a given pair of pictures, the percent of people in Group I who chose picture *A* was 72% and the percent in Group II was 53%. That 19-point difference between the two groups shows much lower between-group agreement than if the Group I figure had been 72% and the Group II figure 67%. Next, the extent of intergroup agreement for all 50 picture-pairs combined can be discovered by treating the 50 percentages from each group as scores and calculating a Pearson-*r* correlation coefficient between Group I and Group II.

Question 3: How closely did one individual participant's preferences match another individual's preferences?

A Pearson-*r* correlation coefficient can be calculated between Individual X's list of 50 choices and Individual Y's list of 50 choices. For instance, a correlation coefficient of *r*= +.88 between an art teacher and one of her students shows that their preferences are far more alike than are the preferences of two artists whose inventory results, when compared, yield an *r* of -.16.

Question 4: How closely did one individual participant's preferences match the overall, average preferences of a group?

To produce a set of 50 choices that typify a group, we can select—for each pair of pictures—the choice (A or B) that the greatest number of group members preferred. This resulting list of 50 most-frequent preferences serves as the *typical group pattern*. We can then compute a Pearson-*r* coefficient between the group pattern and an individual participant's 50 preferences to show how closely the participant and group agreed.

Question 5: What reasons do people offer to account for why they like some pictures more than other pictures?

For each pair of pictures, a table of participants' reasons will first be listed in the descending order of their frequency. Next, the information from those tables will be used to prepare five tables showing the frequency of different reasons bearing on the study's types of art-product characteristics—subject-matter, composition, media, style, and color.

Finally, I will inspect the tables and draw conclusions about likenesses and differences in reasons among the five groups of subjects—fifth-graders, tenth-graders, college students, teachers, and artists—and also between males and females.

Part II: Qualitative Interpretations

Question 6: How can we produce a verbal summary of the characteristics that either an individual or a group prefers in graphic-art products?

An analyst, by inspecting the pattern of a person's choices among the 50 picture-pairs, can offer an estimate of that person's preferences in terms of subject-matter, composition, media, style, and color. The word *estimate* is important here, because the sample of people's preferences has been based on only 50 pairs of pictures. Hundreds of additional pair combinations utilizing other pictures are possible. Therefore, a conclusion drawn from the evidence provided by the inventory is necessarily an estimate rather than a complete, infallible analysis.

The most obvious method of providing such an estimate consists of an analyst inspecting the cluster of picture-pairs that bears on one of the five art-product variables that the inventory was designed to feature, such a variable as *type of subject-matter* (a cluster of 12 picture-pairs). From inspecting the choices that an individual participant made within that cluster, and from that participant's stated reasons, the analyst infers the nature of the participant's subject-matter preferences. The analyst's method is qualitative—a judgment based chiefly on logic and intuition. To illustrate, here are three hypothetical interpretations that might be drawn from the inventory-choice patterns of two artists and one fifth-grade pupil.

Artist M: Likes realistic art—accurate copies of nature—especially outdoor scenes, both landscapes and seascapes. Favors complex compositions in which all the spaces are filled with objects and people. Appears to prefer symmetrical, evenly balanced compositions. Chooses oil painting and watercolor over other media.

Artist W: Favors abstract, stylized art that distorts or ignores forms in nature. Likes bold colors, strong contrasts. Prefers compositions that include a few objects that are composed of straight lines and sharp angles. Favors a dominant center of interest in a picture. Seems to accept all media that produce intense contrasts.

Fifth-Grader: Rather indecisive—often cannot make up his or her mind about which sort of composition or medium to prefer, but does like photographic realism and scenes from nature, such as landscapes, buildings, and animals. Chooses symmetrical, formally balanced compositions. Rejects abstract art and stylized, distorted renditions of natural objects.

The same sort of verbal interpretations about individuals' preferences can also be inferred from group inventory results by means of an analyst inspecting a typical group-preferences pattern that has been constructed from the picture choices of the majority of a group.

Practical applications of the inventory. Ways that the completed inventory could be used include those of

- Estimating an individual's or group's pattern of graphic-art preferences. This information could be useful to a teacher who holds a particular conception of what constitutes "good art" and who wishes to know how closely students' present preferences match that conception.
- Comparing the graphic-art preferences of individuals (or groups). Inventory results could help an analyst recognize likenesses and

differences between individuals (or groups) in their art preferences and to estimate the causes of such similarities and differences.

- Identifying changes in art preferences over time. Students could take the inventory at the beginning of a course in art and also at the end in order to reveal what changes—if any—in taste and judgment occurred for individuals during the conduct of the course.

References. The following sources have been cited in this proposal.

Graves, Maitland. (1948). *Graves Design Judgment Test.* New York: Psychological corporation.

Horn, Charles C. (1953). *Horn Art Aptitude Inventory.* Chicago: C. H. Stoelting.

Knauber, Alma Jordan. (1935). *Knauber Art Ability Test.* Cincinnati, OH: A. J. Knauber.

Lewerenz, Alfred S. (1927). *Tests in Fundamental Abilities of Visual Art.* Los Angeles: California Test Bureau.

Lowenfeld, Viktor. (1957). *Creative and Mental Growth.* New York: Macmillan.

McAdory, Margaret. (1929). *McAdory Art Test.* New York: Bureau of Publications, Teachers College, Columbia University.

Meier, Norman Charles. (1942). *Meier Art Tests: I, Art Judgment.* Iowa City: Bureau of Educational Research and Service, State University of Iowa.

Varnum, William Harrison. (1946). *Selective Art Aptitude Test.* Scranton, PA: International Textbook Co.

Welsh, Geroge S. (1949). *Welsh Figure Preference Test.* Palo Alto, CA: Consulting Psychologists Press.

Appraising Note-Taking Methods

Salient features. In this project, the author hopes to make two sorts of contributions to knowledge: (a) furnish information about how and why people act as they do in emergency situations and (b) describe the effectiveness of different techniques for taking notes during the conduct of research. Thus, the study of people's behavior in emergencies provides an opportunity for investigating the comparative effectiveness of various note-taking methods.

Among the qualitative aspects of the project are a researcher's (a) choice of interview questions to ask people who are involved in emergencies, (b) interpretations of interviewee's answers and actions, (c) inferences drawn from observing emergency incidents, (d) choice of criteria for judging the worth of different note-taking methods, (e) extracting hypotheses and conclusions from notes taken in emergency cases, (f) selecting criteria to use in evaluating different note-taking techniques, and (g) writing an overall comparison of note-taking methods.

Quantitative aspects of the project include (a) tables reporting the frequency of different types of answers people give to interview questions and (b) rating scales that permit the comparative value of different note-taking methods to be expressed both graphically and as numbers.

Dissertation title. An Evaluation of Note-Taking Technologies in a Study of People's Reactions to Emergencies

The project's rationale. As implied in its title, this dissertation is designed to yield two kinds of results. One is substantive, the other methodological. The substantive result consists of information about how and why people behave as they do in emergency situations. The methodological result consists of information about the comparative effectiveness of different note-taking methods during the conduct of research.

Reactions to emergencies. Although much has been written about how individuals respond during emergencies that threaten people's safety, rarely has the analysis of such responses been systematic. Much of that literature is of an anecdotal nature, consisting of the impressions of people who have been personally involved in threatening incidents, or have witnessed such incidents, or have heard about incidents. The purpose of this dissertation is to provide a systematic study of how people react under emergency conditions and of why they behave in such ways.

Note-taking technologies. The expression *note-taking*, as intended in this proposal, refers to a person's recording, in either a detailed or succinct form, the content of a document, of a discourse, or of an observed event. Because taking notes is an activity required in nearly all research projects, it is my belief that researchers can profit from understanding the diverse types of available note-taking techniques and the advantages and disadvantages of each type.

The plan for investigating reactions to emergencies and of assessing note-taking techniques is described in two parts: (1) Investigating Reactions to Emergencies and (2) Evaluating Note-Taking Procedures.

Investigating Reactions to Emergencies

The emergency project's guide questions. The purpose of the emergency-investigation portion of the dissertation is to answer six questions:

- How should the words *emergency* and *reaction* be defined?

- How are people's reactions to emergencies discovered? In other words, how does an observer recognize the nature of someone else's reactions?
- How can such reactions be conveniently classified?
- What conditions apparently influence the thoughts and emotions that people experience and the behaviors that people display in emergencies? In other words, why do individuals think, feel, and act the way they do in different emergency situations?
- How can causes of emergency incidents be conveniently classified?
- What methods might be adopted for improving people's responses to emergencies, that is, for making responses more constructive?

Methods of collecting evidence. For nearly a year, I have been serving as a volunteer, part-time assistant deputy sheriff in the Jefferson County Sheriff's Department. My work there places me in a convenient position to witness many emergencies related to traffic accidents, domestic disputes, fires, drug-abuse cases, robberies, fights, teenage runaways, juvenile crime, and more. I have discussed this proposed research with my superiors in the sheriff's department. They find my plan interesting and useful, so I can count on their cooperation in carrying it out.

I plan to collect information about people's reactions to emergencies by means of

(1) directly observing emergency events,
(2) interviewing participants in, and witnesses of, events,
(3) interviewing deputy sheriffs who have observed emergencies and have spoken with participants and witnesses,
(4) reading sheriff's-department and newspaper reports of emergencies, and
(5) viewing television news broadcasts and videos of emergencies, of participants, and of witnesses.

I have prepared a preliminary description of information to collect about a typical emergency. I recognize that this plan will probably need revision and expansion to suit particular cases. (See Table 1.)

I have already tried out this system on four cases—three auto accidents and one house fire—and found that I cannot expect to get complete answers to the guide questions because people involved in an incident are often either unavailable or unwilling to answer my inquiries. Therefore, I am obliged to draw conclusions from incomplete information. Of course, the same is true of most—if not all—jury trials. Complete, reliable evidence is rarely available. Nevertheless, my trying out the system with the four cases suggests that gathering data in this systematic way leads to more convincing insights than do the typical unsystematic, approaches to understanding how and why people act in emergencies.

Table 1

Guide to Collecting Information about an Emergency

Directions: The following kinds of information should be sought in each case.

1. What was the type of incident (robbery, fire, fight, etc.) and why was it considered to be an emergency?
2. When did the incident occur (date, time of day, how long it lasted)?
3. Who were the principal participants in the incident?
    3.1 What did each participant do before, during, and after the incident?
    3.2 On what evidence was each participant's reported action based?
    3.3 How did each participant explain what had happened and why it happened that way (sequence of events leading up to the incident, sequence of events during the incident, sequence of events following the incident)?
    3.4 What reasons did participants give for the way they had acted?
    3.5 What estimates did participants offer about why other participants in the incident behaved as they did?
    3.6 How much agreement was there between different participants' descriptions of the incident?
    3.7 What were probable reasons for any discrepancies found among the different descriptions of the incident?
    3.8 What emotion did each participant display or report (regret, fear, guilt, shame, distress, hate, sorrow, etc.)?
    3.9 What consequences did each participant expect as a result of the incident?
    3.10 What desirable and undesirable outcomes resulted from participants' actions at different stages of the incident?
4. Who witnessed the incident?
    4.1 What account of the incident did each witness offer?
    4.2 What was the personal relationship between the witness and each participant (friend, relative, stranger, employer, etc.)?
    4.3 What estimates did witnesses offer about why the various participants in the incident behaved as they did?
    4.4 How much agreement was there between different witnesses' descriptions of the incident?
    4.5 What were probable reasons for any discrepancies found among the different descriptions of the incident?

5. What actions did emergency personnel (deputy sheriffs, police, fire fighters, paramedics) take at different stages of the emergency?

    5.1 How did participants respond to those actions?

    5.2 How effective were those actions in resolving the emergency?

    5.3 What estimates did emergency personnel offer about why participants acted as they did?

    5.3 What emotions did emergency personnel display or report at different stages of the incident?

    5.4 What reasons were offered by emergency personnel for the actions they themselves took at different stages of the incident?

    5.5 What desirable outcomes resulted from the actions of emergency personnel at different stages of the incident?

6. At the close of the incident, what was the status of each participant? In other words, what had happened to each participant by the end of the incident?

Types of emergencies to study. In order to reduce the number of variables to a manageable size, I intend to study only two kinds of emergencies—auto accidents and domestic disputes. (The expression *domestic disputes* refers to conflicts within a family or between families that call for the intervention of law-enforcement personnel.) The sheriff's department frequently faces these two kinds of cases, so I should have no difficulty finding material for my project. I will try to include 20 accidents and 20 domestic conflicts in the study.

Analyzing the collected evidence. The analysis of the data is to be conducted in two stages that consist of (1) organizing the information and (2) extracting hypotheses and conclusions from the data.

Organizing the information. I plan to create computer files into which the collected information will be entered. A separate file will be established for each emergency case. Every file will be divided into sections that address each guide question in turn—questions 1, 2, 3, 3.1, 3.2, etc. The collected information bearing on a given guide question will be entered under the appropriate numbered section. Therefore, I will be able to accumulate the data about each case in terms of the guide questions. Furthermore, in order to draw conclusions from the data about a given question (such as participants' stated reasons for their actions) for all 20 accident cases combined, I can copy the information bearing on that question from each of the 20 case files and place that information into a new file bearing the title of that guide question.

This procedure of compiling the evidence in two forms—(1) under separate cases and (2) under separate questions for all 20 cases of the same type—facilitates my examining a large quantity of complex information, summarizing it, and drawing inferences about what it means.

For certain of the guide questions, summarizing information across 20 cases can be rendered more precise if the data can be expressed in quantitative terms. For example, reasons that participants in domestic disputes offer for their own actions can be identified as different "types of reasons" (such as motives, personality traits, carelessness, lack of knowledge, etc.) and the frequency of each type can be tabulated. Then, the frequency of reasons as offered by participants and by witnesses can be compared statistically (Spearman's rank-order correlation method) to determine the level of agreement between participants and witnesses about causes behind domestic disputes. Such a procedure can help answer such questions as "How often do participants give the same reasons for their own actions in domestic disputes as the reasons suggested by witnesses to account for the participants' behavior."

Extracting hypotheses and conclusions. The final stage of the project involves my inspecting all of the organized evidence and, on the basis of my analysis, proposing a series of hypotheses and conclusions about answers to the questions that the project was designed to answer. An *hypothesis,* as that word is intended here, is a statement or summary of what the evidence "likely means," but such meaning is only tentative. That hypothesis requires better support than the available evidence provides before it is accepted as true. In contrast, the word *conclusion* refers to a statement or summary that I am confident is true. The evidence from the present study, and from other studies, is sufficient to warrant accepting conclusions as sound bases for action.

Extracting hypotheses and conclusions is mainly a qualitative activity that involves poring over a great amount of qualitative information, estimating the comparative importance of different factors found in the data, and proposing connections among factors. This qualitative activity is rendered more precise whenever portions of the information can be expressed as quantities (frequencies, amounts) and when relationships (correlations) can be calculated statistically.

Evaluating Note-Taking Procedures

The study of reactions to emergencies requires a great deal of note-taking. Therefore, the study offers an opportunity to evaluate the effectiveness of different note-taking methods, particularly for comparing traditional methods with those made possible by recent technological advances in photocopying equipment, computers, audio- and video-recorders, cell phones, and such computer accessories as scanners, optical-character-recognition (OCR) software, and voice-recognition programs.

In the emergency-case project, notes are taken (a) from written materials (police reports, social-case-workers' reports, witnesses' written accounts), (b) from the researcher directly observing events (the results of an auto accident, family members interacting in domestic settings), and (c) from interviews (of emergency-incident participants, witnesses, emergency personnel). Furthermore, notes can be recorded in various forms: (a) handwritten in a notebook or on the back of an envelope, (b) dictated into a tape recorder, (c) keyed into a computer, (d) photocopied from a document, or (e) entered from a document into a computer with the use of a scanner and OCR software or use of voice-recognition equipment. The purpose of the note-taking-evaluation portion of this project is to compare the effectiveness of different combinations of these techniques under the different note-taking circumstances provided by the emergencies on which the project focuses.

The study procedure. The method of evaluating note-taking techniques will involve two major steps: (1) systematically varying note-taking combinations from one emergency case to another and (2) evaluating each combination by means of a series of criteria.

The 10 note-taking combinations. The word *combination* refers to a particular pattern of (a) the source of note-taking (document, observation, interview), (b) the method of taking notes (handwritten, tape recorded, photocopied), and (c) the method of storing notes (file folders, notebook, computer file).

For example, in the case of one auto accident, all notes may be handwritten at the time of an observation or interview and then accumulated in a series of manila folders stored in a file cabinet.

In the case of another auto accident, all notes about the researcher's direct observations may be dictated into a hand-held audio-recorder at the time of the observations, and witnesses' accounts can be audio-recorded at the time they are interviewed. Summaries of the audio-recordings can later be keyed into a computer file.

The above two combinations will be used for managing note-taking in two or three of the 20 auto accidents and in two or three of the 20 domestic disputes. Six other combinations of note-taking methods and media will be created for use in the project's remaining cases. Therefore, each of the resulting eight combinations of media will be applied in five cases—in two or three accidents and in two or three domestic disputes. As a result, the evaluation of each note-taking combination will be founded on evidence from five cases, so that conclusions about the effectiveness of a type of method will drawn from more than one case.

The evaluation criteria. I plan to appraise each note-taking method in terms of seven efficiency standards. Each standard is defined by a question.

- Cost: How expensive is the method to obtain and use?
- Simplicity: How easy is the method to use?
- Accuracy: How faithfully do the notes resulting from the method represent events that were observed and opinions that were expressed?
- Completeness: In how much detail do the notes resulting from the method describe observed events and interviewees' statements?
- Time requirement: How much time does the method require?
- Acceptability: How acceptable is the method to the people who are involved in an event?
- Dependability: How much can the method be counted on to consistently function as intended?

The ultimate purpose of the note-taking aspect of this project is to produce an easily understood comparison of the eight note-taking combinations by showing each combination's rank on the seven standards. The plan for producing such a comparison involves three steps.

First, after all notes for each of the 40 emergency cases have been compiled, I will review each case in terms of the seven evaluation criteria and write a brief summary of the apparent advantages and disadvantages of the note-taking combination used with that case. For example, in an auto-accident case in which I had used a video camera to record events and interviews, I might write under the *acceptability* criterion that "Over half of the people who were interviewed objected to having themselves videotaped, so I had to take hand-written notes for those interviews instead."

Second, after finishing the written summaries, I intend to translate the content of the summaries for each criterion into points along seven scales. The purpose is to show how the effectiveness of the note-taking method used in one case compared with the method used in another case. Therefore, in filling out the rating scales for each case, I must have in mind a sense of how the effectiveness of the method (combination) in that case compared with the effectiveness of other methods used in other cases. This is a rather simple task for certain of the criteria, such as in judging *cost, accuracy* or *completeness*. For instance, it is easy to realize that taking hand-written notes is far less expensive than videotaping events. It is also relatively easy to recognize that audiotaped interviews will usually produce a more accurate record of what witnesses say than will hand-written notes. However, it can be more difficult—at least in some cases—to judge the *acceptability* of a note-taking method. Therefore, a larger measure of personal judgment is required for determining the appropriate place on a scale to locate some note-taking methods than to locate others.

The intended result of preparing rating sheets for two hypothetical domestic-dispute cases is illustrated in Figures A and B.

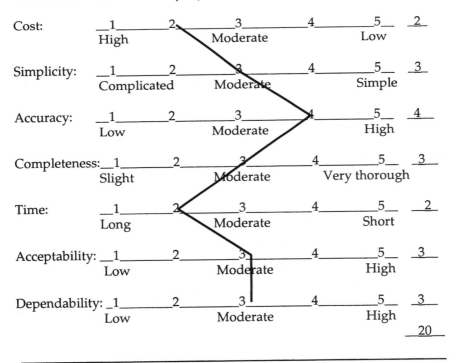

Figure A

Comparative Rating of a Note-Taking Method—Case X

The method: *Interview responses and observations keyed directly into a laptop or hand-held computer at the time that the interviews and observations are conducted.*

The case: *Wife called 911 for help, claimed that drunken spouse had beaten her. Two deputy sheriffs went to the house.*

Cost:	_1_____2	____3____	___4___	__5_	_2_
	High	Moderate		Low	
Simplicity:	_1_____2	___3____	___4___	__5_	_3_
	Complicated	Moderate		Simple	
Accuracy:	_1_____2	___3____	_4__	__5_	_4_
	Low	Moderate		High	
Completeness:	_1_____2	___3__	___4___	__5_	_3_
	Slight	Moderate	Very thorough		
Time:	_1__2	___3___	___4___	__5_	_2_
	Long	Moderate		Short	
Acceptability:	_1_____2	___3_	___4___	__5_	_3_
	Low	Moderate		High	
Dependability:	_1_____2	__3_	___4___	__5_	_3_
	Low	Moderate		High	
					_20_

In the two figures, each variable is represented as a five-level scale, ranging from 1 (the least desirable status) to the 5 (the most desirable status). Thus, on the *cost* scale, "low" is assigned a 5; and on the *dependability* scale, "high" earns a score of 5. Distinguishing levels of desirability with a set of numbers common to all seven scales facilitates comparisons across scales.

Figure B

Comparative Rating of a Note-Taking Method—Case Z

The method: *Printed or typed documents are entered into a computer with the aid of a scanner and OCR software.*

The case: *A bitter disagreement between neighbors over a fence that one of them was building along a disputed property line that divided their lots led one of them to threaten the other with a shotgun. When deputy sheriffs arrived on the scene, the gun-wielding neighbor threatened them and was arrested. The information about the event available to the district attorney consisted of (1) letters exchanged between the neighbors and (2) the two deputies' typewritten reports of the incident.*

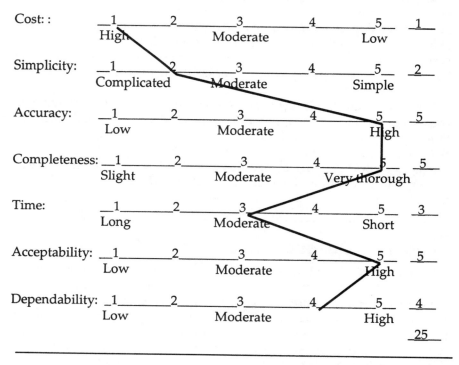

Cost: :	1 High	2	3 Moderate	4	5 Low	1
Simplicity:	1 Complicated	2	3 Moderate	4	5 Simple	2
Accuracy:	1 Low	2	3 Moderate	4	5 High	5
Completeness:	1 Slight	2	3 Moderate	4	5 Very thorough	5
Time:	1 Long	2	3 Moderate	4	5 Short	3
Acceptability:	1 Low	2	3 Moderate	4	5 High	5
Dependability:	1 Low	2	3 Moderate	4	5 High	4
						25

An analyst can summarize the status of different note-taking methods by checking the number along a scale line to suggest the desirability of a particular method as compared with other note-taking methods or combinations. The checked numbers on the seven scales can also be connected with lines to produce a quickly identified profile of the pattern of advantages/disadvantages of the note-taking methods used in a particular emergency.

In effect, condensing qualitative judgments of note-taking methods in a graphic, quantitative form furnishes an easy-to-grasp—though somewhat imprecise—comparison of the effectiveness of various methods. The rating scales can be accompanied by written explanations and examples of factors in that particular case which influenced the ratings assigned on the seven scales.

As shown in Figures A and B, the number from each scale can be recorded in the blank at the right of the scale, so that the numbers for all seven scales can be summed at the bottom, offering an quantitative estimate of the overall desirability of the note-taking combination used in that case. Generally, the higher the total, the greater the overall desirability of the note-taking scheme for the kind of case that was studied. However, the overall total should not be taken at face value but should be interpreted in relation to which factors are most important in the case at hand. For example, if the sheriff's department is well funded, the high cost of videotape equipment may be of no consequence in comparison to the greater accuracy and completeness of the record of events that videotapes provide.

Third, the final step in the process of comparing note-taking methods consists of writing a description of each method's characteristics in relation to different note-taking circumstances and illustrating the description with examples and rating scales from the 40 emergency cases.

It is my hope that the comparative evaluation of note-taking techniques that results from this study will aid other researchers in selecting the note-taking methods they plan to use in their studies.

Improving Questionnaire Rates of Return

Salient features. The researcher's purpose in this proposal is to identify efficient ways to construct and administer questionnaires. The two methods he intends to use are (a) a content analysis of published studies that have included questionnaires and (b) an experiment involving a comparison of three techniques for encouraging questionnaire recipients to return their completed questionnaires to the researcher. The qualitative approaches in this plan include (a) content analysis to identify factors that affect the success of questionnaire surveys and (b) summarizing the results of the analysis in the form of suggestions about how to prepare, administer, and interpret questionnaires under various conditions. The study's quantitative aspects are found in (a) the frequency with which different published studies agree about how to prepare and administer questionnaires, (b) typical rates (percentages) at which completed questionnaires are returned under diverse circumstances, and (c) the comparative rates of return (percentages) of questionnaires under three follow-up conditions.

Thesis title. *The Comparative Effectiveness of Three Follow-Up Techniques in Questionnaire Research*

Introduction. While working on my master's degree in social psychology, I have been employed part-time in the university's alumni-relations bureau. Periodically we mail questionnaires to alumni for various reasons—to collect information about their present lives for the *Alumni Newsletter*, to learn what services and activities the bureau should offer, and to encourage alumni to support the university's fund-raising efforts. When we prepare a new questionnaire to send out, there is usually a debate among members of the bureau about the best way to formulate the questionnaire and administer it so that a large number of alumni will complete the form and return it to the bureau. But during the debate it becomes clear that the members of the bureau do not know enough about questionnaire surveys to do the job most efficiently. Therefore, in order to improve the efficiency of collecting information from alumni and of encouraging their financial support, I am proposing to write my master's thesis on ways of constructing and administering questionnaires.

The specific objectives. The aim of the thesis is to answer three general questions and one specific question.

The general questions—

- What decisions need to be made in the construction, administration, and analysis of questionnaires?
- What kinds of answers or solutions are available at each of those decision points?
- What are the advantages and disadvantages of each answer or solution? In other words, under what conditions is one answer or solution better than another?

The specific question—

One matter of particular interest to the staff of the alumni bureau is how to maximize the rate at which people who receive questionnaires will actually fill out the forms completely and return them to the alumni office. Published studies of this issue show that the percentage of questionnaires returned can vary greatly from one survey to another. In a few studies, over 90% of the forms are completed and sent back to the researchers. In many others, only 30% to 50% of the questionnaires are returned. In still others, no more than 15% or 20% are sent back.

One way to encourage recipients to complete and return questionnaires is to make follow-up appeals. A follow-up consists of a second or third or fourth appeal sent to recipients who did not return the questionnaire after they first received it. When the matter of follow-up is discussed by the alumni bureau staff, a variety of conflicting opinions are voiced about which follow-up method would yield the greatest number of questionnaire returns. Three of the follow-up options that staff members have suggested involve making the appeal via (a) regular mail, (b) e-mail, and (c) telephone calls. Therefore, one question the staff is particularly interested in answering is:

- Which follow-up technique will produce the highest rate of return —regular mail, e-mail, or telephone call?

Methods of answering the research questions. I plan to study the three general research questions by analyzing the contents of books and journal articles that focus on the use of questionnaires in survey research. I have already conducted a preliminary sampling of the following sources: Aiken, 1997; Angleiner & Wiggins, 1986; Berdie, Anderson, & Niebuhr, 1986; Cox, 1996; Foddy, 1993; Labaw, 1981; and Oppenheim, 1992. My review of those sources suggests that I will find valuable information in the professional literature about how decisions regarding "significant variables" influence how effectively questionnaires (a) provide the information desired by the researcher and (b) encourage recipients to complete and return questionnaires.

Significant variables include:
Format (the clarity and attractiveness of the questionnaire's physical layout)
Questionnaire length
Number of decisions required of a recipient in completing the instrument
Complexity of the required responses (check a choice, short answer, write an extended narrative, etc.)
Directions about how to complete and return the questionnaire
Clarity and simplicity of wording
The sequence in which questions appear
Incentives (what the recipient can expect to get out of completing the questionnaire, or what contribution the recipients' answers will make)
Delivery method (sent by mail, sent by e-mail, verbally transmitted in the form of a face-to-face or telephone interviews)
Follow-up methods and their success rates

From the thorough search of the literature that I plan to make, I expect to identify additional variables that should be included in my evaluation of ways to build, administer, and interpret questionnaires.

In my preliminary inspection of the above-mentioned literature sources, I failed to find an answer to the question about the comparative effectiveness of three follow-up methods—regular mail, e-mail, and telephone calls. Therefore, I intend to hunt for an answer by incorporating those three options in the next questionnaire survey that the alumni bureau will send out. That part of the study takes the form of a quasi-experiment.

The intended questionnaire (which solicits information about the present address, e-mail address, phone number, and noteworthy activities of alumni) will be mailed to the 783 alums for which the bureau has mailing addresses and phone numbers. For many of these, we also have e-mail addresses. We will allow three months for the recipients to return the initial questionnaire. After the three-month period, the remaining individuals who did not return questionnaires will be divided into three groups. One group will be sent a follow-up reminder via the regular mail, another via e-mail, and the third via a telephone call.

The analysis and presentation of the results. The final stage of this study will be divided into two parts. For the first part, I will write an interpretation of the content-analysis results to answer the three general questions about the strengths and weaknesses of different ways to create questionnaires and administer them. That part of the thesis will close with suggestions about which ways are best suited to the needs of the alumni-relations bureau.

In the second part of the final stage, I will report the results of comparing the three follow-up methods and will suggest which method—or combination—seems best for the bureau's purposes.

Cited Literature:

Aiken, L. R. (1997). *Questionnaires and Inventories: Surveying Opinions and Assessing Personality.* New York: Wiley.

Angleitner, J. S., Wiggins, J. S. (Eds.). (1986). *Personality Assessment Via Questionnaires: Current Issues in Theory and Measurement.* New York: Springer-Verlag.

Berdie, D. F., Anderson, J. F., & Niebuhr, M. A. (1986). *Questionnaires: Design and Use* (2nd ed.). Metuchen, NJ: Scarecrow Press.

Cox, J. (1996). *Your Opinion, Please!: How to Build the Best Questionnaires in the Field of Education.* Thousand Oaks, CA: Corwin.

Foddy, W. H. (1993). *Constructing Questions for Interviews and Questionnaires.* New York: Cambridge University Press.

Labaw, P. J. (1981). *Advanced Questionnaire Design.* Cambridge, MA: Abt.

Oppenheim, A. N. (1992). *Questionnaire Design, Interviewing, and Attitude Measurement.* New York: St. Martin's.

Conclusion

Each of the proposals described in this chapter was designed to contribute to research methodology. The first example described a new way to appraise people's graphic-art preferences, the second offered a way to appraise note-taking methods, and the third addressed the advantages and disadvantages of ways to construct, administer, and interpret questionnaires. In addition, one of the proposals was intended to make a substantive contribution to knowledge—to describe how people act, feel, and think in emergencies and to estimate why they act, feel, and think in such ways.

Among the qualitative aspects of the proposals were (a) researchers' decisions about which aspects of a phenomenon would receive attention in their project (characteristics of art products, types of emergencies, types of questions to ask emergency participants, questionnaire components); (b) people's expressed opinions (about art preferences, thoughts and feelings during emergencies, types of questionnaire follow-up procedures); (c) researchers' choices of criteria to use in assessing phenomena (such phenomena as art tests, note-taking techniques, questionnaire-construction methods); and (d) processes of extracting hypotheses and conclusions from compiled data (art preferences, reactions to emergencies, questionnaire construction and administration methods).

Quantitative features of the chapter's proposals included (a) the calculation of frequencies within a group (art preferences, responses to emergencies, the comparative success of three questionnaire follow-up procedures) and (b) statistical comparisons among groups and individuals (in art preferences, in reactions to emergencies, in preferences for questionnaire follow-up methods).

12

Replicating Others' Research

A replication study is a project that repeats—either precisely or in large part—the same research methods that were used in an earlier project. A replication study is typically designed to perform one of four functions:

- Assess the results of an earlier investigation in order to confirm or disconfirm the reported outcomes of that investigation.
- Repeat an earlier investigation at a later date in order to judge how stable the results have remained with the passing of time and to estimate the causes of any changes that occurred.
- Alter some aspect of the earlier methodology in order to discover what effect such alteration has on the outcome.
- Apply the earlier method to a different group of people or different set of events in order to learn whether conclusions derived from the earlier study apply equally well to those different people or events.

The following proposals illustrate the last three of these functions.

Readers' Skills in Grade 1 and Grade 7

Salient features. In this example, the author plans to conduct a follow-up study to (a) reveal the degree to which children's comparative standings in selected reading skills is constant between first grade and seventh grade and (b) suggest causal factors that might account for changes in a child's comparative standing over the six-year period.

Qualitative decisions implied in the proposal include the author's (a) choice of items to include on a *Family Background Inventory* and (b) estimate of what factors in pupils' lives caused change—or lack of change—in their comparative positions in four reading skills between grade 1 and grade 7.

The quantitative component of the proposal is found in the test scores and in the analysis of scores by means of computing correlations and calculating the extent to which a group's scores spread out.

Thesis Title: *The Consistency of Pupils' Relative Status in Reading Skills Between Grades 1 and 7*

Introduction: In 1996, Garcia (1998) studied the early reading skills of first-grade children in the school district in which I teach. Garcia's particular interest was in the relative contribution made to reading comprehension by children's phonemic awareness, letter-naming fluency, and vocabulary knowledge. Garcia's results confirmed other authors' findings that those three foundational skills were strong predictors of early reading success.

In my research plan, I am proposing to follow up Garcia's work by studying how consistently pupils' performance in phonemic awareness, letter-naming fluency, vocabulary knowledge, and reading comprehension in seventh grade matches their comparative standing in those four skills when they were in first grade. I hope to answer two questions:

(1) To what extent is a pupil's rank among classmates in phonemic awareness, letter-fluency, vocabulary development, and reading comprehension the same in grade 7 as it was in grade one? In other words, how well does a pupil's performance in the four skills in grade 1 predict that pupil's relative performance in grade 7?

(2) What conditions in pupils' lives are likely responsible for changes, or the absence of changes, in pupils' ranks in the four skills over the six-year period between grade 1 and grade 7?

The components of the proposal are presented as a sequence of four topics: (1) the skills to be studied, (2) the measurement techniques, (3) the subjects, and (4) the analysis of test results.

The skills to be studied. The four reading skills that are the focus of this research are as follows:

Phonemic awareness. The term *phonemic awareness* is usually defined in the linguistic literature as a person's understanding that phonemes (the simplest, most basic speech sounds) exist in spoken language and can be isolated and manipulated. Phonemic awareness is recognized as one of the linguistic skills that gradually develop as children learn to use language. There is a large quantity of evidence suggesting that phonemic awareness is essential for acquiring reading skills, because a person must be aware of the individual sounds that make up spoken words in order to learn the sounds of letters that make up printed words.

Letter-naming fluency. Many research studies have demonstrated that children who are more fluent in naming letters of the alphabet tend to develop reading comprehension sooner than children who are less fluent. It is not just accuracy in naming letters, but ease and fluency in letter-naming that gives children an advantage in early reading.

Vocabulary knowledge. Garcia defined *reading vocabulary* as the number of words that a reader could both decode (identify how it sounds) and understand. She cited studies indicating that the oral vocabulary of first-grade children in the United States was between 2,500 and 5,000 words. Estimates place the growth in recognition vocabulary of school-age children as typically exceeding 3,000 words a year. Once children have mastered skills for decoding printed words, the most important remaining barrier to school success among language-disadvantaged children is their insufficient knowledge of word meanings (Garcia, 1998, p. 39).

Reading comprehension. Pupils' reading comprehension is reflected in their degree of accuracy in telling, or demonstrating in some other manner (gesture, perform an action, point to an object, draw a picture), what printed passages mean.

The results of Garcia's study showed that first-graders who were better than their agemates in the first three skills were usually also better at reading comprehension. In effect, phonemic awareness, letter-naming fluency, and vocabulary knowledge appeared to be foundational skills contributing to reading comprehension.

Not only did Garcia gather data about first-graders' reading skills but also about the socioeconomic status of their families as reflected in such indicators as parents' occupations, parents' levels of education, levels of education of siblings, and quantity of books and periodicals in the home. Her purpose in collecting such information was to estimate how factors in a child's home life might affect the development of the four reading skills.

The measurement techniques. The methods of assessing seventh-graders' reading skills and socioeconomic status will be as follows:

Phonemic awareness. The same sorts of tasks used by Garcia to reveal children's phonemic awareness in grade 1 will be used in grade 7, with the number of items and difficulty of items increased. Those tasks include: (1) categorizing words on the basis of common sounds (example:

mat and *man* go together because both start with *m*), (2) segmenting a word into its elemental phonemes (example: segmenting *cat* into *c*, *a*, and *t*), and (3) deleting phonemes (example, saying *book* without the *b*).

Letter-naming fluency.   Pupils are given a list of letters and a list of words.   The pupils' task is to name the letters as rapidly as possible.

Vocabulary knowledge.   Pupils take a printed multiple-choice vocabulary test to determine how well they select the most common meaning for a word out of four choices.   That is, each item on the test identifies a word that is embedded in a sentence, and the pupil is to select which meaning, out of four choices, is the one intended in the sentence.   At the seventh-grade level, the length of the test and the difficulty of word choices far exceed the length and difficulty at the first-grade level.

Reading comprehension.   Garcia measured first-graders' overall reading ability by use of the first-grade version of the *Gates-MacGinitie Reading Tests* (3rd edition).   I plan to use the junior-high version of the *Gates-MacGinitie* battery (4th edition, 2000).

Socioeconomic status.   An estimate of the socioeconomic level of a pupil's family will be based on a *Family Background Inventory* that the seventh-graders and/or their parents fill out.

The subjects.   The seventh-graders who will participate in this research are ones whom Garcia studied when they were in first grade.   There were 87 first-graders in Garcia's original sample.   Since then, 22 of the original subjects have transferred out of the school district, so that there will be, at most, only 65 seventh-graders in my study.   However, that still should be enough pupils on which to base conclusions about the consistency of individuals' ranks on the reading skills over the six-year interim.

The record of each pupil's test results from grade 1 is still available, so I am able to compare pupil's rankings for the four skills in grade 1 with the rankings in grade 7.

Test results' analysis.   To answer the research question about the consistency of pupils' ranks in the four skills across a six-year interval, I plan to calculate the rank-order correlation (Kendall's *tau*) between their performance (in comparison to agemates' scores) in grade 1 and their performance in grade 7.

I am also interested in learning the extent to which the difference between the more skillful readers and less skillful readers grows larger with the passing to time.   In other words, do the less adept readers lag farther and farther behind the more adept as the years advance, or does the gap between the less skillful and more skillful stay the same or diminish?   To answer this question, I will calculate the degree to which the group's scores on the tests of the four skills spread out (standard deviations) in grade 1 as compared to the distribution of scores in grade 7.

In my attempt to answer the question about what factors in pupils' lives appeared to account for change, of lack of change, in their ranking on the four skills between grade 1 and grade 7, I will examine the patterns of response on the *Family Background Inventory* and will inspect pupils' academic and behavior records as found in the folders in which a cumulative account of each child's elementary-school career is kept.

In summary, the results of this investigation will be reported in two forms—(1) statistical analyses of the consistency of pupils' ranks in four reading skills over a six-year period and of the spread of a group's scores in grade 1 compared to grade 7 and (2) an estimate of what factors appear to have caused changes, or a lack of changes, in pupils' relative status in reading skills between grade 1 and grade 7.

Bibliography:

Garcia, Emilia C. (1998). Phonemic awareness, letter-naming fluency, and vocabulary as predictors of reading ability in young children. *International Language Research Quarterly, 6* (2), pp. 37-44.

MacGinitie, Walter H.; MacGinitie, Ruth K.; Maria, Katherine; & Dreyer, Lois G. (2000). *Gates-MacGinitie Reading Tests,* 4th ed. Itasca, IL: Riverside Publishing.

An Enhanced Boot-Camp Study

Salient features. In this author's plan to replicate an earlier study of the effect of a boot-camp experience on socially deviant teenagers, she intends to alter the earlier researcher's methodology in two main ways. She will study a different boot camp and she will have the teenagers complete a pair of paper-pencil inventories—a *Personality Profile Sketch* (Wentworth, 1998) and an exercise (*What Would You Do?*) in which the youths offer recommendations about how a series of juvenile-crime cases should be handled. The research methods are mainly qualitative, consisting of (a) conversations with teenage participants and with staff members in a three-month boot camp, (b) observations of the youths in different camp situations, and (c) follow-up interviews with school personal, youths' family members, and the youths themselves four months after the end of the camp experience. Quantitative methods to supplement the qualitative findings include (a) individuals' scores on the two inventories as compared to the scores in a normative sample (*Personality Profile Sketch*) and (b) the author's summaries of the rate of success of the boot-camp treatment as revealed in a follow-up investigation of participants' behavior four months after their camp experience.

Dissertation title: *The Effect of Boot Camp on a Group of Teenage Boys*

The source of the project. Susan Annette Meade in 2001 completed a doctoral dissertation entitled *'Look What Boot Camp's Done for Me': Teaching and Learning in Lakeview Academy Boot Camp* (Meade, 2001). My proposed project is modeled on her research aims and methods.

Juvenile boot camps are institutions that provide short-term, high-intensity experiences for teenagers who have displayed sufficiently serious personal/social difficulties to warrant their parents or juvenile-court authorities sending them for special treatment. The camps are structured like highly confrontational military boot camps, intended to alter rebellious youths' attitudes and to instill in them the importance of consistency and obedience. Such camps work best for teenagers who have mild problems of motivation and disrespect for social conventions. The camps are usually located in wilderness-type settings where participants live in tents. The typical duration of a camp's treatment program is between 30 and 90 days.

Meade followed two cohorts of boys at they progressed through a 90-day program at a privately operated Midwestern boot camp to which she assigned the pseudonym *Lakeview Academy*.

> The boys were not casual offenders in the criminal system; they were repeat offenders, drug users, alcohol abusers, and perpetrators of school violence. Their behavior and choices were well known in their schools, their towns, and their counties. With multiple offenses on their records, they had manipulated and mocked the juvenile justice system. For many, Lakeview was their last chance before prison. My intent, as the lone ethnographer, was to capture their voices, understand their lives, and make meaning of their behavior and choices. (Meade, 2001, pp. 1-2)

Drawing on Erving Goffman's work on "total institutions," Meade attempted to determine "how youth who have offended respond to the power and control of the [Lakeview Academy as a total] institution" (Meade, 2001, abstract, p. 1). On the basis of the data that Meade had collected during the boys' stay at the camp and had gathered in a follow-up investigation that she conducted some weeks after the boys returned to their homes, she concluded that

> Most boys realized personal success, were able to develop at least one positive relationship with an adult, and were able to recognize and reform inappropriate thought patterns and behaviors. A great deal of learning occurred while the boys were at the camp. However, because the learning was forced

and under controlled circumstances, for the most part it was not transferred or generalized when the boys were released to their home environment. Unfortunately, the effectiveness of the boot camp, as experienced by the respondents of this study, was determined by the will of the boy, the existence and effectiveness of aftercare programs, and the amount and type of support from the family. (Meade, 2001, abstract, p. 2)

Aims and methods of the proposed project. The two purposes of the project described in this proposal are

(b) to compare the results of my own study of a teenage boot camp with the results of Meade's study in order to see if my findings are similar and

(c) to judge whether the boot-camp participants' scores on Wentworth's *Personality Profile Sketch* and on my own *What Would You Do?* exercise are useful in predicting the boys' behavior over the four-month period following their boot-camp experience.

My method of collecting data will be the same as Meade's, except for the addition of the two paper-pencil inventories. That is, I will spend three months, on nearly a daily basis, at the camp to speak with inmates and staff members and to observe their activities and modes of interacting. The following questions are ones that will direct my conversations and observations.

- How do the youths' act toward people in positions of authority at different stages of their stay at boot camp?
- What techniques do different staff members use in their interactions with the youths? What effect do those techniques have on the youths' subsequent behavior?
- What goals do the staff members hold for the teenagers?
- What goals—both short-term and long-term—do the teens hold for themselves? What goal changes, if any, do the youths make during the boot camp?
- How do the teenagers evaluate their boot-camp experience?
- What judgments do staff members offer about the success—or lack of success—of the boot camp for influencing the teenagers' attitudes and behavior?
- How influential is the boot camp for effecting positive changes in participants' behavior over the weeks following the participants' return home from boot camp?

The results of my conversations with boot-camp participants and staff members, and my observations of their modes of interaction, will be compiled in the form of handwritten notes or descriptions dictated into an audiotape recorder.

The two inventories (*Personality Profile Sketch* and *What Would You Do?*) will be administered to the teenagers during their first week at the camp and again during the final week of their stay.

Near the end of the three–month period following the boys' camp experience, I plan to visit the schools they attend and visit as many of their families as is feasible in order to learn about the boys' post-camp behavior. I also plan to interview as many of the boys as possible. My dual purpose will be to (a) estimate the continuing effect of the camp experience on their post-camp behavior and (b) identify conditions in their post-camp life that apparently influence how well they maintain any improved attitudes and behaviors that they developed at the camp. The results of these visits will be summarized in the form of estimated "improvement scores." That is, I will estimate the extent to which a boy's post-camp attitudes and behaviors improved over his pre-camp attitudes and behavior, reporting my estimate on a 5-point scale—post-camp (a) much worse than pre-camp, (2) slightly worse than pre-camp, (3) same as pre-camp, (4) slightly better than pre-camp, (5) much better than pre-camp.

Analyzing the data. The notes compiled over the nine-week camp will be reviewed in order to provide generalizations in the form of answers to the questions that directed the conversations and observations. Generalizations will be drawn for both (a) individual youths and staff members and (b) the youths and staff members as two groups. Conclusions will be drawn about how closely the results of Meade's study match the results of my own investigation.

The youths' first-week scores on the two inventories will be compared with their last-week scores to judge what effect the camp experience apparently had on the boys' expressed attitudes and perceptions. The boys' scores on the *Personality Profile Sketch* will be compared with the norms of a national sample of teenagers to show how the boot-camp participants (as individuals and as a group) performed in comparison to the sub-groups in the national sample.

I also plan to compute correlations between boys' improvement ratings and their scores on each of the inventories in order to determine how well the inventory scores might predict attitudes and behaviors that the boys exhibited during the weeks following attendance at the camp.

In writing the final outcomes section of the dissertation, I plan to (a) describe how closely Meade's results matched the results of my study, (b) summarize the general trends discovered in my study (mainly in terms of the questions that guided my interviews and observations), and (c) include frequent examples from the lives of individual boys and staff members who participated in the project.

References:

Meade, A. M. (2001). 'Look what boot camp's done for me': Teaching and learning in Lakeview Academy Boot Camp. (Doctoral dissertation, Iowa State University, 2001). *Digital Dissertations,* AAT 3026731, Online. Available: http://wwwlib.umi.com/dissertations/

Wentworth, G. W. (1998). *Personality profile sketch.* Tucson, AZ: Psych Assessment Center.

Hispanics Rather Than American Indians

Salient features. The author's intention in this proposal is to use a research method from a 2001 dissertation for studying a different group of people than had been studied by the author of that dissertation. Whereas the 2001 dissertation focused on stereotypical concepts of American Indians, the present author's study focuses on stereotypical perceptions of Hispanics.

The proposal's qualitative aspects include the author's (a) dividing stereotypes of Hispanics into 16 categories, (b) interviewing 40 respondents to learn what jokes they know about Hispanics and what influence those jokes have on people's lives, (c) interpreting sociopolitical factors that have likely affected the nature of Hispanic stereotypes during different decades over the past century, and (d) describing techniques for correcting invalid stereotypes.

The main quantitative features of the plan are found in (a) frequencies of particular stereotypes during different periods across the past century and (b) the apparent level of success achieved with different methods of combating invalid stereotypes.

Dissertation title. *Images of Hispanics in Mainstream American Folklore and Popular Culture*

Background. In 2001, in the anthropology department at the University of California (Berkeley), Christine Lorine Palmer completed a doctor of philosophy dissertation entitled *Representation of American Indians: The Role of Mainstream Folklore and Popular Culture.* I found a reference to her dissertation on the Internet and obtained a copy of the entire document through the UMI ProQuest-Information website. The aim of Dr. Palmer's research was to compare two sources of American-Indian stereotypes as found in the United States. She called one source *folklore* and the other *popular culture.* In her study, folklore was reflected in jokes, and popular culture was reflected in movies (films). In explaining the nature of her research, she wrote:

This project explores the ways in which ethnic jokes permeate American culture and serve to express culturally embedded beliefs. Additionally, this project examines cinematic contributions to stereotyped images of American Indians to conclude that there are important historical, cultural, and social reasons that specific images of native people in the US persist. (Palmer, 2001, abstract p. 2)

I was very impressed by Dr. Palmer's work, and I believe that valuable insights into popular images of Hispanics in the United States can be gained by applying her methods in a similar study of the impact of folklore and popular culture on stereotypes of Hispanics.

Project goal. The research that I intend to carry out draws on Dr. Palmer's:

- *Focus*—that of identifying kinds of stereotypes, their form, their frequency, the extent to which they change over time, and why they change or fail to change.
- *Sources of evidence*—jokes and films (movies, television programs).
- *Methods of gathering evidence*—content analyses of publications (books, magazines articles, advertisements), interviews with knowledgeable individuals (particularly Hispanics), content analyses of films (movies, television programs).
- *Interpretation*—seeing stereotyped folklore and popular culture within the U.S. American historical/social "cultural landscape of ethnicity."

The two main ways that my approach differs from Dr. Palmer's are in the ethnic group that is the center of attention (Hispanics rather than American Indians) and in my effort to measure—at least roughly—the incidence, strength, and persistence of certain stereotypes.

Key terms. In this dissertation, the definitions assigned to five key terms are as follows:

Stereotype. A stereotype is a characteristic that is believed to typify members of a group and that distinguishes those members from members of other groups.

Hispanic. The word *Hispanic* in the present context refers to people whose native language is Spanish or who trace their heritage to Spanish-speaking cultures in the Western Hemisphere. For example, people whose cultural origins can be traced to Mexico, Puerto Rico, Cuba, Venezuela, or the like are considered to be Hispanic.

Mainstream. The pattern of beliefs and ways of life of the majority of U.S. Americans represents *mainstream U.S.* culture

Folklore. For the purpose of this dissertation, *folklore* consists of jokes (anecdotes that are intended to cause laughter) commonly spread among members of a population.

Popular culture. The words *popular culture,* as used here, apply only to cinematic representations (fictional or documentary) of people's lives in the form of movies, television programs, and videos.

Questions for the purpose of gathering evidence. I plan to adopt three sets of questions to focus my search for information about stereotypes of Hispanics. The first set concerns sources of information. The second set concerns the kinds of content I will seek in those sources. The third is about the effects of such stereotyping on the lives of Hispanics.

Source questions. Where can I find jokes about Hispanics from different periods of time over the past century?

What key terms will best steer my search for ethnic jokes?

Where can I locate and view films (movies, videos, television shows) that include Hispanic characters?

Content questions. How have Hispanics been stereotyped in jokes and films at different periods of time over the past century in terms of:

Face and body appearance?	Typical food and drink?
Modes of speech?	Levels of education?
Modes of dress?	Recreational pursuits?
Social-class levels?	Housing?
Occupations?	Modes of transportation?
Moral values?	Gender roles?
Manners and etiquette?	Religiosity?
Personality traits?	Aesthetic taste?

Effect questions. How valid are the different stereotypes of Hispanics? In what ways have stereotypes influenced the lives of Hispanics? What steps have been—or can be—taken to eliminate invalid stereotypes?

Compiling the evidence. My plan for collecting information about jokes and movies includes the following methods. (I expect to add further methods and sources that I discover during the process of gathering evidence.)

Finding jokes. I intend to hunt for jokes about Hispanics through (a) library books that contain collections of jokes from different eras, (b) bookstores that specialize in second-hand books, (c) websites on the Internet, and (d) interviews with both Hispanics and non-Hispanics.

I plan to visit university libraries and public libraries that are nearby and also search the holdings of more distant libraries by means of the Internet.

Local bookstores that sell used books will be visited, while booksellers in distant locations can be contacted via the Internet. I am particularly interested in joke books from past decades.

There are many Internet sources of jokes about Hispanics, as illustrated by the following websites:

www.wcotc.com/comedy/_j_hispanic.html
www. comedyemails.com
ldp42.home.texas.net/joke.htm

I do not intend to select a random sample or systematic sample of individuals to interview. Instead, I will use convenience sampling—talking with acquaintances and people I casually meet who are willing to be interviewed. I plan to interview 20 Hispanics and 20 non-Hispanics in order to (a) solicit examples of jokes, (b) ask what effect stereotypes in jokes exert on the lives of Hispanics, and (c) collect opinions about the validity of 10 such stereotypes.

Finding films. Such television channels as *American Movie Classics* and *Turner Classic Movies* show films from different eras, extending from the first years of the 20th century to the present time. The types of movies in which I will most likely find older Hispanic stereotypes are Westerns and historical films, such as *The Magnificent Seven, The Cisco Kid, Zoro,* and *Viva Zapata.* Films that focus on ethnic conflicts (*West Side Story, Border-line*) can also be useful, along with television channels that rebroadcast more recent series, such as *Law and Order* and *NYPD Blues.*

Library books and Internet sources that offer brief reviews of films should prove useful in my identifying which movies are likely to include Hispanic characters. The TV movie channels' periodicals that tell which films will be broadcast during the coming weeks can inform me of when I will be able to view a particular film. I can then tape-record the most helpful of the films in order to view them more than once for the purpose of extracting stereotypes. I can also borrow films from the past that have been recorded on videodisks (DVD) or videotapes.

Organizing the findings. As I collect stereotypes from jokes and films, I will enter each stereotype into a computer file that bears the title of a content question (see above list of content questions). I will not only list the kinds of stereotypes—such as "farm laborer" or "bandit" or "mayor" under *occupations*—but will also note the frequency with which that stereotype has appeared in jokes and films, thereby suggesting how prominently such a stereotype has figured in folklore and popular culture at different times.

Personal/social effects of stereotyping in jokes. During the 20 interviews with Hispanics and 20 with non-Hispanics, I will present a joke and ask: (a) Do you find that joke funny? (b) Do you think people should be telling that kind of joke? Why or why not?

Here are samples of the sorts of jokes, in the form of riddles, which I could use in the interview.

Question— Why do you never hit a Hispanic on a bike?
  Answer— Because the bike might be yours.
Question— Why did the Mexicans fight so hard to take the Alamo?
  Answer— So they could have four clean walls to write on!
Question— What do you get when you cross a Hispanic with an octopus?
  Answer— I don't know, but it sure can pick lettuce.

The purpose of those items is to discover how interviewees believe such jokes can affect people's self-perceptions, ethnic identities, and social relationships.

The validity of stereotypes. Some stereotypes are more accurate than others. For example, a widespread stereotype about human beings is that humans typically have two legs and can walk upright. Although there are exceptions to this stereotype (a leg can be severed, and newborns cannot walk upright), it is true that *most* humans have two legs and can walk upright. Therefore, a stereotype which validly applies to *most* individuals in a particular group is not only considered to be true most of the time, but it is also useful in preparing people for what to expect of individuals who are seen as members of the stereotyped group. Therefore, in order to discover which stereotypes of Hispanics that my 40 interviewees believe are valid, I plan to pose 10 true/false statements. Here is a sample of six such statements, which respondents will be asked to identify as either true or false (or they may say they don't know).

Most Hispanics have black hair.
Most Hispanics are Catholics.
Most Hispanics are lazy.
Most Hispanics can speak Spanish.
Most Hispanics drink a lot of alcohol, like beer and tequila.
Most Hispanics don't do well in school.

The aim of this part of the interviews is to learn (a) the extent to which respondents consider different stereotypes of Hispanics to be valid and (b) how my samples of Hispanics and non-Hispanics compare in their beliefs about the validity of particular stereotypes.

Efforts to combat and correct stereotypes. As a final step in collecting information, I plan to search for methods of correcting invalid stereotypes along with evidence about the success rate of those methods. I intend to use such keywords as *stereotypes, prejudice,* and *ethnic characteristics* to direct my hunt for books, articles in academic journals, and Internet websites that describe efforts to alter people's stereotypes.

Summary. Compiling the foregoing sorts of information should equip me to write a dissertation that (a) identifies kinds of stereotypes of Hispanics in American folklore and popular culture, (b) estimates the incidence of different Hispanic stereotypes during different periods over the past century, (c) proposes how certain sociopolitical conditions have caused changes (or lack of changes) in stereotypes from one era to another, (d) compares Hispanics and non-Hispanics in the ways they view typical stereotypes, and (e) suggests methods for correcting or reducing the types and incidence of invalid stereotypes.

Cited Dissertation: Palmer, Christine Lorine. (2001). *Representation of American Indians: The role of mainstream folklore and popular culture.* Berkeley, CA: University of California. Unpublished doctoral dissertation, available as Publication Number AAT 3044621 from UMI ProQuest Information and Learning Company (website: http.//wwwlib.umi.com/dissertations/preview_all/3044621)

Conclusion

Among the qualitative aspects of this chapter's three research proposals are (a) the way of choosing which items to include on an inventory or test or in an interview (readers' skills, boot camp, Hispanic stereotypes), (b) estimated causes of an observed outcome (readers' skills, boot camp, Hispanic stereotypes), (c) participants' expressed opinions (boot camp, Hispanic stereotypes), (d) examples of individuals' behaviors and opinions (boot camp), and (e) the outcomes of a research project as expressed in generalizations (readers' skills, boot camp, Hispanic stereotypes).

Quantitative features of the chapter's proposals have been (a) individuals' test scores and inventory scores (readers' skills, boot camp), (b) a group's average performance level (readers' skills, boot camp), (c) the correlation between individuals' performances at different times (readers' skills, boot camp), (d) the extent of variability within a group (readers' skills, boot camp), (e) rating-scale rankings of observed events (boot camp), (f) comparisons of a group's inventory scores with nationwide norms (boot camp), and (g) trends over the decades in the incidence of a phenomenon (stereotypes of Hispanics).

13

Publishing the Results

Upon completing their thesis or dissertation, students often wish to share their research with an audience that extends beyond the faculty members of the committee that supervised their work. The purpose of this chapter is to describe a variety of ways to fulfill that wish.

Research results can be disseminated in either oral or written form. Typical settings in which to report research orally are college seminars, professional inservice workshops, meetings of service clubs, conferences of academic associations, and radio or television talk shows or news programs. Printed media in which to report research results include professional and academic journals, books, book chapters, magazines, newspapers, newsletters, computer Internet websites, and an author's own desktop publications. The following pages offer brief descriptions of those resources in terms of (a) how to employ them and (b) their advantages and limitations.

Oral Presentations

Seminars, workshops, and service clubs. University departments sometimes hold seminars in which students describe their thesis or dissertation project for the benefit of fellow students and faculty members. During such gatherings, the author typically describes (a) the purpose of the project, (b) the methodology, (c) the results, (d) problems encountered during the conduct of the project and how the problems were solved, and, perhaps, (e) further kinds of research that seem warranted. The oral presentation is often accompanied by a projected slide show that displays statistical tables, diagrams, and principal stages of the research process. The presenter is also expected to answer questions from the audience.

Similar presentations may be made at workshops and inservice-training sessions sponsored by school systems, by professional associations (architects, dentists, lawyers, motel operators, physicians, realtors, and the like), or by businesses (an accounting firm, a chain of restaurants, a large automobile agency). To make available the opportunity to give such a presentation, a student can phone or write to the head of the organization whose business is within the domain of the thesis or dissertation and describe the nature of the project, including the benefit that the members of the organization might derive from hearing the project's results and practical applications.

Such service clubs as Rotary, Kiwanis, Lions, and Optimists are always on the lookout for individuals who can give an interesting, useful speech at their weekly luncheon meetings. Students who believe that their research might interest club members can write or phone to the club president or program planner, briefly describing the nature of the project and offering to present it during a club meeting.

Conferences of academic associations. Within all academic disciplines there are associations or societies whose members sponsor national and regional conferences at which speakers address topics related to the members' professional interests. Examples of such bodies are the *American Educational Research Association, American Psychological Association, American Sociological Association, International Political Science Association, National Council for Black Studies, National Science Teachers Association, Pacific Coast College Health Association,* and *Society for Neuroscience.* There are many dozens of such groups whose names and addresses can be found on the Internet.

Future conferences to be held by an academic association are typically announced on the organization's Internet website, along with instructions about how a person can apply to contribute a research report. The presentation at such events can be of various kinds—lectures, panels organized around themes, debates, question/answer sessions, open discussions, and poster displays. Poster presentations are relatively recent innovations that consist of researchers being assigned positions in a room or hallway where each presenter exhibits key elements of her or his project and discusses the work with whatever interested individuals choose to stop by.

The size of the audience reached by a speech, a panel, or a debate depends on several factors—the number of people attending the conference, the reputation of the presenter, the popularity of the research topic, the time of day (mid-morning, mid-afternoon, and early evening tend to draw larger crowds), and the number of parallel sessions going on at the same time so that the total audience is divided among multiple sessions.

The length of time allotted to a speaker can vary form five minutes to an hour or so, depending on the eminence of the researcher and the number of presentations that the conference organizers have chosen to include. Fifteen minutes is a rather typical length of time allowed each presenter, thereby offering an author the opportunity to describe no more than the highlights of the research methods and results.

The chance of having a research paper accepted for delivery at a conference is usually far greater than the chance of having it accepted for publication in a journal or as a chapter in a book. Conference planning committees, compared to journal and book editors, are typically more lenient in the standards they apply when judging submissions; and competition for having a paper accepted for a conference is usually less than for a journal. Sometimes the opportunity to present a paper is limited to members of the association that sponsors the conference.

If the conference proceedings are subsequently published as a collection of abstracts of conference papers, then students who gave a conference account of their thesis or dissertation project can be credited with a brief print publication in addition to an oral presentation.

Radio and television. Two potential broadcast outlets for oral research reports are radio or television newscasts and talk shows.

Whenever the results of a student's research could be of interest to the general public, the student can phone or write to a radio or television station, informing the news editor of the topic and research outcomes. An editor who decides that the research is, indeed, a worthy news item will usually assign a reporter either to read a brief description of the project or to interview the author. The research then becomes a short item in a news broadcast, perhaps with the student appearing to answer queries the broadcaster asks.

Talk shows are usually half-hour programs during which one or more visitors are interviewed. Students may receive an opportunity to describe their research on a talk show if they write or phone to the show's host and describe the nature and significance of their research. The matters discussed on the show are usually determined by the host's sequence of questions rather than by the student.

Print Presentations

Professional and academic journals. Frequently, the same occupational and academic organizations that conduct training workshops and conferences also sponsor journals that publish research studies. The world's journals number in the thousands. They can be issued monthly, bimonthly, quarterly, semiannually, or annually. The most common schedule is probably quarterly. Each journal accepts articles in a defined realm of interest that may be quite narrow (*Oral History Review, Rural Special Education Quarterly*) or quite broad (*Journal of Thought, Education*). The journal's subject-matter focus can be of a particular kind, such as:

- A professional specialization (*Journal of Correctional Education, Journal of the Association for the Severely Handicapped*)
- An academic discipline (*Analytical Biochemistry, Historica Mathematica, American Political Science Review, Social Context of Education*)
- An ethnic group (*Black Issues in Higher Education*)
- A region (*The Middle East Journal, Journal of Asian and African Studies*)
- A sociogeographic entity (*Research in Rural Education*)
- A gender category (*Women's Studies Quarterly, Women's Rights Law Reporter*)
- A religious denomination (*U. S. Catholic, Lutheran Theological Journal, Muslim Education Quarterly, Journal of Jewish Communal Services*)

Lists of journals and descriptions of their sources and contents are readily available on the Internet. Entering the key words *academic journals* or *professional journals* into a computer via such a search engine as Google generates more than a million websites, most of which list numerous journals bearing on the topic of the particular website. At an increasing pace, journals are being published electronically on web pages rather than printed in traditional paper form. Such journals are therefore easily accessed from a user's own computer rather than requiring a trip to a library.

The size and type of a journal's reading audience are influenced by several factors—the publication's subject-matter focus, its reputation, its cost, how widely it is advertised, and whether it is issued by a professional association. Whenever a journal is a key publication of a professional group or scholarly society, every individual in the society usually receives the journal as a right of membership. Thus, the larger the membership, the larger the guaranteed reading audience. However, many journals—not published by an association or not automatically distributed to an association's members—must depend solely on paid subscriptions for their distribution. Because subscription prices are frequently high, individuals often avoid buying such publications and depend, instead, on using copies in a college library. However, in recent years, as library funds have shrunk, many libraries have stopped subscribing to journals that are seldom used or are especially expensive, so the reading audience reached by those publications has dwindled.

Journals can vary markedly in the proportion of submitted manuscripts they will publish. The most prestigious and popular journals may accept as few as 15% or 20% of the papers they receive. In contrast, journals of low status or ones with a small potential audience may publish 80% or more of the submitted items. Journal editors usually maintain strong control over the form, topics, and scholarly quality of the articles they accept, so authors are obliged to abide strictly by editors' preferences. Consequently, authors enjoy far less freedom and control over journal articles than they do over conference presentations and—in many cases—book manuscripts.

The acceptable length of articles can differ considerably from one journal to another. Some editors limit entries to ten printed pages or less. Others accept reports as long as 40 or 50 pages. Frequently a periodical's policy regarding length is described on the journal's inside cover (front or rear) in a notice to potential contributors and on the journal's Internet website.

At a rapidly increasing pace, journal editors are requiring that manuscripts be submitted via the Internet rather than on paper via the postal service. An example of guidance for potential authors is the following set of directions about sending articles to the Society for Research in Child Development to be considered for publication in the society's flagship journal, *Child Development*.

Please follow submission requirements carefully, as deviations may slow processing. *Child Development* will not consider for publication any manuscript under review elsewhere or substantially similar to a manuscript already published. (Please note that papers posted on the world-wide web are considered to be "published.") Editors retain the right to reject manuscripts that do not meet established ethical standards.

Manuscripts should be submitted to cdev@umich.edu as an electronic attachment in a Word or WordPerfect file. The transmittal e-mail should contain (a) the name(s) of the author(s) and affiliation(s), and the street address, telephone, fax, and electronic mail address of the corresponding author; (b) a statement that warrants that all co-authors are in agreement with the content of the manuscript and that the study has been conducted in accordance with the ethical standards of SRCD (see the *Child Development* website or pp. 283-284 of the 2000 *SRCD Directory*). The corresponding author is responsible for informing all co-authors, in a timely manner, of manuscript submission, editorial decisions, reviews, and revisions.

The manuscript file should be formatted with double spaced, 12-point type, and should include a single paragraph abstract of 100-120 words. Please follow all guidelines on format, style, and ethics provided in the Publication Manual (5th ed.) of the American Psychological Association. Original figures should be submitted only with final versions of accepted manuscripts. Authors should keep a copy of all files and figures to guard against loss. (Manuscript submission, 2000)

The time lag between an author's submitting a paper to a journal and the paper's actually appearing in print can differ significantly from one journal to another. The time lapse can be affected by several conditions —the number of steps in the publishing process, the efficiency of the journal's personnel, the number of submissions the journal receives, the backlog of accepted papers, the frequency with which the journal is issued, and the number of pages in each issue of the publication. In some cases, the journal's editor determines which manuscripts to accept, so authors must wait only two or three months to learn whether their paper will be published. But far more often, editors send manuscripts out to reviewers, such as college professors who teach in the area of the manuscripts' subject-matter. Such reviewers are frequently quite tardy in appraising a paper's worth, so that the publishing process is much delayed. Consequently, the time between an author's submitting an article and the time it is published can be two, three, or four years.

Journals are not all alike in their policies regarding the costs that authors are expected to bear and the payments authors may receive. Most journals neither charge authors for publishing their articles nor pay authors for their work. Some journals require that authors contribute to the expense of publication (usually paying a given amount per printed page), whereas others pay writers a nominal sum for articles.

Books. Occasionally a dissertation is of sufficient interest and quality to warrant its publication as a book. However, rarely is the work published in the exact form it appeared as a dissertation. Instead, the original research report is usually refashioned into a shorter, more appealing version designed to interest a wider reading audience than would be attracted to the original.

For the purpose of this chapter, books can be divided into two categories—trade and academic/professional. Trade books are intended for the general reading public and are available in regular bookstores, public libraries, and on the Internet. Academic/professional books are intended for such specialized audiences as students and faculty members in colleges and universities, teachers and administrators in elementary and secondary schools, accountants, architects, engineers, industrialists, lawyers, physicians, and the like. Such books are most often found in college and university bookstores and libraries, and on the Internet.

Although most dissertations are best suited for publication as academic/professional books, a few may appeal to the general public and thus qualify for the trade market.

The procedure for offering manuscripts to publishers can be different for trade and for academic/professional books. Especially in the case of trade fiction, publishers are not likely to accept submissions directly from authors. It is thus necessary for an author to hire a literary agent to provide the initial screening of the manuscript. The agent first reviews the author's product, estimates its potential, and offers advice about changes needed. Only then will the agent seek a publisher who is willing to consider the work. An agent either charges the author a fee or else takes a percentage of the royalties paid to the author by the publisher, with the total amount of royalties determined by the number of books sold. Typically, the royalty for each book is 10% or 12% of the book's selling price.

In the case of academic/professional publishing, although an agent might be useful, agents are really not necessary. An author can negotiate directly with publishers. Most publishers maintain websites on the World Wide Web, so authors can find on that site the directions about how to submit proposals. Editors seldom want to receive an entire manuscript at the outset. Instead, they want a description of what the book is about, what unique attractions it offers, the intended reading audience, a detailed outline or table of contents, and one or two completed chapters that reveal the author's writing style. The editors may send those materials to experts in the field of the manuscript's subject-matter for opinions about the worth of the work and its likely sales appeal. On the basis of the reviewers' opinions and the editors' own assessment, the author either (a) will be offered a contract to publish the work (or perhaps first asked to send more chapters) or (b) will be told something like "We regret to inform you that your proposed book does not fit into our present publication schedule, but we wish you success with publishing it elsewhere."

Editors can differ in the amount of control they attempt to wield over the content, structure, and format of the books they issue. For instance, at the *least-control* end of the control scale are editors who conduct what are essentially printing-and-marketing services. In effect, they leave decisions about the subject-matter content, structure, and writing style entirely in the hands of the authors. The responsibility of such publishers is thus limited to ensuring that the final printed book is free from typographical errors, is bound attractively, and is advertised to potential readers. In contrast, publishers at the *most-control* end of the scale conceive their responsibility to include verifying and—if judged necessary—changing the technical content of the work, revising the structure (altering the sequence of chapters, moving paragraphs, eliminating portions), revising the writing style (changing phrasing and vocabulary), dictating the book's type font and format, binding the work, and marketing the finished product. Some publishers adjust their degree of control to the characteristics of the author and of the submitted manuscript. The work of a prestigious, highly influential researcher is less likely to be altered than is that of a newly graduated doctoral student. A brilliantly crafted manuscript can pass through the editorial process unscathed, whereas an awkwardly written one can be subjected to major editorial changes.

Book chapters. A thesis or dissertation, more often than being issued as an entire book, will be accepted in a much-abbreviated form as a chapter in someone else's book. There are several ways that a student may receive such an opportunity. In the first way, a person who is editing a volume on a particular topic selects the authors who will be asked to submit chapters for the volume. In the second way, an editor selects a variety of already-published journal articles to be reissued as chapters of a book. In the third, papers presented at a conference are collected to comprise the book's contents.

Editors of collections can vary considerably in the amount of control they attempt to exert over the content and quality of contributors' chapters. Some editors publish the offerings without change, except for correcting spelling and grammar errors. Other editors return manuscripts to authors with directions for substantial changes, or else an editor may choose to rewrite submissions quite substantially.

Authors usually receive a free copy of the volume in which their chapter appears, but they seldom are paid for their work.

Popular periodicals. Theses and dissertations that treat topics of interest to the general public are suitable sources of articles in magazines, in newspapers, and in newsletters distributed to members of organizations.

To write a short account of a research project for publication in such periodicals, a student can (a) identify the central question or questions that the research project attempted to answer, (b) briefly sketch the methodology used, and (c) describe in more detail the research results and the implications those results hold for the community, the nation, or the lives of individuals or groups.

The task of identifying which periodicals would be suitable outlets for a research report can consist of the author browsing through the magazines in a public library, in a bookshop, or at a magazine stand. Upon locating what seems to be a fitting publication, the student can inspect its contents to find the usual length of articles and to identify the writing style. This information is used for fashioning a version of the thesis or dissertation suitable for such a publication. The resulting article can be mailed to the magazine's editorial office, accompanied by a letter explaining the background of the research and suggesting why an account of the project might appeal to the magazine's readers. A similar approach can be used for submitting an article to a newspaper or an organization's newsletter editor, with the newspaper version typically a good deal briefer than the one intended for a magazine.

Self-published research reports. Thanks to the widespread availability of personal computers and sophisticated word-processing software, researchers can now create book and journal pages that appear to be professsionally typeset. In effect, desk-top publishing has come of age. This means that the author, rather than the editors in a publishing house, maintains complete control over the format and quality of the final product.

However, there are several important disadvantages of self-published books and articles. When a professional publisher is involved, editors, copyreaders, and proofreaders assume responsibility for helping ensure that a manuscript's structure, grammar, and spelling are accurate. But even though authors can easily do the typesetting, few have the equipment and skill needed to bind a book or periodical successfully. Thus, the task of binding must be contracted out to professionals, with the author paying the cost that would be borne by the publisher if the book or article were issued by a publishing house.

Then there is the problem of disseminating the finished work to a suitable audience. This is one of the most important functions of commercial publishers, who typically maintain a complex marketing program, complete with (a) specialists in writing advertising copy, (b) lists of libraries and members of professional societies who are potential buyers, (c) displays of books at conferences, and (d) a system for shipping books to booksellers and individual buyers. But when authors themselves publish their theses and dissertations, they are obliged either to market the products personally or else contract the distribution task to a company that provides such service for a price.

Whether books, pamphlets, or audiotapes are issued by a publisher or by researchers themselves, authors can attempt to enhance the dissemination of their works through several media—presentations at conferences, announcements in newsletters and journals of professional societies, articles in newspapers and magazines, and appearances on radio and television talk shows. But for authors who do not wish to spend the time and bother that such efforts require, issuing their work through a professional publisher is a better method than self-publishing to introduce their work to a wide audience.

Internet Publishing

The Internet, with its World Wide Web, provides an outlet for thesis and dissertation research that enjoys a variety of advantages over print publishing.

First, the Internet provides several ways to disseminate information—as an e-mail attachment, as a document on a bulletin board, or as an entry on the author's own webpage. As is now widely recognized, e-mail (electronic mail) consists of messages sent over the computer Internet rather than by a postal mail carrier. An entire dissertation or a summary can be sent either to selected individuals or to a large audience of a particular type, known as an *interest group*, by the author's assigning the document to an electronic bulletin board or mailing list.

> A single message posted on a popular bulletin board or sent to a mailing list might reach and engage millions of people. . . . Each bulletin board or news group has a name, and anyone interested can "hang out" there. . . . Almost any topic you can name has a group communicating about it on the network. (Gates, 1995, p. 123-125)

Or a student can create his or her own web page on which the thesis or dissertation is displayed, either in full or in part. Internet users locate that page by means of a search engine and key words that are associated with the topic of the research.

As a further option, a publishable version of the research project can be sent via the Internet to the editor of one of the journals that issue their products on the World Wide Web rather than on paper. With the costs of print publishing rising and the number of subscribers to many scholarly journals declining, traditional journals are increasingly encountering financial difficulties. Thus, a growing number are turning to electronic publishing as a solution to their money problems.

For students who have newly completed their thesis or dissertation, one of the most attractive features of electronic publishing is its ability to provide readers immediate access to the research report. In the case of books and journals, a year or more can elapse between the time a completed manuscript is submitted to editors and the time the work is finally in print. With electronic publishing, there is no wait between the time that the author puts the report on the network and the time the report is available to readers. Furthermore, electronic publishing eliminates problems of distance, since the Internet reaches virtually all parts of the world in which computers are available, so readers anywhere can access the researcher's report as soon as it is placed on the web.

Whereas traditional journals and books cannot be conveniently altered once they are in print, materials on the web can be revised at any time—corrected, lengthened, updated. Publishing on the Internet also enables an author to receive rapid feedback from readers who send their comments to the author by e-mail. Documents placed on the World Wide Web can include full color illustrations, which is a feature that is expensive in print media but is included at little or no cost on the Internet. Finally, in electronic publishing, the author maintains complete control over the form of the report, because no editors are involved, except in the case of formal Internet journals and books that must pass through the editorial process before being issued on the web. However, a disadvantage of shortcutting the editorial process is that the author then lacks the professional aid with the writing style and the elimination of errors that editors usually provide.

Conclusion

As illustrated in this chapter, there are many ways graduate students can share the results of their research with audiences beyond the members of their supervising committee. Oral presentations can be given during seminars, professional workshops, service-club meetings, conferences of academic associations, and radio or television talk shows or news programs. Printed reports can be issued in professional journals, books, magazines, newspapers, newsletters, computer Internet websites, and an author's own desktop publications.

14

Reviewing the Themes

The purpose of this brief final chapter is to recognize five themes—in the form of convictions—that have determined the content of Chapters 1 through 12.

- Qualitative research methods involve gathering and interpreting information from the viewpoint of *kinds* of objects, ideas, or events. Quantitative research methods involve collecting and interpreting information from the viewpoint of *amounts, frequencies,* or *magnitudes* of objects, ideas, or events. (Chapters 1–12)

- Qualitative methods are neither inherently nor generally superior to quantitative methods, and vice versa. Which type of method is more suitable in a particular research project depends on the question—or questions—that the research is supposed to answer. Some questions call for a qualitative approach. Others call for a quantitative approach. Questions frequently call for combining qualitative and quantitative methods. Consequently, controversies which, in general, pit qualitative against quantitative methods are ill-founded and a waste of time. (Chapter 1)

- The term *research methods* commonly encompasses a diversity of procedures, including general approaches to data collection (historical, biographical, case study, and more), information-gathering techniques (content analysis, interviews, tests, and more), and ways of interpreting data (cause, comparison, prediction, and more). It is useful for students to be acquainted with these varieties when they are planning their thesis or dissertation research so they can make an informed choice of the methods they will employ in their own projects. (Part I)

- There are many ways that qualitative and quantitative methods can be blended. Students can profit from analyzing numerous examples of such blends in order to identify the strengths and limitations of ways they might combine qualitative and quantitative methods in their own work. (Part II)

- There are numerous alternative forms in which students can cast their thesis and dissertation proposals. Which form will be most appropriate in a given instance depends on such factors as (a) the nature of the questions the research is intended to answer, (b) how much information the student has already collected, and (c) faculty members' preferences in terms of methodology, the sequence in which ideas are presented, and the amount of detail that a proposal should include. Therefore, at the proposal-preparation stage, students can profit from comparing a diversity of proposals that are organized in different patterns so they can choose the combination of elements from those examples that they wish to adopt in designing their own research plans. (Part II)

References

Aiken, L. R. (1997). *Questionnaires and inventories: Surveying opinions and assessing personality.* New York: Wiley.

Almond, G. A. (2002). *Ventures in political science: Narratives and reflections.* Boulder, CO: Lynne Rienner.

American Psychiatric Association. (2000). *Diagnostic and statistical manual of mental disorders—IV.* Washington, DC: American Psychiatric Association.

Anderson, L. R. (1997). *Women and autobiography in the twentieth century: Remembered features.* New York: Prentice-Hall & Harvester Wheatsheaf.

Andrews, W. L. (Ed.). (1993). *African American autobiography: A collection of critical essays.* Englewood Cliffs, NJ: Prentice Hall.

Angleitner, J. S., Wiggins, J. S. (Eds.). (1986). *Personality assessment via questionnaires: Current issues in theory and measurement.* New York: Springer-Verlag.

Arthur, M., Bridenthal, R., Kelly-Gadol, J., & Lerner, G. (1976). *Conceptual frameworks for studying women's history: Four papers.* Bronxville, NY: Sarah Lawrence College.

Aubel, J. (1994). *Guidelines for studies using the group interview technique.* Geneva: International Labour Office.

Babbie, E. R. (1990). *Survey research methods* (2nd ed.). Belmont, CA: Wadsworth.

Ball, S. (1985). Reactive effects in research and evaluation. In T. Husén & T. N. Postlethwaite (Eds.). *International encyclopedia of education: Research and studies* (1st ed., vol. 7, p. 4200). Oxford: Pergamon.

Barnett, V. (1991). *Sample survey principles and methods.* New York: Oxford University Press.

227

Bentley, M. (Ed.) (1997). *Companion to historiography.* New York: Routledge.

Berdie, D. F., Anderson, J. F., & Niebuhr, M. A. (1986). *Questionnaires: Design and use* (2nd ed.). Metuchen, NJ: Scarecrow Press.

Brady, J. J. (1976). *The craft of interviewing.* New York: Vintage.

Braverman, M. T., & Slater, J. K. (Eds.). (1996). *Advances in survey research.* San Francisco: Jossey-Bass.

Broomsedge chronicles writing samples. (2002). Online. Available: www.wku.edu/Dept/Academic/AHSS/ English/pub/bwritsam.htm.

Brydon-Miller, M. (1991). Education, research, and action. In D. L. Tolman, & M. Brydon-Miller, M. (Eds.). *From subjects to subjectivities* (pp. 77-89). New York: New York University Press.

Byrne, B. M. (1996). *Self-concept across the life span: Issues and instrumentation.* Washington, DC: American Psychological Association.

Campbell, D. T., & Stanley, J. C. (1966). *Experimental and quasi-experimental designs for research.* Chicago: Rand McNally.

Cannell, C. F. (1977). *A Summary of research studies of interviewing methodology.* Rockville, MD: U.S. Government Printing Office.

Carspecken, P. F. (1996). *Critical ethnography in educational research: A theoretical and practical guide.* New York : Routledge.

Chase, S. E., & Rogers, M. F. (2001). *Mothers and children: Feminist analyses and personal narratives.* New Brunswick, NJ: Rutgers University Press.

CLCWeb Library: A Website of research and information in comparative culture and media studies and comparative culture and literature studies. (2002). Online. Available: http:// clcwebjournal. lib.purdue. edu/ library. html>

Cone, J. D., & Foster, S. L. (1993). *Dissertations and theses from start to finish: Psychology and related Fields.* Washington, DC: American Psychological Association.

Cox, J. (1996). *Your opinion, please!: How to build the best questionnaires in the field of education.* Thousand Oaks, CA: Corwin.

Cresswell, J.W. (1998). *Qualitative inquiry and research design: Choosing among five traditions.* Thousand Oaks, CA: Sage.

Daniels, D. H. H., Doolin, C. A., Beaumont, L. J., & Beaumont, F. (2001) *Understanding children: An interview and observation guide for educators.* New York: McGraw-Hill.

Denzin, N. K. (1989). *Interpretive biography.* Newbury Park, CA: Sage.

Denzin, N. K. (1997). *Interpretive ethnography.* Thousand Oaks, CA: Sage.

Denzin, N. K., & Lincoln, Y. S. (Eds.). (1994). *Handbook of qualitative research.* Thousand Oaks, CA: Sage.

Dewalt, B. R., & Dewalt, K. M. (2002). *Participant observation.* Lanham, MD: Rowman & Littlefield.

Dey, I. (1999). *Grounding grounded theory.* San Diego: Academic.

Douglas, J. D. (1985). *Creative Interviewing.* Beverly Hills: Sage.

Eakin, P. J. (Ed.). (1991). *American autobiography: Retrospect and prospect.* Madison, WI: University of Wisconsin Press.

Elder, G. H., Jr. (1996). Human lives in changing societies: Life course and developmental insights. In R. B. Cairns, G. H. Elder, Jr., & E J. Costello, *Developmental science.* Cambridge, England: Cambridge University Press.

Elder, G. H., Modell, J, & Parke, R. D. (1993). Studying children in a changing world. In G. H. Elder, Jr., J. Modell, & R. D. Parke. *Children in time and place.* Cambridge, England: Cambridge University Press.

Erickson, K. C., & Stull, D. D. (1998). *Doing team ethnography: Warnings and advice.* Thousand Oaks, CA.: Sage.

Ethnography. (1994). *The new Encyclopaedia Britannica* (vol. 4). Chicago: Encyclopaedia Britannica.

Fabian, A. (2000). *The unvarnished truth: Personal narratives in nineteenth-century America.* Berkeley, CA : University of California Press.

Fetterman, D. M. (1998). *Ethnography: Step by step* (2nd ed.). Thousand Oaks, CA: Sage

Fink, A., & Kosecoff, J. (1998). *How to conduct surveys: A step-by-step guide* (2nd ed.). Thousand Oaks, CA: Sage.

Foddy, W. H. (1993). *Constructing questions for interviews and questionnaires.* New York: Cambridge University Press.

Follman, J. (1984). Cornucopia of correlations, *American Psychologist, 39,* 701-702.

Fowler, F. J. (1990). *Standardized survey interviewing: Minimizing interview-related errors.* Newbury Park, CA: Sage.

Frank, C., & Bird, L. B. (2000). *Ethnographic eyes: A teacher's guide to classroom observation.* Portsmouth, NH: Heinemann.

Gates, B. (1995). *The road ahead.* New York: Viking.

Glaser, B. G. (1978). *Theoretical sensitivity.* Mill Valley, CA: Sociological Press.

Glaser, B. G. (1992). *Emergence v. forcing: Basics of grounded theory analysis.* Mill Valley, CA: Sociology Press.

Glaser, B. G., & Strauss, A. (1967). *The discovery of grounded theory: Strategies for qualitative research.* Chicago: Aldine.

Glass, G. V., & Hopkins, K. D. (1996). *Statistical methods in education and psychology* (3rd ed.). Boston: Allyn & Bacon.

Glass, G. V., McGaw, B., & Smith, M. L. (1981). *Meta-analysis in social research.* Beverly Hills, CA: Sage.

Glatthorn, A. A. ( ) *Writing the winning dissertation: A step-by-step guide.*

Glesne, C., & Peshkin, A. (1992). *Becoming qualitative researchers.* Thousand Oaks, CA: Sage.

Goodall, H. L. (2000). *Writing the new ethnography.* Lanham, MD: AltaMira.

Graham, J. R. (1984). *Psychological testing.* Englewood Cliffs, NJ: Prentice-Hall.

Gronlund, N. E. (1998). *Assessment of student achievement* (6th ed.). Boston: Allyn & Bacon.

Guenzel, P. J. (1983). *General interview techniques: A self-instructional workbook for telephone and personal interviews training.* Ann Arbor, MI: Institute for Social Research, University of Michigan.

Gutiérrez-Jones. C. (2001). *Critical race narratives: A study of race, rhetoric, and injury.* New York : New York University Press.

Hambleton, R. K., & Zaal, J. N. (Eds.). (1991). *Advances in educational and psychological Testing.* Boston: Kluwer.

Hays, W. L. (1994). *Statistics* (5th ed.). Fort Worth, TX: Harcourt Brace.

Heckhausen, J., & Schulz, R. (1999). Selectivity in life-span development. In J. Brandstädter & R. M. Lerner (Eds.), *Action and self-development* (pp. 67-103). Thousand Oaks, CA: Sage.

Hodson, R. (1999). *Analyzing documentary accounts.* London: Sage.

Hofstede, G. (1980). *Culture's consequences: International differences in work-related values.* Thousand Oaks, CA: Sage.

Hunter, J. E., Schmidt, F. L., & Jackson, G. B. (1982). *Meta-analysis: Cumulating research findings across studies.* Beverly Hills, CA: Sage.

Hurst, J. (1995). *Popular education.* Online. Available: http://www-gse.berkeley.edu/Admin/ExtRel/educator/spring95texts/popular.ed uc.html.

Jaccard, J., & Becker, M.A. (1990). *Statistics for the behavioral sciences* (2nd ed.). Belmont, CA: Wadsworth.

Kendall, M. G., & Gibbons, J. D. (1990). *Rank correlation methods* (5th ed.). New York: Oxford University Press.

King, G., Koehane, R. O., & Verba, S. (1994). *Designing social inquiry: Scientific inference in qualitative research.* Princeton, NJ: Princeton University Press.

Kirk, J., & Miller, M. L. (1986). *Reliability and validity in qualitative research.* Thousand Oaks, CA: Sage.

Kreppner, K. (1989). Linking infant development-in-context research to the investigation of life-span family development. In K. Kreppner & R. M. Lerner (Eds.). *Family systems and life-span development* (pp. 33-64). Hillsdale, NJ: Erlbaum.

Kridel, C. (Ed.). (1998). *Writing educational biography.* New York: Garland.

Krippendorf, K. (1980). *Content analysis: An introduction to its methodology.* Beverly Hills, CA: Sage.

Labaw, P. J. (1981). *Advanced questionnaire design.* Cambridge, MA: Abt.

Larocca, M. (2002, June). *Narrative and dialogue—A contrast in writing styles.* (2002, June). Online. Available: www.freereads.topcities.com/narrativedialogue.html.

Lesage, J. (2002). *Making a difference: University students of color speak out.* Lanham, MD: Rowman & Littlefield.

Loevinger, J. (Ed.). (1998). *Technical foundations for measuring ego development.* Mahwah, NJ: Erlbaum.

Macsporran, I (1982). Hermeneutics: An alternative set of philosophical assumptions for comparative education? In R. Cowen & P. Stokes (Eds.). *Methodological issues in comparative education* (pp. 47-51). London: Routledge.

Madsen, D. (1991). *Successful dissertations and theses: A guide to graduate student research from proposal to completion.* San Francisco: Jossey-Bass.

Magarey, S., Guerin, C., & Hamilgon, P. (Eds.). (1992). *Writing lives: Feminist biography and autobiography.* Adelaide, Australia: University of Adelaide.

Mannien, J. & Tuomela, R. (Eds.) (1976). *Essays on explanation and understanding.* Dordrech, Neterhalnds: D. Reidel.

Manuscript submission. (2000). Ann Arbor, MI: Society for Research in Child Development. Online. Available: www.srcd.org/cd.html.

Marcus, G. E. (Ed.). (1999). *Critical anthropology now: Unexpected contexts, shifting constituencies, changing agendas.* Santa Fe, NM: School of American Research Press.

McArthur, D. L. (Ed.). (1987). *Alternative approaches to the assessment of achievement.* Boston: Kluwer.

McCaw, N. (2000). *George Eliot and Victorian historiography: Imagining the national past.* New York: St. Martin's.

McGaw, B. (1985). Meta-analysis. In T. Husén & T. N. Postlethwaite (Eds.), *International encyclopedia of education: Research and studies* (1st ed., vol. 6, pp. 3322-3330). Oxford: Pergamon.

Miles, M. B., & Huberman, A. M. (1994). *Qualitative data analysis* (2nd ed.). Thousand Oaks, CA: Sage.

Nazarea, V. D. (Ed.). (1999). *Ethnoecology: Situated knowledge/located lives.* Tucson : University of Arizona Press.

Neuendorf, K. A. (2001). *The content analysis guidebook.* Thousand Oaks, CA: Sage.

Oppenheim, A. N. (1992). *Questionnaire design, onterviewing, and attitude measurement.* New York: St. Martin's.

Palafox, J. C., Prawda, J., & Velez, E. (1994). Primary school quality in Mexico, *Comparative Education Review, 38* (2), 167-180.

Parke, C. N. (1996). *Biography: Writing lives.* St. Leonards, Australia: Allen & Unwin.

Patten M. Q. (2001). *Qualitative research and evaluation methods.* Thousand Oaks, CA: Sage.

Popping, R. (2000). *Computer-assisted text analysis.* Lanham, MD: University Press of America.

Reed-Danahay, D. E. (Ed.). (1997). *Auto/ethnography: Rewriting the self and the social.* New York: Berg.

Riffe, D., Lacy, S., & Fico, F. (1998). *Analyzing media messages: Using quantitative content analysis in research.* Hillsdale, NJ: Erlbaum.

Roberts, C. W. (Ed.) (1997). *Text analysis for the social sciences: Methods for drawing statistical inferences from texts and transcripts.* Mahwah, NJ: Lawrence Erlbaum.

Roid, G. H., & Haladyna, T. H. (1982*). A technology for test-item writing.* New York: Academic.

Rudestam, K. E., & Newton, R. R. (1992). *Surviving your dissertation: A comprehensive guide to content and process.* Thousand Oaks, CA: Sage.

Scholz, R. W., & Tietje, O. (2002). *Embedded case study methods: Integrating quantitative and qualitative knowledge.* Thousand Oaks, CA: Sage.

Schultz, E. (1965). *Proverbial expressions of the Samoans.* Wellington, New Zealand: The Polynesian Society.

Seidman, I. (1997). *Interviewing as qualitative research: A guide for researchers in education and the social sciences* (2nd ed.). New York: Teachers College Press.

Siegel, S., & Castellan, N. J., Jr. (1988). *Nonparametric statistics for the behavioral sciences* (2nd ed.). New York: McGraw-Hill.

Sirkin, R. M. (1995). *Statistics for the social sciences.* Thousand Oaks, CA: Sage.

Skinner, B. F. (1974). *About behaviorism.* New York: Knopf.

Slavin, R. E. (1984). *Research methods in education.* Englewood Cliffs, NJ: Prentice-Hall.

Sohng, S. S. L. (1995). *Participatory research and community organizing.* Online. Available: http://www.interweb-tech.com/nsmnet/docs/sohng.htm.

Sprinthall, R. C. (1997). *Basic statistical analysis* (5th ed.). Boston, MA: Allyn & Bacon.

Sternberg, D. (1981). *How to complete and survive a doctoral dissertation.* New York : St. Martin's Press.

Stewart, A. J., & Shields, S. A. (2001). Gatekeepers and change agents. In D. L. Tolman & M. Brydon-Miller, (Eds.). *From subjects to subjectivities* (pp. 304-318. New York: New York University Press.

Stewart, P. J., & Strathern, A. (Eds.) (2000*). Identity work: Constructing Pacific lives.* Pittsburgh, Pa. : University of Pittsburgh Press.

Stone, A. E. (Ed.). (1981). *The American autobiography: A collection of critical essays.* Englewood Cliffs, NJ: Prentice-Hall.

Strauss, A., & Corbin, J. (1990). *Basics of qualitative research.* Newbury Park, CA: Sage.

Stringer, E. (1997). *Community-based ethnography: Breaking traditional boundaries of research, teaching, and learning.* Mahwah, NJ: Lawrence Erlbaum.

Stuchtey, B., & Wende, P. (Eds.) (2000). *British and German historiography, 1750-1950: Traditions, perceptions, and transfers.* New York: Oxford University Press.

Stutzman, R. L. (2001). *WEB links to participatory action research sites.* Online. Available: http://www.goshen.edu/soan/soan96p.htm.

Tashakkori, A., & Teddlie, C. (1998). *Mixed methodology: Combining qualitative and quantitative approaches.* Thousands Oaks, CA: Sage.

Taylor, Y. (Ed.) (1999). *I was born a slave: An anthology of classic slave narratives.* Chicago: Lawrence Hill Books.

Thomas, R. M. (1974) "A pattern for teaching indigenous culture. *Comparative Education,* Vol. 10, No. 1, pp. 49-55.

Thomas, R. M. (1995). *Classifying reactions to wrongdoing: Taxonomies of misdeeds, sanctions, and aims of sanctions.* Westport, CT: Greenwood.

Thomas, R. M. (1998). *Conducting educational research.* Westport, CT: Bergin and Garvey.

Thomas, R. M. (2001). *Recent theories of human development.* Thousand Oaks, CA: Sage.

Thomas, R. M., & Brubaker, D. L. (2000). *Theses and dissertations: A guide to planning, research, and writing.* Westport, CT: Bergin & Garvey.

Thomas, R. M., & Brubaker, D. L. (2001). *Avoiding Thesis and Dissertation Pitfalls.* Westport, CT: Bergin & Garvey.

Titscher, S., Meyer, M., Wodak, R., & Vetter, E. (Eds.). (2000). *Methods of text and discourse analysis.* Thousand Oaks, CA: Sage.

Tolman, D. L., & Brydon-Miller, M. (Eds.). (2000). *From subjects to subjectivities.* New York: New York University Press.

Tong, R. P. (1998). *Feminist thought* (2nd ed.). Boulder, CO: Westview.

Toulmin, S. E. (1994). Philosophy of science. In *Encyclopaedia Britannica,* Vol. 25, 652-669. Chicago: Encyclopaedia Britannica.

Wallace, D. B., & Gruber, H. E. (Eds.). (1989). *Creative people at work: Twelve cognitive case studies.* New York: Oxford University Press.

Weisberg, H. F., Krasnick, J. A., & Bowen, B. D. (1996). *An introduction to survey research, polling, and data analysis.* Thousand Oaks, CA: Sage.

West, M. D. (Ed.). (2000). *Theory, method, and practice in computer content analysis.* Norwood, NJ: Ablex.

Whyte, W. F. (Ed.). (1991). *Participatory action research.* Newbury Park, CA: Sage.

Whyte, W. F., Greenwood, D. J., & Lazes, P. (1991). Participatory action research. In W. F. Whyte (Ed.). *Participatory action research* (pp. 19-55). Newbury Park, CA: Sage.

Wolcott, H. F. (1988). Ethnographic research in education. In R. M. Jaeger (Ed.), *Complementary methods for research in education* (pp. 187-210). Washington, DC: American Educational Research Association.

Wolcott. H. F. (1999). *Ethnography: A way of seeing.* Walnut Creek, CA : AltaMira.

Young-Bruehl, E. (1998). *Subject to biography: Psychoanalysis, feminism, and writing women's lives.* Cambridge, MA: Harvard University Press.

Index

**CORWIN
PRESS**

The Corwin Press logo—a raven striding across an open book—represents the happy union of courage and learning. We are a professional-level publisher of books and journals for K-12 educators, and we are committed to creating and providing resources that embody these qualities. Corwin's motto is "Success for All Learners."